THE BEGINNING OF WISDOM

DENNIS R. AYERS

eLectio Publishing
Little Elm, TX
www.eLectioPublishing.com

The Beginning of Wisdom
By Dennis R. Ayers

Copyright 2017 by Dennis Ayers. All rights reserved.
Cover Design by eLectio Publishing, based on *The Conversion of St. Paul* (oil painting) by Nicolas-Bernard Lépicié (public domain).

ISBN-13: 978-1-63213-360-1

Published by eLectio Publishing, LLC
Little Elm, Texas
http://www.eLectioPublishing.com

Printed in the United States of America

5 4 3 2 1 eLP 21 20 19 18 17

The eLectio Publishing creative team is comprised of: Kaitlyn Campbell, Emily Certain, Lori Draft, Court Dudek, Jim Eccles, Sheldon James, and Christine LePorte.

Publisher's Note

The publisher does not have any control over and does not assume any responsibility for author or third-party websites or their content.

*In honor of my beloved wife, Elizabeth,
my parents, Roy and Eskie Ayers,
and the many people who have given me
friendship and encouragement across the years.*

Contents

Preface—The Rules of Life Never Change

The beautiful painting on the cover of this book, by Nicolas-Bernard Lépicié, depicts the Apostle Paul's conversion to Christianity on the road to Damascus (Acts 9:3-8). It could be argued that Western civilization, as we know it, was born at that moment. The Apostle Paul would go on to preach the gospel of Jesus Christ to the Gentiles until martyred by the Emperor Nero in AD 67. The Judeo-Christian faith with its values, ethics, and morality would spread throughout the lands of the West and order the lives of successful individuals and the societies of successful nations across the subsequent centuries. The concept of the importance of the individual would slowly flower and eventually give rise to a civilization unique in history for its peace, security, freedom, tolerance, and opportunity. Paul's words still hold power over the multiple levels of our lives as he urges us to "Stand fast therefore in the liberty by which Christ has made us free, and do not be entangled again with a yoke of bondage" (Galatians 5:1 NKJV).

From the time of exploration and initial settlement, America has been a land of faith. Even in the primarily commercial settlement of Jamestown, one of the first acts in 1607 was to erect a wooden cross in keeping with its ancillary purpose of propagating the "Christian Religion to such Peoples as yet live in darkness . . ."[1] This simple rough-hewn cross was erected by men generally acknowledged to be less godly than the Puritans who would later settle New England, but such apparent contradictions have often been the case in the countries of the West. Even in times of folly, failings, and transgression, the ideal has always been the faith and the values of our Judeo-Christian heritage. Together with the faith and Judeo-

---

[1] Peter A. Lillback and Jerry Newcombe, *George Washington's Sacred Fire* (Bryn Mawr, Pennsylvania: Providence Forum Press, 2006), 64; *See also*, Virginia Charter of 1606.

Christian values it symbolized, that simple cross has cast its blessings and beneficent influence across all the years that followed.

Alexis De Tocqueville[2] observed in 1835 that "... America is still the country in the world where the Christian religion has retained the greatest real power over people's souls and nothing shows better how useful and natural religion is to man, since the country where it exerts the greatest sway is also the most enlightened and free."[3] The spirit of our prevailing common wisdom, as documented by Tocqueville, once soared high upon wings of faith, reverence, and obedience; but it was always grounded in a respectful fear of the Lord and a firm belief in divine reward and judgment. These values formed the framework of the faith-based wisdom of the common man which served both the individual and the nation well from pioneer days through the comparatively recent past.

The modern world is now largely secular. It is a place often filled with complexity, distraction, temptation, and unhealthy compromise which together obscure many truths once obvious. God's path is no longer as clearly marked as perhaps it was in former times. Today, in the United States, it is increasingly easy to forget that we are all common men and women standing upon the shoulders of ancestors who bequeathed to us a Judeo-Christian legacy that has enriched our institutions, laws, and culture from the time the first settlers set foot upon the shores of the New World. This legacy forms the bedrock upon which our unique society of peace, opportunity, security, and freedom rests. This legacy even safeguards the right of those who do not share its beliefs to worship

---

[2] Alexis De Tocqueville (1805-1859): French statesman, philosopher and historian. In 1831 Tocqueville spent nine months touring the young United States of America covering some 7,000 miles in the process. In 1835 he published his account of this epic journey in his monumental treatise, *Democracy in America*. This famous work is considered an invaluable unbiased account of what the United States and its people were like in the early years of the democracy.

[3] Alexis De Tocqueville, *Democracy in America and Two Essays on America*, trans. Gerald E. Bevan (New York: Penguin Group (USA) Inc., 2003 [1835, 1840]), 340.

peacefully as they please in a manner that is still incomprehensible to much of the rest of the world. This is a simple reflection of the fact that, in many cases, our forefathers came to America in search of religious freedom and, in the process, eventually created one of history's most uncommon nations.

It is a tenet of this book that the basic rules of life never change, and we forget this at our peril. Belief in God, freedom, accountability, discipline, and self-reliance is now disparaged by growing segments of contemporary society. In a time much given to the revision of both history and the Bible, we are losing sight of the basic values that have made us a people of unique blessings. Far too many Christians in the countries that are home to Western civilization no longer know what they believe or why they believe it. The purpose of this book is to recall to mind principles that were once unquestioned by which previous generations successfully governed their lives. These principles constituted a common wisdom, derived from our Judeo-Christian heritage, which formed the foundation of our previous success.

The term *common man* is utilized in this book not as a divisive or populist device, but simply as a phrase that best describes the mass of average, honest, and well-intentioned individuals of faith and good will from all classes that form the backbone of this or any other nation. It was in the spirit of the common man and woman that our nation was created by individuals who rejected the concept of aristocracy. It is in the spirit of the common man and woman that this book is written.

The varied life experiences of most people will readily attest to the fact that there are hardworking, innovative individuals at every layer of our society contributing to its success. During my college years, I had the opportunity to work in a grocery store, a construction firm, a university maintenance department, and various university departmental assistant positions in order to defray educational expenses. Later, I worked as an attorney and then spent most of my career as an executive in a community hospital on the wild and woolly frontier of modern healthcare.

3

Bright and intelligent people illuminated my work history regardless of the job or its nature. No level in our society has a monopoly on smarts, virtue, or vice. Both the failings and the triumphs of the human psyche are present at all layers of our society. This personal journey confirmed my belief in the conservative principles at the heart of our often-maligned common wisdom. This book is written from the Christian perspective because I am proud to claim that as my faith. Most scriptural quotes are taken from the *New American Standard Bible*.[4]

The Bible states that "Jesus Christ is the same yesterday and today and forever. Do not be carried away by varied and strange teachings . . ."[5] Many modern critics often forget that God is timeless and eternal. The things God honored and valued thousands of years ago, as well as the things He disliked, are the same today as they were when He inspired the individuals who penned the Bible and selected the texts it contains. In this light, T. S. Eliot[6] believed that Christian morality is unchanging because it is based upon fixed beliefs which cannot change. In his view, if the Church were to formally accept the highly variable morality of secular society, it would have "to abandon its task of evangelizing the world."[7] The degree to which both Christian truth and morality are viewed as relative, or constantly evolving, terms in the modern world is a reflection of the degree to which the contemporary church has failed in one of its most basic and primary missions.

---

[4] Scripture taken from the *New American Standard Bible*®, Copyright ©1960, 1962, 1963, 1968, 1971, 1972, 1973, 1975, 1977, 1995 by The Lockman Foundation. Used by permission.

[5] Hebrews 13:8-9; Malachi 3:6; Isaiah 40:8; Isaiah 46:8-10; Psalm 117:2; 119:160.

[6] Thomas Stearns Eliot (1888-1965): Influential American-British poet, playwright, intellectual, editor, and critic. A member of the Anglican Church, he became an advocate of orthodox Christianity and traditional values.

[7] T. S. Eliot, *Christianity & Culture*, (Lexington, KY.: A Harvest Book, Harcourt, Inc., 2014 [1948, 1939]), 72.

It is the premise of this book that just as the basic truths contained within the Bible never change,[8] neither do the principles of our common wisdom. This wisdom or cultural memory has been a source of strength and sound judgment for the citizens of this nation since the Founding Fathers looked to the wisdom of the Bible when they founded our country. Ultimately, there is no easy way or slide way through this life for those who want to experience the best that God and this great nation have to offer. The rules of both the Bible and our ethnic common wisdom developed over millennia for a purpose, and we stray from them at great risk to our individual and national future.

Most of us will never be called upon to defend the Alamo for our nation, or walk out into an arena of hungry lions for our faith. We have, however, come to a time when it is now evident that if we do not take the time to read the Bible, learn our nation's history, and affirm the values of our Founding Fathers, a heritage of individual liberty and religious freedom, unique in the annals of the world, could fade into the twilight shadows of history. If others cannot see the Judeo-Christian values, to which most of us are heir, reflected each day in the decisions we make as individuals and as a nation, we can hardly expect the world, which so often threatens us, to one day share those values.

Out of misguided deference to the secular norms imposed by political correctness or other reasons known only to the individual heart, we have long been complacent while the foundations of our religious heritage and the dreams of the Founding Fathers have slowly become obscured by the mists of time and erroneous teaching. Every sincere Christian of faith has been touched by the finger of the living God, through the indwelling presence of the Holy Spirit, and gifted with the light of the ultimate spiritual truth. It was the command of Jesus that our light not be hidden under a basket.[9] It was His desire that we let our light shine forth before all

---

[8] Isaiah 40:8.

[9] Matthew 5:14-19; Mark 4:21; Luke 8:16.

men in such a manner that our Father who is in heaven might be glorified.[10]

We, the living, sometimes forget that we are Christ's body[11] on earth charged with defending the faith and spreading His message of love, repentance, forgiveness of sins, and eternal life. In the respect just described, all Christians are, or should be, missionaries witnessing to the truth of our faith in the commonplace venues of ordinary life. This can be done by example, action, or deed wherever fortune or circumstance may take us, even though most of us may never set foot in a foreign land.

In an ancient time of spiritual drift and national peril, when the "word of the Lord" had become "an object of scorn,"[12] and the people had forgotten "how to blush," God issued a dire warning to the people of Judah. He demanded simply that they seek "the ancient paths" of His covenant and teachings and walk in them that they might find rest for their souls.[13] Although His warning was not heeded at that time, it is still valid today. In the following pages, we will seek the ancient paths and common wisdom of our Judeo-Christian heritage that we might walk successfully amid the pitfalls and distractions of modern life.

If we will but embrace our almost lost common wisdom and retrace our steps to a time of faith in the promise, principles, discipline, accountability, and success of our Judeo-Christian heritage, we may yet find that hope still shines brightly for the United States of America and the countries of the West. As has always been the case from the dawn of mankind's relationship with God, as chronicled in the Bible, this journey begins with the efforts of the individual of faith.

---

[10] Matthew 5:14-17.

[11] 1 Corinthians 12:27.

[12] Jeremiah 6:10 (NRSV).

[13] Jeremiah 6:15-16.

The common wisdom we seek to renew and preserve in our daily lives might best be described, in the spirit of Edmund Burke,[14] simply as that "ancient permanent sense of mankind"[15] embodied in the values of traditional morality, decency, established law, truth, justice, honor, and liberty derived from centuries of orthodox Christian belief, tradition, manners, and custom.[16] This cultural wisdom, together with the values contained within it, serves to protect both the individual and the institutions of civilized society from the consequences of mankind's weaker nature. Although the fire of our fathers has long suffered from indifference, the embers of this wisdom still glow brightly upon our hearth awaiting only our renewed attention and faith.

---

[14] Edmund Burke (1729-1797): British statesman, intellectual, and philosopher. A devout Christian, Burke resolutely opposed the politically correct atheism fashionable in revolutionary France and the intellectual circles of the Age of Enlightenment.

[15] Edmund Burke, *Reflections on the Revolution in France*, ed. L.G. Mitchell (Oxford University Press, New York, 2009 [1790]), 165.

[16] *See*, Alexis De Tocqueville, *Democracy in America*, 335-336.

Chapter 1: Your Greatest Adventure

Most of us have, at one time or another, wished that we could be part of a grand adventure such as those we have seen in the movies, or read about in the great novels or annals of history. Most individuals wish that they could at least once pit themselves against almost impossible odds for a noble ideal or to accomplish some great deed. We might think of David and Goliath; King Arthur, facing Mordred before his last battle; and Frodo and Sam in J. R. R. Tolkien's work, *The Lord of the Rings*. In our more flamboyant moments, we might even remember John Wayne[1] in the original film *True Grit*[2], galloping alone across an open meadow, firing his pistol in one hand and his Winchester in the other, to meet the charging onslaught of an entire band of outlaws.

We tend to forget that we are each the star, hero, or heroine of the greatest saga each of us will ever know—the story of our own lives. This is a story of truly epic proportions to each of us. The decisions and choices we make each day determine whether we will be heroes, villains, footnotes, or supporting characters. As we think within our hearts, so we become (Proverbs 23:7). Shakespeare was correct when he noted that we each strut and fret upon life's stage but for a brief hour.[3] Life is precious and fleeting. The parable of the barren fig tree is a reminder that we are given life to be fruitful, and if we waste that opportunity there will be

---

[1] John Wayne (Marion Robert Morrison) 1907-1979: With a career spanning five decades, Wayne was for much of that time one of Hollywood's most successful stars. While best known for his western films such as *Stagecoach*, *Red River*, *The Searchers*, and *True Grit*, he also received acclaim for his work in other genres; e.g., *The High and the Mighty* and *The Quiet Man*. Wayne received an Oscar for his performance in *True Grit*.

[2] Joseph H. Hazen, Hal B. Wallis (Producers), Henry Hathaway (Director), *True Grit*, Paramount (1969).

[3] William Shakespeare, *Macbeth*, V, v, 25.

consequences.[4] We will each be held accountable for the use we have made of the gift that is our own life.

The Apostle Paul tells us to "be careful how you walk, not as unwise men but as wise, making the most of your time, because the days are evil."[5] We must always remember that the playwright of the play in which we star is far greater than even Shakespeare. The author of our story is none other than God, and He wants to help each of us make the play in which we have the starring role a hit if only we will allow Him to direct us.

Each of us, regardless of our station in life, has someone depending upon us to do our best whether it is God, a spouse, family members, co-workers, fellow soldiers, or our country. Our failure to attempt our best always injures someone besides ourselves. Even if one is inclined to discount this, it is certain that our nation is harmed each time one of its citizens fails to at least make the attempt to do their best—when any of us makes a conscious decision to become a taker rather than a producer.

The Roman Emperor Hadrian's successor, Antoninus Pius, is credited with the statement that "nothing is meaner, indeed more heartless, than to nibble at the property of the state without adding to it by one's own efforts."[6] Some sixteen hundred years later the great English jurist, Sir William Blackstone, noted, "There is not a more necessary or more certain maxim in the frame and constitution of society, than that every individual must contribute his share, in order to the well-being of the community. . . ."[7] When speaking of the universal benefit often derived from actions of individual self-interest, Adam Smith would comment, "Nobody but a beggar chuses [sic] to depend chiefly upon the benevolence of his

---

[4] Luke 13:6-9.

[5] Ephesians 5:15-16.

[6] Jane R. Baun et al. *After Jesus-The Triumph of Christianity,* ed. John A. Pope, Jr. et al (Pleasantville: The Reader's Digest Association, Inc., 1992), 127.

[7] 1 W. Blackstone, *Commentaries,* Chapter 9, VI, 353.

fellow-citizens."[8] Tocqueville wrote in 1835 that "Anyone living in the United States learns from birth that he must rely upon himself to combat the ills and obstacles of life; he looks across at the authority of society with mistrust and anxiety, calling upon such authority only when he cannot do without it."[9] Clarence Thomas, associate justice of the Supreme Court, has wisely noted, "If we are content to let others do the work of replenishing and defending liberty while we consume the benefits, we will someday run out of other people's willingness to sacrifice—or even out of courageous people willing to make the sacrifice."[10]

The primal need to belong and make one's contribution to a worthwhile endeavor is a fundamental element of human happiness. Jesus taught, "It is more blessed to give than to receive."[11] Clearly, Jesus himself was a giver and not a taker, because He voluntarily made the ultimate sacrifice that we might be ransomed from our sins. He saw himself as a servant and desired that His followers emulate His example.[12]

As we have seen, the rules of life by which God governs this existence never change. Jesus told the parable of the talents (Matthew 25:14-28) wherein each individual was held accountable for how he had used his time and ability. Each of us has been blessed with a gift or gifts[13] which constitute talents or abilities that can be used productively and to good purpose. The list of such gifts is as varied as the individuals that exert their influence upon our lives. Faith, wisdom, courage, strength, compassion, charity,

---

[8] Adam Smith, *The Wealth of Nations,* ed. Edwin Cannan (New York: Bantam Dell, 2003 [1776]), 24.

[9] Alexis De Tocqueville, *Democracy in America,* 220.

[10] Clarence Thomas, "Freedom and Obligation—2016 Commencement Address," Imprimis, A Publication of Hillsdale College 45, no.5/6 (May/June 2016):5.

[11] Acts 20:35.

[12] John 13:5-17.

[13] 1 Peter 4:10; 1 Corinthians 7:7; 12:4-11, 28; Romans 12:4-8.

leadership, prophecy, healing, exhortation and ministry, creativity, and invention are examples of such gifts, but the list is as broad as the human spirit and intellect. We will be held accountable if we do not make the attempt to use the gifts, with which we have been blessed, to do our best, and, hopefully, leave the world a little better than we found it.[14] In his commentary on this parable, New Testament scholar D. A. Carson notes, "Grace never condones irresponsibility; even those given less are obligated to use and develop what they have."[15] As Christians, we destroy our witness to others when we project less than our best effort to the world, and place the light we have been given under a basket of indifference.

Being a Christian does not mean that we will never suffer adversity or persecution. Jesus was himself persecuted and warned that those who followed Him could also expect periods of persecution.[16] The Christian knows that, although we may not always be responsible for the negative fortunes of life, we are responsible for the use we make of our time during that hour. Jesus placed His blessing and the promise of heaven upon those who stand firm in the faith and endure to the end during such trials.[17] Most people find themselves forced to live through times or circumstances that they wish had never come upon them. J. R. R. Tolkien, speaking through his character Gandalf, simply says ". . . so do all who live to see such times. But that is not for them to decide. All we have to decide is what to do with the time that is given us."[18]

---

[14] Luke 12:48; 1 Peter 4:10.

[15] Carson, D.A. "Matthew." In *Matthew and Mark*. Vol. 9 of *Expositor's Bible Commentary*, rev. ed., edited by Tremper Longman III and David E. Garland, p. 581. (Grand Rapids: Zondervan, 2012).

[16] Mark 13:9-13; Luke 21:12; John 15:18-21.

[17] Matthew 5:10.

[18] J. R. R. Tolkien, *The Fellowship of the Ring: Being the First Part of The Lord of the Rings*, (Boston: Houghton Mifflin Company, 2003 [1954]), 50.

Tolkien was speaking from experience. He had served in World War I and suffered the loss of virtually all of his boyhood friends in that horrific conflict. He lived on to experience the Great Depression and see the world threatened by Fascism and Nazism culminating in World War II. During this most desperate of modern wars, his country of Great Britain was very nearly defeated. Yet, notwithstanding the unmitigated darkness of the times in which he was fated to live, he used the gifts that God had given him to write *The Lord of the Rings*. Although not an overtly religious work, its spiritual theme consistently radiates an abiding faith in the ability of good to ultimately triumph over evil. This epic novel in three parts[19] stands today as one of literature's great works of courage, hope, and resolve, depicting the importance of standing against evil regardless of the odds. Its story arc chronicles the great good that can flow from the earnest attempts of average people to do the right thing in times of crisis and tyranny.

On life's journey, everyone encounters obstacles, difficulties, and even defeat from time to time as is the case with Tolkien's heroic characters. Many times, the odds will seem to be against one. Sometimes we will be betrayed by those we are entitled to trust. Sometimes even those with a moral, ethical, or fiduciary obligation to support or assist us will betray or fail us. And yet, we press on, even though the possibility of success may seem at times remote, out of self-respect and because there is someone somewhere depending upon us.[20] Sometimes God simply calls upon us to stand up for what is right—win or lose.

If we try our best, many times success will surprise us even in desperate moments. Sometimes, even an apparent failure on our part can expose the evil in others, or accomplish some end which meets God's purpose, though we may not be able to discern it at the time. There is no way to determine the ultimate impact of our lives upon others who we may never even know. The bottom line is that

---

[19] *The Fellowship of the Ring; The Two Towers;* and *The Return of the King.*

[20] Philippians 3: 12-14.

the God-given gift of life itself calls upon us to make the attempt to utilize what talents and abilities we have been given to make the most of our lives.

Just as our life is our greatest adventure, it is also a personal expedition of exploration. We will find that the future into which we travel is indeed an uncharted land of endless possibility both for good and for evil, but it need not be a frightening place. For those wise enough to study them, the Bible, history, and the previous events of our own lives can yield valuable insights as to what form our future is likely to take. As long as we live, course corrections are always possible.

Even the darkest moments in our lives often contain positive lessons of infinite value for those with the eyes to see. It is one of life's greatest paradoxes that success without wisdom can contain the nucleus of future defeat, while disaster, examined with an open mind, can yield the seeds of future triumph. The ability to persevere and the willingness to learn the positive lessons that life has to teach hold the keys to future wisdom, success, and godly fulfillment.

At the institution where I worked for many years, three people come to mind, none of whom had a college education. All three of these individuals greatly enriched our organization. There was Mary (not real name), who joined our dietary department and worked her way up over a long career to the position of dietary supervisor. She always did her best, worked hard, and cared about our patients, her department, and our organization. She had a passion for doing the right thing and an abiding wisdom, born of many years of dedicated service, which many of far greater education found difficult to emulate. She had values and solid judgment. When she ventured an observation or opinion within her areas of expertise, she was virtually never wrong. I always listened when she spoke and weighed her words carefully.

There was Luke (not real name), who worked as a grounds man. Although his job kept him outside in all sorts of weather, he was always cleanly shaven and well groomed, usually in a neatly pressed khaki shirt and pants, even though he was advanced in years. He had an easy air of natural dignity and self-worth about him. His job was so obviously important to him that it never occurred to anyone who knew him to think that he might be of less significance than one of our surgeons or even the leader of our organization. He always had a kind word for everyone and was always willing to take time to assist others. His was a simple dignity, a steady hand, and a wise word that warmed the hearts of all who knew him. He was the type of gentleman that made those who knew him feel clean and good and want to do their best also.

The third person was Paul (not real name). He was in many respects a brilliant man, though he was not blessed with a personality that was always easy to like. He was serious, intense, and definitely not easygoing. He never had the opportunity to go to college and always seemed to regret the lack of a formal degree. He, like so many others of his generation, went to Vietnam, but, unlike many, he learned the positive lessons that experience had to teach and used them to enrich our organization.

Paul was recruited from a for-profit healthcare chain to head our Engineering/Plant Operations department. When it came to patient or employee safety, it quickly became apparent that Paul had the courage of a Knight Templar. He was truly lionhearted. His energy, commitment, zeal, and expertise led to the redrafting of our environment of care and safety policies, the expansion of our Engineering/Plant Operations department, and the creation of a Bio-medical Engineering department at our hospital.

One of the primary lessons that Vietnam had taught him was that once someone is killed by accident, malpractice, or some other misadventure, they cannot be brought back to life in this world. While many in the healthcare world over time become numb to its harsher realities, Paul never forgot and would not let anyone else in the organization forget that healthcare is a life-or-death matter. It is impossible to know how many lives Paul's vigilance may have saved and how many injuries and other mishaps it may have prevented.

15

All three of the individuals described above had their flaws and deficits like all of the rest of us, but they rose above their limitations and circumstances to make something of their lives. They all died rich in years, with the respect and gratitude of our organization, and full of God's purpose. In the end, their lives counted for something. We should all hope to do as well. One does not have to be famous or rich to make important contributions with his or her life. As noted by J. R. R. Tolkien in his work, *The Fellowship of the Ring*:

> This quest may be attempted by the weak with as much hope as the strong. Yet such is oft the course of deeds that move the wheels of the world; small hands do them because they must, while the eyes of the great are elsewhere.[21]

Virtually everyone is a leader, role model, or example for someone. In the mantra of executive leadership, Jesus expects each one of us to walk the talk so as to exemplify the type of individual He has asked us to become. Jesus did walk the talk, but in today's rough and tumble world, this is not something that every leader can be counted upon to do. Many bind heavy burdens that they do not carry, and set out expectations for others which they do not themselves follow.[22]

Part of maximizing the impact of our own lives entails realizing that we are each a leader within our spheres of influence with the potential to set a positive example for those around us. That example can touch the world and positively impact the future in ways that might astonish us. As noted elsewhere in this book, sometimes the part which we play in the script before us is not

---

[21] J. R. R. Tolkien, *The Fellowship of the Ring: Being the First Part of The Lord of the Rings*, 262.

[22] Matthew 23:4; Luke 11:46.

about us. We are meant to be servants[23] serving a greater purpose that may not always be readily apparent.

In summary, we are not always the best judges of what God will ultimately deem most significant in our lives. We are each created for a particular moment, opportunity, or situation wherein we will be given the chance to utilize the unique talent, resolve, ability, or gift[24] given to us by God to make a difference, set an example, and realize God's purpose—if we but have the loyalty, courage, and the faith to do so. For those who believe, our God is the God of both history and the moments of daily life, "declaring the end from the beginning, and from ancient times things that are yet to unfold" (Psalm 46:10). He plucks individuals out of time and circumstance to place them where they are needed most to meet His particular purpose—whether for epic deeds or simple acts of Christian courage, honor, and truth in the home, workplace, or boardroom. Examples of this are Moses, King David, the Apostle Paul, Charles "The Hammer" Martel, John III Sobieski, George Washington, Abraham Lincoln, and Winston Churchill. Had these individuals not picked up the gauntlet of destiny which God threw down at their feet, today's world would be a much darker place.

We often forget that individuals like Winston Churchill went through long periods of failure, depression, and defeat. We know of them today because they persevered, used the gifts God had given them, and never gave up. No one should underestimate the power that one's simple attempt to lead an honorable life and set a Christian example can have upon others, the world, and the future we cannot see.

Sometimes it takes fortitude and courage to remain loyal to ourselves, our values, and to the Word of God. In fact, God asks that we "be strong and very courageous."[25] We are not to turn from

---

[23] Luke 22: 25-26; John 13:12-17.

[24] Romans 12:4-8; 1 Corinthians 7:7; 12:4-11, 28; 1 Peter 4:10.

[25] Joshua 1:6-7.

His law, either "to the right or to the left," if we are to expect success.[26] The Bible tells us that everyone who desires to live a godly life that honors Jesus Christ will be persecuted from time to time.[27] Everyone will, however, have a day that will prove to be the best day of his or her life. It is both a bane and a blessing of this existence that we are not often fated to know which day that will be until many years after the fact—if ever. We should, therefore, approach each day as a grand adventure that could define the rest of our lives, and perhaps present an opportunity for us to fulfill God's ultimate purpose for our creation.

One of the most courageous defenses of Jesus Christ during His lifetime came from the blind beggar whom Jesus had healed on the Sabbath. The poor man and his parents were hauled before a powerful tribunal of Pharisees and repeatedly interrogated as to whether he had in fact been blind and how he came to be cured of his blindness. Both the beggar and his parents knew that there was a real danger of being "put out of the synagogue" or effectively excommunicated if their answers were found too supportive of Jesus and His ministry. Nonetheless, the beggar, who had been healed by Jesus, uttered the now immortal words "though I was blind, now I see." Throwing caution to the wind, the poor beggar then bravely engaged his learned inquisitors in a debate in defense of Jesus' righteousness, which he clearly won (John 9:1-34).

When Jesus heard that the beggar had been put out of the synagogue for his courageous words, Jesus sought him out and ultimately revealed Himself as the Son of Man to this poor, brave man whom He had earlier healed. The only other instance prior to the events leading up to His crucifixion in which Jesus affirmed his status as the Messiah so bluntly to one outside His immediate circle

---

[26] Joshua 1:7; *See also*, Deuteronomy 28:1-15; 1 Kings 2:1-3.

[27] 2 Timothy 3:12; John 15: 18-21; Matthew 10: 16-25.

of disciples was his confession to the Samaritan woman.[28] Little did the blind man know, when he went out to beg at the start of this story, that we would still be talking about him two thousand years later. Each new day is a treasure chest of possibilities awaiting only our good faith effort to live our lives according to God's will and purpose. The example for others of simple acts of basic honesty, honor, hard work, courtesy, love, reverence, courage, and faithfulness can live on to touch the future in ways that we can scarcely imagine. We each have the ability to control whether we will waste our lives in trivial pursuits and spiritual indifference, or use our lives for good as we move away from the things of darkness and into the light.

One of history's great lessons is that the opportunities that God gives us to do the right thing should be taken as they come or they may be lost forever. In fact, much of history is often but a sad commentary on the fatal consequences of ignoring the good that can be accomplished today in the vain hope of perhaps doing some supposedly greater good tomorrow. The Bible tells us that when one "knows the right thing to do and does not do it, to him it is sin" (James 4:17). The future is a surprisingly fragile place. It is very vulnerable to infection by those evils of the current day which are permitted to escape across its borders. The great teacher and theologian William Barclay warned, "There are three things which do not come back—the spent arrow, the spoken word and the lost opportunity."[29]

---

[28] Mounce, Robert H. "John." In *Luke - Acts*. Vol. 10 of *The Expositor's Bible Commentary*, rev. ed., edited by Tremper Longman lll and David E. Garland, p.497. (Grand Rapids: Zondervan, 2012).

[29] William Barclay, *The Letter to the Romans*, 195.

Chapter 2: Wisdom

Life is much more than an initial accident followed by a series of random events governed by luck or chance. As we have seen, it is an epic adventure and the ultimate individual quest for each of us. How we use the gift that is our life is of critical importance to our eternal future, our family, our faith, our nation, and our culture. God has a special purpose for everyone, and He is willing to reveal that purpose to those who come to Him seeking to know it (Psalms 139:13-16; Ephesians 2:10).[1] This is an important early step in developing an ongoing personal relationship with God.

While life is indeed an adventure, it is not meant to be lived recklessly without prayer, reflection, prudence, or planning. The precious gift of life was never meant to be frittered away or squandered. Jesus states that we are to be shrewd as serpents and innocent as doves.[2] The message of the Bible is that life is serious business and is meant to be lived with love, faith, obedience, discipline, humility, and wisdom.

The beginning of wisdom, and the foundation upon which everything else rests, is simply the fear of the Lord.[3] With this fear or respect comes knowledge[4] and the ability to discern righteousness, justice, equity, and every good course.[5] To fear the Lord is to hate evil, pride, and arrogance.[6] The fear of the Lord is both the fountain of life[7] and longevity.[8] This fear is simply an

---

[1] Proverbs 3:5-6; Psalm 32:8; Matthew 7:7-8; 11:28-29; 1 Peter 4:10; Romans 12:4-8; 1 Corinthians 12:4-26; Revelation 3:20; Jeremiah 29:11-13.

[2] Matthew 10:16.

[3] Proverbs 9:10; Psalm 110:10; Job 28:28.

[4] Proverbs 1:7.

[5] Proverbs 2:9.

[6] Proverbs 8:13.

[7] Proverbs 14:27; 19:23.

attitude of profound respect, faith, and dependence upon the will of God. The fear of the Lord should, therefore, be a guiding principle of everyone's life and an attribute of anyone who would seek a leadership role.[9] Virtually everything currently going awry in our personal lives, our culture, and the rest of Western civilization can be traced back to a single root cause. Simply put, far too many among us no longer know the actual God of the Bible or fear Him. T. S. Eliot once noted, "We need to recover the sense of religious fear, so that it may be overcome by religious hope."[10]

Today, many have become accustomed to thinking of God as a God of love and convenience who will obligingly go along with almost anything modern man desires, including the amendment and revision of the Bible. It is often forgotten that the God actually described in the Scriptures is also a God of justice, accountability, and discipline as well as love. It is God who defines truth, sin, justice, and the rules for a life within His will—not mankind. Were it not so, there would have been no need for Jesus Christ to die upon the cross for the sins of humanity. The God of the Bible has never been a god of convenience.

To fear God, therefore, implies faith in a God who actually exists and rewards those who seek Him.[11] This faith is accompanied by love, respect, reverence, humility, obedience, voluntary self-discipline, accountability, and an acknowledgement of God's supreme holiness. Fear of the Lord also requires an acceptance of God's authority, and an obligation to honor God's commandments, laws, and rules for life as set forth in the Bible.[12] God states that He will "look upon those who are humble and contrite of spirit, and

---

[8] Proverbs 10:27.

[9] Exodus 18:21.

[10] Eliot, *Christianity and Culture*, 49-50.

[11] Hebrews 11:6.

[12] Deuteronomy 4:5-6.

who tremble at My word."[13] "The Lord favors those who fear Him, those who wait for His loving kindness."[14] Indeed, those who "fear the Lord" will be blessed, "the small together with the great" (Psalm 115:13). "The angel of the Lord encamps around those who fear Him, and rescues them" (Psalm 34:7). Ultimately, God's mercy will be upon those who fear Him from generation to generation.[15]

The Scriptures are very clear that there are few things God dislikes more than pride and the arrogance it represents.[16] C. S. Lewis went so far as to state, "As long as you are proud you cannot know God."[17] Humility is, therefore, an important component of wisdom.[18] Edmund Burke wrote, "True humility, the basis of the Christian system, is the low, but deep and firm foundation of all real virtue."[19]

The Lord leads the humble in justice and teaches the humble His way.[20] He shares the secret of His covenant with those who fear Him.[21] Moses experienced the closest relationship with God of any Old Testament figure, and he was said to be "very humble, more than all men who were on the face of the earth." [22] God has stated what is required of us. It is to do justice, to love kindness, and to

---

[13] Isaiah 66:2; 57:15.

[14] Psalm 147:11.

[15] Luke 1:50.

[16] Proverbs 3:34; 6:17; 8:13; 16:5, 18; 18:12; Isaiah 2:11; Philippians 2:3; James 4:6; 1 Peter 5:5-6.

[17] C. S. Lewis, *Mere Christianity* (New York: HarperCollins Publishers, 2001), 124.

[18] Proverbs 11:2; 15:33; 16:5; 16:18-19; 22:4; 29:23; Luke 18: 14; 1 Peter 5:5-6.

[19] Edmund Burke, *Reflections on the Revolution in France*, Appendix: *Letter to a Member of the National Assembly* [1791], 270.

[20] Psalm 25:9; Psalm 10:17-18; James 4:6, 10.

[21] Psalm 25:14.

[22] Numbers 12:3.

walk humbly with God.[23] While it is often forgotten in modern times, an important characteristic of our humble walk with God involves obedience to His commandments free of stubbornness and rebellion (1 Samuel 15:22-23). If one is willing to humble oneself in the sight of the Lord, He will lift you up (James 3:10). Jesus thus invites us to "Take my yoke upon you and learn from Me, for I am gentle and humble in heart, and you will find rest for your souls."[24]

In hindsight, it is thus not entirely surprising that Jesus Christ was born in some sort of stable[25] and humbly entered Jerusalem mounted upon a donkey at the climax of His earthly ministry.[26] Jesus did not conduct his ministry in the power center of Rome or in the highly erudite intellectual hubs of Athens or Alexandria. He was drawn to humble and contrite people who appreciated what they did not know and actively sought to learn more about God and their faith. His message was not for the proud of heart who were supremely confident of their salvation. He sought to bring hope to those who feared God, acknowledged their sinfulness, and despaired of mercy.[27] He came as the Son of Man to teach and provide a path to salvation for mankind. Few have expressed this point better than the early church father Irenaeus, when he said of Jesus: "He became what we are, to make us what He is."[28]

Though He was the Son of God, Jesus chose to live His life on this earth as a common man. After His resurrection and ascension into heaven, Jesus entrusted the building of His church and the spreading of His message to common men and women. Two thousand years ago, the common men and women of that time

---

[23] Micah 6:8; Deuteronomy 10:12-13.

[24] Matthew 11:29.

[25] Luke 2:7-16.

[26] Zechariah 9:9; Matthew 21:5; Mark 11:2-8; Luke 19-35; John 12:14-15.

[27] Luke 18:9-14; Matthew 9:13.

[28] William Barclay, *The Letter to the Romans*, rev. 3rd ed. (Louisville, Kentucky: The Westminster John Knox Press, 2002), 16; 2 Corinthians 5:21.

understood the message of Jesus far better than the elite of their day. Experience would seem to indicate that the same is frequently true in our time as well. Jesus warned that "many who are first will be last; and the last first" (Matthew 19:30).

A successful life and even greatness always involves an element of humility. Regardless of their station in life, those who are truly great never forget that they are at heart common men and women subject to the will of God. The legendary American pioneer Daniel Boone was reputed to have stated late in life, "With me the world has taken great liberties, and yet I have been but a common man."[29] Although Boone opened up large areas for settlement, had many great adventures, and, against all the odds for a man of his background, achieved great fame, he never forgot that he was but a common man. When one begins to think of one's self as truly important, to substitute one's own desires and moral preferences for the guidance of the Bible, and to believe that debating God will be a viable option on the day of judgment, then all hope of true greatness fades.

During college, I had the privilege of working in the maintenance department of a major university to help meet my educational expenses. It was at this time that I met an individual who exemplified the principles just discussed. He more closely personified the perfect Christian gentleman than anyone else I have ever known. He was a carpenter in his sixties named David (not real name). Still a physically strong and imposing man, he walked with shoulders back and spine ramrod straight in a manner very reminiscent of the cowboy star Randolph Scott.[30] He had the perfect blend of intelligence, gentle humor, honor, wisdom, quiet strength,

---

[29] Lyman C. Draper, *The Life of Daniel Boone*, ed. Ted Franklin Belue (Mechanicsburg: Stackpole Books, 1998), 3.

[30] Randolph Scott (1898-1987): American movie actor. Although Scott starred in virtually every type of movie, he was best known for his classic tall-in-the-saddle cowboy or western roles. His very erect posture in the saddle marked him as one of Hollywood's most picturesque and effective horsemen.

and gracious Christian humility. Although he was one of the best carpenters in the department, David was always modest and self-deprecating with respect to his considerable talents and abilities. He never showed off, but he was always willing to assist anyone else who might need help.

The university was a benevolent employer and David's position was one of trust, responsibility, and considerable freedom. It has been said that there is a slide way to do any job, but David never took it. He always did each job in the correct manner even if it involved greater difficulty or took more time. This work ethic, common to all of the older gentlemen in the shop, sometimes made them somewhat unpopular with some of the younger workers, but no one ever messed with David. He was courteous and polite, but firm and steady with respect to his beliefs and moral code. He would not conform to the diminished standards of contemporary society in a time and place where such values often demanded courage and fortitude. He took pride in every aspect of his job and always tried to give an honest day's work to his employer.

One day a younger co-worker was completing an application for another position while seated at the lunch table. He asked David how honest one should be with respect to his level of work experience. David looked down at the table, chuckled, and volunteered to tell a story that might be helpful. After the Great Depression, a major airport in his part of the state had embarked upon a large expansion project. The salary scale on this project was considerably higher than what was normal for construction work in the area, and David was fortunate enough to be offered a position as a carpenter. After the low salaries of the Depression, David had needed this job badly.

David recalled, "On the very first day of work, the foreman directed all twenty or thirty carpenters to line up on the tarmac with our tool boxes in front of us. He then asked anyone who considered himself to be a first-class carpenter to take one step forward. It may have been because of the higher salary, or it may have been that each one of those guys was smarter than I, but every one of them stepped forward . . . except me. I don't mind telling you that I felt pretty small as the foreman walked down that long line of carpenters until he reached me. He looked me up and down and said, 'Everyone here apparently thinks they are first-class carpenters but you. What do you have to say?'

"I said, 'Well sir, I have worked as a carpenter for many years, and I know how to do a lot of things, but I still feel like I learn something new on every job I take. I am a very good carpenter, but I would not be comfortable telling you that I was a first-class carpenter because there are probably still many things that I do not know.' The foreman smiled and pushed his hat back on his forehead, so he could take a better look at me, I guess, and said, 'It sounds to me like you need to take a step forward along with the rest of the men.' That foreman and I had a great working relationship for the duration of that project, which could not be said for some of the other guys who had so quickly taken their step forward that day. It was a good thing that I had told the truth though, because the first job he asked me to do was something that I had never encountered before. So I'd say that honesty is still the best policy when talking about your experience or virtually anything else."

Today, it is difficult to fully appreciate David's courage that day on the tarmac unless one has had the opportunity to know someone who experienced the dream-crushing despair and deprivation of the Great Depression. It has been said that the future course of one's entire life can hinge upon such small, defining moments turned to great purpose. Clearly, David believed that God is real and a "rewarder of those who diligently seek Him."[31] He took his faith seriously and allowed it to actively motivate his life.

David was an excellent example of that type of individual who fears God, but absolutely nothing else. His attempt to faithfully

---

[31] Hebrews 11:6.

represent, to the best of his ability, his Christian beliefs had, over the course of his life, transformed him into an individual so imposing that I still remember his example almost forty years later. As he tried to live out his Christian principles in the activities and circumstances of daily life, he became, without even realizing it, a very effective ambassador and role model for his faith. In today's world, it is often difficult to discern the difference between many who claim to be Christians and those who are not. In David's case, the positive difference that Christ can work in the life of a believer was very apparent. David never became rich or famous, but he did become a great man in the eyes of those fortunate enough to know him.

Chapter 3: Believe

The writer of the 14th Psalm notes that "The fool has said in his heart, 'There is no God.'" The evidence of God's existence is evident all about us in the incredibly intricate and beautiful world in which we live. The fingerprint of the divine is, perhaps, most discernible in the unique nature of our own souls which animate our physical bodies with a light beyond that of other creatures. The Apostle Paul stated, "For since the creation of the world His invisible attributes, His eternal power and divine nature have been clearly seen, being understood through what has been made . . ."[1] In short, there is an obvious intelligence, although many prefer to ignore it, behind the endless symmetry and intricacy of creation. It was Paul's opinion that those who do not believe are thus "without excuse."[2] Paul believed, without question, that we are, in fact, special God-created creatures, living on a special God-created planet, in a wonderful God-created universe. The intelligence, order, care, and beauty so discernable in the creation means that there must be intelligence, order, care, and beauty behind it at its source. This intelligent, ordered, caring, and beautiful source is what we know as God.

We often forget that some of our most famous scientists were Christians including: Copernicus, Kepler, Galileo, Descartes, Boyle, Newton, Pascal, Faraday, Lavoisier, Priestly, Pasteur, Mendel, and many others.[3] With respect to science and religion, Wernher von Braun, one of the fathers of our space program, felt there was no conflict, because science seeks only to understand the creation, whereas, religion seeks to understand the Creator. Of those today that would challenge science to prove the existence of God, he

---

[1] Romans 1:20.

[2] Romans 1:20.

[3] Dinesh D'Souza, *What's So Great About Christianity* (Carol Stream, Illinois: Tyndale House Publishers, Inc., 2008), 99.

somewhat incredulously asked, "But, must we really light a candle to see the Sun?"[4] Dr. von Braun further noted:

> Science, for instance, tells us that nothing in nature, not even the tiniest particle, can disappear without a trace ... Nature does not know extinction. All it knows is transformation! Now, if God applies this fundamental principle to the most minute and insignificant parts of His universe, doesn't it make sense to assume that He applies it also to the masterpiece of His creation—the human soul? I think it does. And everything science has taught me—and continues to teach me—strengthens my belief in the continuity of our spiritual existence after death. Nothing disappears without a trace.[5]

Wernher von Braun had survived evil times that were dangerous both physically and spiritually in World War II Germany.[6] His Christian journey (both as a Lutheran and later as an Evangelical) is a story of revelation, ongoing personal growth, faith, and redemption. He learned the positive lessons that his negative wartime experiences had to teach and went on to help make the fledgling American space program a success. The fact that he dreamed of reaching the stars did nothing to weaken his faith in God.

Few of those who are inclined to doubt God's existence would deny that evil exists in the world, and that it seems to be at war with all things good. While bad things do happen, if one looks across the span of history, God never allows evil to triumph in the long run. Epidemics eventually fade, tyrants like Hitler are defeated, and oppressive systems such as communism ultimately

---

[4] Dr. Wernher Von Braun, *The Voice of Dr. Wernher von Braun An Anthology*, ed. by Irene E. Powell-Willhite (Burlington: Apogee Books, 2007), 223.

[5] Ibid., 78.

[6] Bob Ward, *Dr. Space, The Life of Wernher von Braun* (Annapolis, Maryland: Naval Institute Press, 2005), 31-53.

fail. Evil may sweep across the world's landscape like a wildfire, but often, within a few years, green shoots and flowers are flourishing in a new life that appeared impossible during the heat and terror of the fire. Order always seems to prevail over chaos and ruin in a beautiful, wondrous, and ultimately benevolent universe. The existence of God, therefore, can almost be proven by inference from the negative.

There are those who will now state that, to the contrary, the existence of evil, pain, and suffering actually proves that God does not exist. There has been an enormous amount of ink spilled on this subject by great intellects such as St Augustine, Thomas Aquinas, David Hume, John Laird, and others. Some have speculated that perhaps the possibility of evil must exist to allow good to be recognizable as a virtue. Others have recognized that much pain has a purpose. Some pain at times renders moral instruction while other instances of pain serve to protect us from harming ourselves. If there were no suffering would we be fully capable of appreciating the good in the world?

The Judeo-Christian tradition teaches that mankind has free will. God created every human being with the potential to become a sheep or a goat in the moral sense. Free will permits each of us to voluntarily separate ourselves into one of the two herds—the sheep into the light and the goats into darkness (Matthew 25:31-46; John 17:3-26). In this sense, we are thus each given the freedom to both determine our own eternal destiny and, to a certain extent, judge ourselves. Significantly, Jesus Christ refers to Himself as the good shepherd who gives his life for the sheep who know His voice that they might be saved (John 10:9-15).

If we are free to choose to do *good,* then we are equally free to choose to do *evil.* In this world, such a choice frequently has consequences that result in pain and suffering. This suffering is clearly not God's desire because He goes to great lengths in the Bible to instruct humanity how to avoid many behaviors that result in suffering. Indeed, an incredible amount of evil, pain, suffering, and general misfortune could be avoided if all of mankind simply

31

honored God's commandments and refrained from worshipping false gods, lying, murder, covetousness, stealing, sexual sin, and otherwise "doing whatever seems right in one's own eyes."

It is also arguable, along the lines intimated by C. S. Lewis, that this existence was created so that free beings, through confrontation with the rigors of life, would have their souls matured and tempered. Thus, shaped, sanded, and polished in the streamed of life, they would move closer to becoming worthy of God's gift of eternal life through faith in Jesus Christ.[7] In a world free of pain, suffering, and consequences would it be possible to distinguish right from wrong and would attributes such as faith, love, kindness, self-sacrifice, prudence, courage, accountability, and strength of character develop?[8] If Lord Acton was correct when he suggested that "power tends to corrupt, and absolute power corrupts absolutely,"[9] would we not become insensitive elitists without the instruction that the possibility of suffering, pain, defeat, failure, danger, sorrow, and ultimately death represent?

If one believes in the God of the Judeo-Christian tradition, the sanctity of freedom, and the reality of eternal life, then a world such as that in which we live can be seen to effect the fulfillment of God's ultimate purpose. In our world, the greatest evil in human history, the crucifixion of Jesus Christ, can also be seen as history's greatest good. It was the crucifixion that made it possible for Jesus to, as noted by C. S. Lewis, "infect" the world with goodness that all men might catch it.[10]

Since the dawn of man there has been a fairly consistent belief in god(s) and an afterlife. It can be argued that an almost instinctive

---

[7] C. S. Lewis, *Mere Christianity* (New York: HarperCollins Publishers, 2001), 74-75; 2 Thessalonians 1:4-5.

[8] *See,* Romans 5:3-5.

[9] Lord Acton (John Emerich Edward Dalberg-Acton), *Historical Essays and Studies*, ed. John Neville Figgis and Reginald Vere Laurence (London: Macmillan, 1907), Appendix: Letter to Bishop Mandell Creighton, April 5, 1887.

[10]Lewis, *Mere Christianity*, 177, 221.

belief in an afterlife even predates civilization itself. After the flowering of civilization, some cultures have gone to truly enormous lengths in the quest for eternal life as in the case of Egypt and the pyramids. In short, a belief in something beyond ourselves, accompanied by a belief in some sort of existence beyond this one, seems to stretch back to that mist shrouded time, "beyond which the memory of man runneth not to the contrary," to use a phrase from Sir William Blackstone.

There simply does not appear to be a downside to believing in God. Christians know that after death they will enter into the kingdom of heaven having, through faith, accepted God's freely given gift of eternal life through Jesus Christ. Our attempts to live life according to the principles of the Christian faith will generally (although not always) afford us a healthier, less complicated, and less stressful life than we might otherwise have had pursuing our first impulses as pagans. And, by attempting to love God and our fellow man, and pursue the quest to do unto others as we would have them do unto us,[11] we might just leave the world a slightly better place.

Those who deny God, on the other hand, bet all of eternity on the correctness of this arrogant, prideful, and ultimately fatal assumption. If one believes in a soul that survives death, as did Dr. Wernher Von Braun, then it follows that, as Charles F. Stanley[12] frequently notes, "We are all going to spend eternity somewhere." If death is not the end, then those who renounce God will be in deep trouble indeed.

In conclusion, a story relayed to me by my old rafting buddy Jim (not real name) comes to mind. Jim was a friend who truly loved rugged outdoor adventure. Jim is in heaven now, but in 1996

---

[11] Matthew 7:12.

[12] Dr. Charles F. Stanley is pastor of the First Baptist Church of Atlanta, Georgia and founder of In Touch Ministries. Stanley's practical, inspirational, and highly motivational sermons are still televised weekly and can be purchased at reasonable cost from the store at www.intouch.org

he was in his prime. So it was that we had just rafted the Colorado River from Potash, Utah, through Cataract Canyon, to Hite, Utah, on Lake Powell with Western River Expeditions. After the wonderful raft trip, we had rented a car in Grand Junction, Colorado, and driven back into the canyon country to visit Arches National Park. That evening, after feasting on buffalo at a local restaurant in Moab, Utah, we drove up to Dead Horse Point State Park to try our luck at filming a western sunset. As we left the park in the growing darkness, a western storm blew in replete with thunder claps and very impressive bolts of lightning.

While driving back down the winding road in the rain, Jim unfolded his tale. Jim ran a business in a small town, so he knew many of the life stories in his community. I cannot recall what brought it up, but I suspect that it related to the overwhelming grandeur of God's creation in which we had been immersed that week. Jim stated that he could not help but recall a man he had once known who, in the pride of his intellect, had decided there was no God. In the course of time, that man married a woman of like mind and they had children, grandchildren, and great-grandchildren. His family eventually totaled some thirty-five members. Such was the force of that man's personality that most of his large family followed him into atheism. Then that man died. Jim then looked at me, as he concluded his story, and said, "Can you imagine, after the wonder of the creation we have witnessed today, dying and facing your final judgment having led thirty-five souls into unbelief?"

Today, unfortunately, there are many in our culture more than willing, for their own purposes, to take upon themselves the spiritual consequences of leading others astray.[13]Jesus characterized these false shepherds as thieves who sneak into the sheepfold "only to steal and kill and destroy," and who are not willing to lay down their own lives for the flock as Jesus was prepared to lay down His

---

[13] Matthew 18:6-7; Luke 17:1-2.

life.[14] Other folks (like the well-intentioned Apostle Peter) sometimes think solely in human rather than godly terms, thereby giving Satan the opportunity to speak through them as when Peter tried to convince Jesus that His death in Jerusalem was not necessary.[15]

Perhaps due to intellectual pride, ambition, or other reasons more difficult to discern, many of these false shepherds seek to weave an earthly wisdom into the intrinsically otherworldly story of New Testament salvation. This earthly wisdom is often unrelated to individual salvation and is calculated to appeal to the perceived weakness of the audience that the false shepherd is attempting to sway. Such earthly or conventional wisdom may relate to the flashpoint sexual, entitlement, political, or social issue of the day, but it will always differ from the plan for New Testament salvation preached by Jesus Christ, the Apostles, and the fathers of the orthodox, traditional Christian church.

In response to such false teachings, the Apostle Paul would ask, "Where is the wise man? Where is the scribe? Where is the debater of this age? Has not God made foolish the wisdom of the world?"[16] For Paul, "The word of the cross is foolishness to those who are perishing, but to us who are being saved it is the power of God."[17] Paul understood that "God has chosen the foolish things of the world to shame the wise, and the weak things of the world to shame the things which are strong."[18] For him the false shepherd's attempts at earthly or conventional wisdom compromised the truth, the miracle, and the elegant simplicity of the salvation offered by Jesus Christ. He warned the faithful against those who would seek to preach a gospel different from that received and preached by

---

[14] John 10:7-13.

[15] Matthew 16:22-23.

[16] 1 Corinthians 1:20.

[17] 1 Corinthians 1:18.

[18] 1 Corinthians 1:27.

Paul and the other apostles.[19] This warning is still valid today. Obedience to God always trumps the conventional wisdom of contemporary culture.

Today many forget that Jesus stated that "the Scripture cannot be broken" (John 10:35). When the advice, theology, or policy espoused by false shepherds adds to, subtracts from, or contradicts God's word as revealed in the Bible, it can never be inspired by the Holy Spirit, Jesus Christ, or God.[20] This is true notwithstanding the various claims made to that effect by many of those who have lost their way.[21] Speaking through Jeremiah, God made his disapproval of such practices very clear when he stated, "An appalling and horrible thing has happened in the land: The prophets prophesy falsely, and the priests rule on their own authority; and My people love it so!"[22] Jesus emphasized, "He who speaks on his own authority seeks his own glory; but he who seeks the glory of Him who sent him is true, and in him there is no falsehood"(John 7:18 RSV).

God is ancient beyond the concepts of time or memory, and He is holy beyond the capacity of the modern mind to fully grasp. Unlike the gods of many other religions, the God of the Judeo-Christian faith is not made in mankind's image reflecting attributes, virtues, and weaknesses common to humanity. The God of the Judeo-Christian faith imposes standards of behavior, morality, ethics, and—most importantly—solutions which are, in many cases, beyond those which could be characterized as intuitive or

---

[19] Galatians 1:8-9.

[20] Mounce, Robert H. "John." In Luke - Acts. Vol. 10 of *The Expositor's Bible Commentary*, 569, 589; Kieffer, René, "John." *The Oxford Bible Commentary*, edited by John Barton and John Muddiman, 990. (Oxford, New York: Oxford University Press, 2001).

[21] Deuteronomy 4:2; 12:32; Joshua 1:7-8; Isaiah 40:8; Proverbs 13:13; 30:5-6; Psalm 119:160; Matthew 5:19; John 10:35; 1 Corinthians 4:6; Galatians 1:8-9; 2 Peter 1:20; Titus 1:9-11; Revelation 22:18-19.

[22] Jeremiah 5:30-31; See also, Isaiah 30:9-11; Matthew 15:7-9.

instinctive to mankind, as demonstrated by the lack of such scruples in much of the world outside the influence of the Judeo-Christian faith. Our God is timeless and eternal because He exists outside the realms of space and time as we know them. He does not contradict Himself or change His mind. Yet, many rush to the bookstores to buy the books of the false shepherds while ignoring the Bible inspired by God through which we will all eventually be judged.[23] Jesus warned that if a blind person chooses to follow a guide who is also blind, then both will ultimately "fall into a pit."[24]

We live in a society where the concept of sin has become repugnant to the sinner. Proverbs 30:20 states, "This is the way of an adulterous woman: She eats and wipes her mouth, and says, 'I have done no wrong.'" This describes the modern attitude of many towards any sin. In previous times, one might try to justify or rationalize inappropriate behavior, but, increasingly, in our culture there are strident voices demanding that we sanction, approve, and ratify inappropriate or unacceptable behavior in the name of human diversity. When we do this, we take those sins, for which formerly only the sinner was accountable, upon ourselves and our nation. Would we not do well to ponder whether the utterly holy God of justice, accountability, and love, who cast Satan out of heaven for pride and rebellion, is likely to admit into heaven those who seek to rewrite the Bible to suit declining standards of contemporary morality? Should we not pause to consider what God might think of those who worship a god whom they have fashioned in their own image?[25]

The famous biblical scholar William Barclay noted that "the biblical history of Israel" constitutes "the demonstration in the events of history that ultimately life turns out well for the good, but evil comes to the wicked."[26] He goes on to clarify that God's path is

---

[23] John 12:48.

[24] Matthew 15:14; Proverbs 28:10.

[25] Isaiah 14:13; 2 Peter 2:4-9; Jude 1:6; Revelation 12:7-9.

[26] William Barclay, *The Letter to the Romans*, 230.

not always the easy way, "but in the end, it is the only way to everything that makes life worthwhile in time and in eternity."[27] The God of the Judeo-Christian faith is a God of definite and delineated moral standards and expectations. These moral standards are set forth in both the Old and New Testaments. Nowhere does God state that these moral standards are negotiable. God promises positive consequences for honoring His moral code and negative consequences for dishonoring that code on both a personal and national level. God is in effect stating that, with respect to the unfolding story of His will on earth, we are each expected to be active participants on His team, or soldiers in his army, against evil rather than mere spectators. In this life, God's hope is that we will not take a seat in the stadium or a place on the opposing team, but rather fill a place on His team and actively strive to make a difference in the outcome of the great cosmic struggle between right and wrong and good and evil.

While "all have sinned and fallen short of the glory of God,"[28] most of us recognize sin and inappropriate behavior by viewing them through the prism of the Ten Commandments and associated commentary, such as the Law of Moses,[29] the prophets, and the teachings of Jesus Christ as chronicled in the New Testament. It is for this reason that the Bible, in general, and Christianity, in particular, have come increasingly under attack.[30] The ethics and morality of our Judeo-Christian heritage cramp the style of powerful constituencies in our modern, increasingly pagan world.[31] Jesus warned that those who do evil hate the Light for fear that their deeds will be exposed, while those who practice the truth are drawn to the Light, so that their deeds may be seen to be of God (John 3:20-21).

---

[27] Ibid.

[28] Romans 3:23.

[29] The first five books of the Old Testament also known as the Pentateuch.

[30] John 3:19-20.

[31] John 3:36; Matthew 25:31-46; 1 Corinthians 6:9-10.

For the thoughtful person of faith, there can be little doubt that what we choose to believe and the example we choose to set in this life have serious consequences. Most common men and women know instinctively that once on the other side of this life, we will each be faced with a final reckoning that will determine our eternal destiny. Everyone passes through a life of joy, sorrow, success, and misfortune to finally face the great darkness that lies beyond the final frontier. This final, lonely moment holds no comfort or solace for the atheist or those who have otherwise renounced their Christian faith. For them the Bible says this will be a time for "weeping and gnashing of teeth" (Matthew 8:12). For those without faith, the life in which they have placed all glory dissolves into the cold, dark, grim abyss of an unknown and unpleasant future.

With this sobering prospect in view, we would all do well to take ourselves and the decisions we make in this life much more seriously than has been our custom in recent decades. One of the great strengths of Christianity is that it does offer hope, answers, and comfort in times of tragedy, heartbreak, and death. For the believer, the darkness beyond the final frontier is neither black nor cold or lonely, and it holds no terrors. It is simply the twilight before the dawn of a wonderful new life filled with light, love, joy, and happy reunions.

Chapter 4: The Indispensable Guide

As recently as the 1950s there were few houses in America that did not contain a Bible. The Bible was read, actively preached in our churches, and many people had a relatively good understanding as to what was in the Bible. We prayed enough in school to impress upon us that honoring God was important. We sang Christmas carols like "Silent Night" during the Christmas season, and the girls took turns placing their dolls in the Christmas manger scene.

These memories are not just an impression. When I was in the second grade, I was a quiet, shy little boy. My teacher was a godly woman who actually seemed to love all of her students. She asked me one day if I would ask my father, who was a carpenter at that time, if he would build a manger for our classroom nativity scene at Christmas. I proudly took the request home to my father, and he graciously accepted the assignment. The entire family searched through all of our biblical reference books to learn what a manger might have looked like, and my father went to work.[1] The end result was a beautiful manger sized big enough to accommodate the largest of dolls. Looking back across the years through the eyes of memory, it still seems almost big enough to have been a real manger. Whatever the case, it was certainly almost as big as I was. My father's craftsmanship made me very proud indeed.

The beautiful, but large and awkward, manger had to be taken to school on the school bus. My mother did not have a driver's license at that time, and my father had to be at work much too early to be able to take me to school. It was a considerable distance to the bus stop, and, with the additional burden of my books, carrying the manger was almost overwhelming. I managed to get the manger to the bus stop and struggle up the bus steps with it only to find that there were no vacant seats. I would have to stand with the manger

---

[1] In the ancient Middle East, mangers for the feeding of livestock were crafted from a variety of materials including wood, stone, masonry, clay mixed with straw or even carved out of natural rock formations. Since my father was a carpenter, our manger was constructed of wood.

all the way to school. I was mortified to feel tears of exasperation begin to sting the corners of my eyes. Suddenly, a boy several years older than me, who I did not know, asked me what it was. I replied that it was a manger for the baby Jesus. He then said, "You just hold your books, and I will carry the manger to your classroom for you." It was an act of kindness that I have never forgotten. That boy may have been an angel for all I know. I have no memory of ever seeing him again.

The manger became the focal point of the nativity scene situated in front of the class Christmas tree. That Christmas season each girl in my class was given the opportunity to place her favorite doll in the manger to represent the baby Jesus. The face of each young girl was illuminated with the soft glow of earnest reverence as she placed her doll in the manger with as much tender care and love as if it were indeed Jesus. We sang Christmas carols, enjoyed the beauty of the tree with its multicolored lights, and learned the true meaning of the Christmas season.

The simple faith of a second-grade teacher in a public school had reached out and touched the heart of every child in her class, and given them a Christmas memory to warm their hearts for the rest of their lives. After Christmas, my teacher asked if she could keep the manger to use with future classes, which I imagine she did until she either retired or the Supreme Court told that good woman that it had decided that such actions violated separation of church and state.

As can be seen from the vignette above, those were very different times on multiple levels of innocence and faith. Pretty much everyone believed in God, an eventual judgment, and heaven and hell. Our society, as a whole, was better for these beliefs. Sadly, this is no longer true. Today, when we speak of God, the Bible, or Jesus Christ we can no longer assume, even in America or the other countries of the West, that our audience understands our frame of reference. Virtually everyone thinks they know what is in the Bible (the Old and New Testaments) because they may know bits and pieces of the story, but few have actually read it. It has become one of the most misquoted and abused works in our culture, and yet it is arguably the cornerstone of Western civilization.[2] It is at the foundation of our modern concepts of justice, freedom, liberty, virtue, and how we treat our fellow man (man, woman, and child), and, yet, it is often pilloried in the media and our popular culture.

Many in our time erroneously believe that the New Testament was written down so long after the events narrated that no one could possibly know what Jesus really said. These individuals also believe that there are so many mistakes and variations in the transcription and translation of the New Testament that no one can know the truth of Jesus' message. It is also assumed by some that the doctrines of the traditional, orthodox Christian church have been weakened, compromised, or superseded by later scientific, archeological, theological, or philosophical insights. And lastly, there are those that believe that Jesus was a radical who distanced himself from the great moral and ethical themes laid out by God in the Old Testament. As we will soon learn, none of these statements are true, but it would be difficult to discern this from the media or many pulpits.

Today, using terms such as *fundamentalist* or *evangelical* in a condescending or contemptuous manner, many in academia, the media, and the liberal pulpit attempt to discourage the general public from reading the Bible because its truth often conflicts with the contemporary secular message. Given the confusion wrought by this cultural war against our Judeo-Christian heritage, there are, however, few moral obligations more important than reading the Bible for one's self and learning what it really does say. This is no longer a difficult task as there are now many excellent translations of the Bible such as the *New American Standard Version*, the *New King James Version*, and the *New Revised Standard Version* which are written in modern English and very easy to read. It is virtually impossible to maintain a life of faith while ignorant of the true

---

[2] Jean-Pierre Isboults, *The Biblical World An Illustrated Atlas* (Washington, D.C.: National Geographic Society, 2007), 11; *See also*, Eliot, *Christianity & Culture*, 200.

43

contents of the Bible and without regular Bible study. This fact constitutes one of the paramount themes in this book. Jesus warned that even though one may receive the word of God with joy and believe for a while, it is still possible to fall away in times of temptation if one's faith has no firm root.[3]

Biblical scholarship, by virtue of the Dead Sea scrolls and the discovery of biblical sources more ancient than those available to the translators of early English Bible translations such as the original *King James Version* of the Bible, has established that the biblical Scriptures we have today are faithful to the earliest known documents yet discovered. In his fascinating book, *Searching for the Original Bible*, Randall Price speaks of the abundance of textual evidence as putting the "New Testament in a class by itself, distinguishing it as having the most and the earliest manuscripts of any literary document from the ancient world."[4] Price notes:

> Recall that we have all of the variants that make up the Original Bible somewhere in our vast number of manuscripts, and that textual criticism has so far been able to bring our state of the text very close to the wording of the original (95 percent for the Old Testament and 99 percent for the New Testament). This clearly indicates Divine Providence has preserved the text for us to an amazing degree. By comparison with secular literature, we have in the Bible, hands down, the best and most complete text in all of human history. This cannot be by random chance![5]

---

[3] Luke 8:13.

[4] Taken from: *Searching For The Original Bible* by Randall Price, p.113, Copyright© 2007 by World of the Bible Ministries, Published by Harvest House Publishers, Eugene, Oregon 97402, www.harvesthousepublishers.com. Used by Permission.

[5] Randall Price, *Searching For The Original Bible*, 247-248; See, J. D. Douglas and Merrill C. Tenney, rev. Moisés Silva, "Bible." *Zondervan Illustrated Bible Dictionary*, 200 (Grand Rapids: Zondervan, 2011); William J. Federer, *What Every American*

William J. Federer came to the same conclusion when he, citing many sources, refuted the Islamic claim that the Bible has been "corrupted" in his book, *What Every American Needs To Know About The Qur'an, A History of Islam and The United States*. The accuracy of the preservation of the text of the Bible, documented by Price, Federer, and many others, is nothing less than a miracle when one considers the span of years involved and the number of times the Bible's pages had to be copied by hand. It is also a miracle worthy of note that we even have the Bible today given the efforts by some of history's most totalitarian regimes to suppress it.

How remote from the time of Jesus is the origin of the Scriptures accepted as authoritative in the New Testament we have today? We learn that the temple in Jerusalem had been under construction for forty-six years during the time of Jesus' active ministry (John 2:20). We know that the temple was begun by Herod the Great in 20 BC,[6] so this tells us that Jesus was still conducting his ministry, which appears to have lasted at least three years, in AD 26. The traditional date for Jesus' crucifixion is AD 30, but a credible case has also been made for AD 33.[7]

There is now considerable consensus that all of the books of the New Testament were completed before the end of the first century AD. There are even facts that suggest that the New Testament may have been completed before AD 70, because the cataclysmic destruction of the Jewish temple (a wonder of the ancient world) and Jerusalem in AD 70 by the Romans is not mentioned in the New Testament. This omission seems strange, given the fact that Jesus had prophesied that event,[8] unless the New Testament

---

Needs To Know About the Qur'an-A History of Islam & The United States (St. Louis: Amerisearch, Inc., 2011), 37.

[6] Isbouts, *The Biblical World An Illustrated Atlas*, 262.

[7] Carson, D.A. "Matthew." In *Matthew and Mark*. Vol. 9 of *The Expositor's Bible Commentary*, rev. ed., edited by Tremper Longman III and David E. Garland, p. 593. (Grand Rapids: Zondervan, 2012); Douglas and Tenney, rev. Silva, "Chronology (NT)." *Zondervan Illustrated Bible Dictionary*, 283.

[8] Luke 19:41-44; Matthew 24:1-2; Mark 13:1-2.

documents were completed prior to Jerusalem's destruction. Additionally, we know that the entire corpus of Christian thought and theology comprised by the New Testament writings of the Apostle Paul was complete before AD 70, because Paul is believed to have been martyred by the Emperor Nero who died in AD 68. The Apostle Peter is also thought to have died in the Neronian persecutions, and yet neither his death (other than Jesus' prophecy of his death, John 21:18-19) nor Paul's are mentioned in the New Testament, although both deaths would have been highly significant events.

Also, it is generally accepted that the Gospel of Luke and The Acts of the Apostles were both written by Luke, the "beloved physician," friend, and traveling companion of the Apostle Paul on some of his missionary journeys.[9] These two books were written together and viewed by the early church as a single two-volume work. Together both books account for approximately thirty percent of the New Testament.[10] The New Testament scholar, Richard N. Longenecker, has made a very persuasive case for the completion of Acts (and by implication the Gospel of Luke) by AD 64, citing factors beyond the obvious fact that Acts ends with the Apostle Paul apparently still very much alive.[11] Since most modern

---

[9] Longenecker, Richard N. "Acts." In *Luke ~Acts*. Vol. 10 of *The Expositor's Bible Commentary*. rev. ed., edited by Tremper Longman III and David E. Garland, pp. 665,702-703 (Grand Rapids: Zondervan, 2012).

[10] Ibid., 665.

[11] Longenecker, Richard N. "Acts." In *Luke ~ Acts*. Vol. 10 of *The Expositor's Bible Commentary*, pp.699-701: (1) Longenecker notes that the depiction of the status of Jews in the Roman world seems to predate the destruction of the Jewish nation in AD 70; (2) the concept of Roman justice is relatively favorable and positive with respect to the future of Christianity which could hardly have been the case after the Neronian persecutions which were initiated in AD 65; (3) the descriptions and nature of the language in Acts appears to reflect the usage of the earliest days of the church. For another example, the description in Acts of the border between Phrygian Iconium and the Lycaonian cities of Lystra and Derbe (Acts 14:6) was only accurate for the years between 37 and 72 AD; (4) Acts reflects no knowledge of Paul's letters or their later importance to the church community.

scholars now believe that Luke relied, at least in part, upon the Gospel of Mark when he wrote his gospel, this is another indication that the Gospel of Mark must have been in circulation prior to AD 64. In short, there is serious biblical scholarship attesting to the strong possibility that most of the New Testament was written prior to the Roman sack of Jerusalem in AD 70 or within less than forty years of the crucifixion.

Even if the last of the books of the New Testament (probably the Gospel of John) was not completed until near AD 100, this still means that all of the materials that comprise what we now know as the New Testament were completed within sixty-seven to seventy years of the time of Jesus, most probably by people who either knew Jesus or had access to people who had known Jesus or his original disciples.[12] In his thoughtful, well-researched, and highly illuminating book, *Jesus and the Eyewitnesses: The Gospels as Eyewitness Testimony*, Richard Bauckham states:

> The Gospels were written within living memory of the events they recount. Mark's Gospel was written well within the lifetime of many of the eyewitnesses, while the other three canonical Gospels were written in the period when living eyewitnesses were becoming scarce, exactly at the point in time when their testimony would perish with them were it not put in writing. This is a highly significant fact, entailed not by unusually early dating of the Gospels but by generally accepted ones . . . the period in question is actually that of a relatively (for the period) long life time.[13]

That is in fact what the orthodox histories of the early church tell us. In these we learn, for example, that the early church father

---

[12] 2 Peter 1:16-18.

[13] Richard Bauckham, *Jesus and the Eyewitnesses: The Gospels as Eyewitness Testimony* (Grand Rapids: William B. Eerdmans Publishing Co., 2006), p. 7.

Irenaeus was a student of Polycarp who knew John who was an Apostle of Jesus.

In his work, *In Search of the Trojan War,* Michael Wood is able to demonstrate a surprising degree of factual detail, which has been substantiated by archeology, in Homer's *Iliad.* This was possible even though the *Iliad* is thought to have been entirely orally composed and only reduced to writing hundreds of years after the events described.[14] Indeed, a firm belief in an actual historical basis for many of the descriptions in Homer's *Iliad* ultimately led the controversial businessman turned archeologist Heinrich Schliemann to a windy hill in Turkey named Hissarlik in 1871, which has since been accepted as the site of Homer's Troy.

In an ancient world steeped in oral tradition as well as a Roman/Judaic society where writing and even shorthand[15] were not all that uncommon, a time window for the completion of all the New Testament books of a mere sixty-seven to seventy years or much less from the events narrated is very short indeed. If the *Iliad,* composed hundreds of years before the birth of Jesus Christ, can point archeologists to ancient sites long lost to history, is it really so difficult to accept that the Bible can point the way to heaven?

No less a luminary than William Barclay made a strong case, based on the testimony of early church sources and his own literary analysis, that the Apostle John actually did dictate the Gospel of John near the end of his long life[16] and that, according to the early church father Papias, the Gospel of Matthew was actually based upon the sayings of Jesus originally collected by Matthew in

---

[14] Michael Wood, *In Search of the Trojan War* (New York: Facts on File Publications, 1985), p. 130,132,134-136.

[15] Douglas and Tenney, rev. Silva, "Gospel of Matthew." *Zondervan Illustrated Bible Dictionary,* 910.

[16] William Barclay, *The Gospel of John,* rev. ed. (Philadelphia: The Westminster Press, 1975) vol.1, p. 24; *See also,* Mounce, Robert H. "John." In *Luke - Acts.* Vol. 10 of *The Expositor's Bible Commentary,* rev. ed., edited by Tremper Longman III and David E. Garland, p. 360. (Grand Rapids: Zondervan, 2012).

Hebrew.[17] There are those who contest the authorship of Matthew by the Apostle Matthew, but famed New Testament scholar D. A. Carson affirms that "there are solid reasons in support of the early church's unanimous ascription of this book to the apostle Matthew, and on close inspection the objections do not appear substantial."[18] Carson goes on to state that the AD 60s are the most "likely decade for Matthew's composition."[19] Richard Bauckham makes a compelling argument that the eyewitness testimony of Peter is the primary source for the Gospel of Mark and a significant source for Luke.[20] The early church universally accepted that Luke who wrote both the Gospel of Luke and Acts was the physician companion of the Apostle Paul.[21]

It is true that many contemporary scholars question traditional assertions of authorship with respect to various New Testament books based upon current approaches to textual criticism. It is asserted that certain texts like the Second Epistle of Peter are *pseudepigraphical*, meaning, in this example, that it is felt that this text was authored by a disciple or follower of the Apostle Peter who placed Peter's name on the document to give it greater authority.

---

[17] William Barclay, *The Gospel of Matthew*, rev. ed. (Philadelphia: The Westminster Press, 1975) vol. 1, p. 4-5; *See also*, Carson, D.A. "Matthew." In *Matthew and Mark*. Vol. 9 of *The Expositor's Bible Commentary*, rev. ed., edited by Tremper Longman III and David E. Garland, pp. 40-43.

[18] Carson, D.A. "Matthew." In *Matthew and Mark*. Vol. 9 *of The Expositor's Bible Commentary*, rev. ed., edited by Tremper Longman III and David E. Garland, p. 43. (Grand Rapids: Zondervan, 2012).

[19] Ibid., 45.

[20] Bauckham, p. 124-126.

[21] William Barclay, *The Gospel of Luke*, rev. ed. (Philadelphia: The Westminster Press, 1975), p. 1-2; *See also*, Liefeld, Walter L. and Pao, David W. "Luke." In *Luke ~ Acts*. Vol. 10 of *The Expositor's Bible Commentary*, rev. ed., edited by Tremper Longman III and David E. Garland, pp. 23-24. (Grand Rapids: Zondervan, 2012); Longenecker, Richard N. "Acts." In *Luke ~ Acts*. Vol. 10 of *The Expositor's Bible Commentary*, pp. 665,702-703.

Many other equally credible scholars state bluntly that there is insufficient evidence to show that the practice of pseudepigraphy was ever tolerated within the context of New Testament literature. New Testament scholar William W. Klein states that early Christians followed the example of the Jews who "never admitted their pseudepigrapha into their canon." In support of this point, Klein quotes the ancient church historian, scholar, and bishop of Caesarea, Eusebius, who wrote in his early history of the church, *Ecclesiastical History*, "For we, brethren, receive both Peter and the other apostles as Christ; but we reject intelligently the writings falsely ascribed to them, knowing that such were not handed down to us."[22]

This longstanding debate with respect to the authorship of various New Testament texts is ultimately explained in the context of the old internal evidence versus external evidence controversy in biblical scholarship. Given the fact that we know that one's writing style can change over time, and that both Josephus and the Apostle Paul used scribes/secretaries,[23] the arguments based primarily on internal textual criticism without supportive external evidence (such as corroborating ancient texts and archeology, etc.) may not always be fully entitled to the weight that they are frequently given in modern times.

Regardless of one's stance with respect to the issues just discussed, as previously noted, few scholars now question the fact that all of the materials contained in the New Testament were

---

[22]Klein, William W. "Ephesians." In *Ephesians ~ Philemon*. Vol. 12 of *The Expositor's Bible Commentary*, rev. ed., edited by Tremper Longman III and David E. Garland, p. 32. (Grand Rapids: Zondervan, 2012); Charles, J. Daryl. "2 Peter." In *Hebrews ~ Revelation*. Vol. 13 of *The Expositor's Bible Commentary*, rev. ed., edited by Tremper Longman III and David E. Garland, pp. 367, 369. (Grand Rapids: Zondervan, 2012).

[23] Romans 16:22; Galatians 6:11; 2 Thessalonians 3:17; Jane R. Baun et al. *After Jesus-The Triumph of Christianity*, 56; Charles, J. Daryl. "2 Peter." In *Hebrews ~ Revelation*. Vol. 13 of *The Expositor's Bible Commentary*, rev. ed., edited by Tremper Longman III and David E. Garland, p. 370.

completed by AD 100. As we have seen, this dating places the penning of all New Testament books within the lifespan of those who personally experienced Jesus and the original Apostles, some of whom would have no doubt survived to question inaccurate information, forgeries, and misplaced assertions of authorship. No book written after the time of the apostles was included in the New Testament.[24] Although there were other writings from this period, no books other than the twenty-seven books currently contained in the New Testament ever received a wide or general consensus for inclusion in the official canon of the New Testament.[25] The earliest records surviving today indicate that the four Gospels, Acts, and the thirteen letters of Paul were accepted by the early Church without reservation. The remaining books in the New Testament appear to have been universally accepted before AD 180.

Randall Price notes that in various permutations, these twenty-seven books were recognized as authoritative from the beginning in the works of early church fathers such as Clement of Rome, Ignatius of Antioch, Polycarp, Irenaeus, and Hippolytus, each of whom acknowledged various books in the years AD 95-235.[26] The bishop of Alexandra, Athanasius, issued a list of all twenty-seven books contained in the New Testament as part of his Easter festival letter for the year AD 367.[27] The authority and general acceptance accorded these books by the early church fathers meant that the need for an official list or canon was apparently not felt until the Council of Laodicea (AD 363) with later affirmations at the Council of Hippo (AD 393) and the Council of Carthage (AD 397).[28] The

---

[24] Ronald F. Youngblood, F.F. Bruce, R.K. Harrison, "The Bible." *Nelson's New Illustrated Bible Dictionary*, 190 (Nashville: Thomas Nelson Publishers, 1995).

[25] J. D. Douglas, Merrill C. Tenney, rev. Moisés Silva, "Canonicity." *Zondervan Illustrated Bible Dictionary*, 248 (Grand Rapids: Zondervan, 2011).

[26] Price, *Searching For The Original Bible*, 153-154, 193; *See*, Douglas, "Canonicity." *Zondervan Illustrated Bible Dictionary*, 248.

[27] Jane R. Baun et al., *After Jesus—The Triumph of Christianity*, 83.

[28] Price, *Searching For The Original Bible*, 154. A copy of an earlier ancient document called the Muratorian Fragment, commonly dated AD 170 (albeit not

New Testament canon had evolved as a result of broad consensus among the church fathers and churches across the Roman Empire. Thus, contrary to recent fictional accounts, neither the Council of Nicaea nor the Emperor Constantine selected the books contained in the New Testament.[29]

The tradition of the church is that the authors of the Gospels were original Apostles or had access to the Apostles or to people who had known the Apostles.[30] There have been no new discoveries in archeology or other external evidence that can definitively refute this ancient claim. Richard Bauckham makes a very strong case that:

> [I]n the period up to the writing of the Gospels, gospel traditions were connected with named and known eyewitnesses, people who had heard the teaching of Jesus from his lips and committed it to memory, people who had witnessed the events of his ministry, death and resurrection and themselves had formulated the stories about these events they told. These eyewitnesses did not merely set going a process of oral transmission that soon went its own way without reference to them. They remained throughout their lifetimes the sources and, in some sense that may have varied for figures of central or more marginal significance, the authoritative guarantors of the stories they continued to tell.[31]

In the sense described above, the authentic sayings and teachings of Jesus and his disciples were orthodox from the very

---

without some challenge), lists 22 of the 27 books now accepted in the New Testament (Price, 152-153).

[29] Price, *Searching For The Original Bible*, 154-156; *See also*, Billy Graham, *The Holy Spirit, Activating God's Power In Your Life* (Nashville, Tennessee: Thomas Nelson, 1988), 36.

[30] Youngblood, "The Bible." *Nelson's New Illustrated Bible Dictionary*, 190.

[31] Bauckham, *Jesus and the Eyewitnesses*, 93.

beginning.[32] Heresies sprang up even during the lifetimes of the original disciples, but they were vigorously refuted from the beginning by living witnesses such as Peter and Paul (who had experienced Jesus on the road to Damascus and met Peter and many of the original eyewitnesses). Later, heresies continued to be strongly refuted by the early church fathers such as Irenaeus who, as we saw, drew knowledge from a chain of witnesses known to them stretching back to the original disciples and hence Jesus himself. It is for this reason that so-called lost gospels like those of Thomas and Judas, written many years after the fact with heretical agendas, ended up buried in the desert.

In short, the leaders of the early church were intelligent individuals who had sound reasons for their belief in the veracity of the materials, which they recognized as authoritative for inclusion in the Bible we have today. These reasons were grounded in traditions of authorship running back through known individuals to Jesus himself. The Roman world was neither naïve nor stupid. It was, in many respects, as sophisticated as our own modern world.[33]

Two of the more famous ancient, external references to Jesus Christ occur in the writings of Josephus and Tacitus. Josephus, the first-century Jewish general, diplomat, and historian, made respectful reference to Jesus in his famous history, *Jewish Antiquities*, written in AD 94. Although certain aspects of the passage's phraseology have long been the subject of scholarly debate, most modern scholars now accept that, although the possibility of some later tampering by Christian copyists cannot be entirely excluded, this passage does, in fact, contain authentic historical reference by Josephus to Jesus' life, ministry, crucifixion, reports of post-death appearances, claim that he was the Messiah, and the continued existence of the "tribe of Christians." Critics often forget that, during the Jewish revolt against Rome of AD 66-73, Josephus was commander of the Jewish forces in Galilee, so he could easily have

---

[32] Price, *Searching for the Original Bible*, 193.

[33] Douglas and Tenney, rev. Silva, "Canonicity." *Zondervan Illustrated Bible Dictionary*, 248.

obtained firsthand knowledge of Jesus' ministry which had occurred no more than thirty-three years earlier. In the most common text of this passage, Josephus mentions Jesus' ministry, that "he was the Christ," his crucifixion under Pilate, that Jesus appeared alive to those who loved Him after the third day as foretold by the prophets, and that "the tribe of Christians, so named for him," was not extinct.[34] Josephus also mentions the arrest and death of John the Baptist as well as the arrest and stoning of James, the brother of Jesus, "who was called the Christ."[35]

Tacitus, a Roman politician and renowned historian, also mentioned Jesus in his famous work entitled *Annals* written in either AD 116 or 117. Tacitus' work refers to "Christus" who was executed by Pontius Pilate during the reign of Tiberius. He describes how the Emperor Nero blamed the Christians for starting a great fire which destroyed much of Rome to divert suspicion from himself. Although clearly no fan of Christians, Tacitus notes that Nero's persecution of them was so vicious that it eventually aroused "a feeling of compassion" among the Romans; for their destruction was "not, as it seemed, for the public good, but to glut one man's cruelty . . ."[36]

In summary, claims that the Bible was written too long after the events described to be credible; that its text is hopelessly corrupted; that its canon was selected arbitrarily by disreputable sources; or that Jesus Christ never lived are more the stuff of urban legend than scholarly fact.

---

[34] Josephus, *Jewish Antiquities* 18.3.3. Although this material appears in Josephus texts as early as the third century, the authenticity of parts of it have been challenged by some scholars while the majority position remains that, while it may contain some evidence of later Christian tampering, it does contain authentic historical reference to Jesus, His ministry, crucifixion under Pilate, the reports of His post-death appearances, the possibility that he might have been the Messiah, and the continued existence of "the tribe of Christians."

[35] Josephus, *Jewish Antiquities* 18.5.2; 20.9.1. These passages have generally been accepted as entirely authentic.

[36] Tacitus, *Annals* 15.44.

Chapter 5: Hearing the Voice of God

Beginning with the Creation and descending through the centuries—from the plains of ancient Sumer in the time of Abraham to the events of the New Testament—the Bible records the consistent variety of the human condition and mankind's relationship to God.[1] As stated in Ecclesiastes 1:9, "That which has been is that which will be, and that which has been done is that which will be done. So there is nothing new under the sun." Both Edmund Burke and George Santayana are credited with words that gave rise to the famous maxim regarding the value of history's lessons: "Those who do not know history are destined to repeat it."[2] It is for this reason that regular Bible study is of critical importance. The pages of the Old and New Testaments document mankind's triumphs, failures, and God's response to both. These books were written by individuals inspired by the Holy Spirit to convey God's message.[3] In fact, the New International Version translation of the Bible states that "All Scripture is God-breathed and is useful for teaching, rebuking, correcting and training in righteousness" (2 Timothy 3:16). As one studies the Scriptures, in a very real sense, one can almost hear the voice of God speaking across time and

---

[1] Sumer was an ancient land located in lower Mesopotamia (Babylonia) in the plain between the Tigris and Euphrates Rivers. One of its major cities, Ur, is mentioned in Genesis 11:28 as the original home of Abraham before he was directed by God to migrate to Canaan (Genesis 12:1-4).

[2] Russell Kirk, *Edmund Burke, A Genius Reconsidered*, (Wilmington, Delaware: Intercollegiate Studies Institute, 1997), 25; Edmund Burke, *Reflections on the Revolution in France*, 33: "People will not look forward to posterity, who never look backward to their ancestors."; George Santayana, *The Life of Reason*, Vol. 1, "Reason in Common Sense", 1905: "Those who cannot remember the past are condemned to repeat it."

[3] 2 Timothy 3:16-17: In this passage, the Apostle Paul states, "All Scripture is inspired by God and profitable for teaching, for reproof, for correction, for training in righteousness; so that the man of God may be adequate, equipped for every good work."

history with respect to His promises and the great moral and ethical themes of the Bible.

By reading the Bible we gain valuable insights as to what God is really like, how He responds to various behaviors, and what actions on our part will likely be successful in this life as opposed to those which will not. Sometimes individuals bemoan the fact that life does not come with an owner's manual. In fact, life does come with an owner's manual and that owner's manual is the Bible which was inspired by our Creator.[4] When Jesus recounts the sad fate of the rich man in torment and contrasts it with the joy of Lazarus in heaven, He is warning us that the Scriptures are to be taken seriously and we ignore them at great peril.[5] The message is that what we choose to believe and our conduct in this life will have eternal consequences that cannot be undone after we pass to the other side.

The Bible tells us that the word of God is "living and active."[6] As Creator of the cosmos, the means by which God can communicate with us are unlimited. Today, many times He communicates through the Scriptures with which He has provided us. If one actively seeks God's will for his or her life and seeks to learn more about God by reading the Bible, many times God will, through the Holy Spirit, give us the insight[7] we need by leading us to the Scriptures that express His will on that topic. For example, most believers have experienced instances when certain verses of the Bible virtually leap off the page with meaningful insight related to a problem at hand when they had previously read those verses at other times with no such insight. In this respect, one is not looking up a topic in a concordance and consciously trying to locate Scriptures to support a specific view or desire. To the contrary, if

---

[4] 2 Timothy 3:16; 2 Peter 1:20-21.

[5] Luke: 16:29-31.

[6] Hebrews 4:12.

[7] John 14:26; 16:13; Luke 12:12; 1 Corinthians 2:12-16

one accepts that the Scriptures are truly "living and active;" it is an article of faith that God can and often does use them to communicate to the sincere of heart who seek to know His will. This is what the believer means when it is said that the Bible constitutes the "living" word of God.[8]

It is important to know what the Bible actually says because of the amount of pseudo-religious misinformation becoming part of our popular culture. Based on most people's small amount of biblical knowledge, such erroneous information often sounds plausible enough to be believed, when in fact there is little or no basis for such beliefs in the actual Scriptures. A certain element of humility is always wise when one attempts to discern moral, ethical, and spiritual issues. God's thoughts and ways are not our thoughts and ways, for His ways are infinitely higher.[9]

Jesus warned that those who attempt to discern spiritual issues with purely earthly wisdom without the assistance of the Spirit of Truth (also called the Holy Spirit, Helper, or Counselor) will be proven wrong with respect to sin, righteousness, and judgment.[10] He had earlier explained to his critics among the Pharisees that they were attempting to judge by the standards of this world "according to the flesh."[11] His examples would ultimately prove to be the most prominent religious figures of Jesus' time who were proven wrong with respect to sin because they did not believe in Jesus and had condemned a sinless man; wrong with respect to righteousness because these priests had thought that they were doing a good deed by having Jesus killed; and wrong with respect to judgment because Jesus was vindicated by His resurrection thereby bringing judgment upon the powers of this world.[12] Those who do not

---

[8] Graham, *The Holy Spirit*, 41-45.

[9] Isaiah 55:8-9; Romans 11:33-36.

[10] John 16:8-13.

[11] John 8:15.

[12] John 12:31.

acknowledge Jesus Christ can never have or experience the Spirit of Truth or Holy Spirit and the wisdom that comes with Him. This is one reason why it is so very unwise to shut Jesus out of one's life whether on a personal or a national level.

There are many false and utterly futile religions, philosophies, and creeds in the world because, at some point, fallible human beings tried to probe the mind of God with purely earthly wisdom without the assistance of the Holy Spirit or Spirit of Truth. It is for this reason that Jesus instructed the Apostles to wait in Jerusalem until the power of the Holy Spirit came upon them before going out into the world to spread the gospel making disciples of all nations (Luke 24:49; John 14:26; Acts 1:4). Christianity was not to be a product of mankind's earthly wisdom. Christianity was to be based upon divine revelation through Jesus Christ and the power of the Holy Spirit. Jesus' message of love, repentance for the forgiveness of sins, grace, redemption, and eternal life was from the beginning contrary to the wisdom of the world because it was not of this world (1 Corinthians 1:18-27; 3:19-20). With the teachings of Jesus Christ and the additional promptings of the Holy Spirit, the full nature of God's true views on love, morality, justice, discipline, and accountability gradually came to light in the mind of man and slowly began to transform the world.

God's word is truth[13] and it is documented in the Scriptures. The Spirit of Truth or Holy Spirit does not reveal new truths,[14] but helps us to understand more fully the truth revealed in the Bible and "brings to our remembrance the teachings of Jesus Christ."[15] In this sense, the true work or revelation of the Spirit of Truth or Holy

---

[13] John 17:17.

[14] Mounce, Robert H. "John." In *Luke ~ Acts*. Vol. 10 of *The Expositor's Bible Commentary*, 569, 589; Kieffer, René, "John." *The Oxford Bible Commentary*, edited by John Barton and John Muddiman, p. 990. (Oxford, New York: Oxford University Press, 2001); Kevin L. DeYoung, *The Holy Spirit*, ed. D. A. Carson and Timothy Keller (Wheaton, Illinois: Crossway, 2011), 17; Graham, *The Holy Spirit*, 171, 222.

[15] John 14:26.

Spirit cannot contradict the teachings of Jesus Christ or the Scriptures.[16] As Billy Graham[17] has noted, "God no longer directly reveals "new truth"; there is now a back cover to the Bible. The canon of Scripture is closed."[18]

Today, many who wish to amend the Bible or abolish aspects of traditional, orthodox Judeo-Christian morality sometimes claim to be inspired by the Holy Spirit. The Holy Spirit's name should, however, only be evoked with caution and reverence. Both the Bible and history have repeatedly taught us that human feelings, desires, and passions are famously untrustworthy gauges of God's will and should not be mistaken for promptings of the Holy Spirit. The fact that an earnest desire for theological change is politically correct, convenient, and deemed expedient does not mean that the desire is from the Holy Spirit. The Bible, in fact, warns us "not to believe every spirit, but to test spirits to see whether they are from God, because many false prophets have gone out into the world."[19] It also warns that there will be "false teachers" who will secretly seek to introduce destructive heresies into the church (2 Peter 2:1). Charles F. Stanley wrote, "The Holy Spirit will never lead you

---

[16] Charles F. Stanley, *The Spirit-Filled Life* (Nashville, Tennessee: Nelson Books, 1995, 2014), 236-240; Graham, *The Holy Spirit,*171-173, 222.

[17] William Franklin "Billy" Graham, Jr: Billy Graham was born in Charlotte, NC on November 7, 1918. Before his retirement due to declining health, he was one of the most prolific and successful Christian evangelists and preachers in history. He established a worldwide Christian ministry, authored books illuminating various aspects of the Christian faith, and was noted for his televised Billy Graham crusades. His life and ministry are memorialized at the impressive Billy Graham Library in Charlotte, NC where the admission is free. Graham's timeless, powerful, and, inspirational sermons are still available on Billy Graham Classics DVD at reasonable price at www.billygraham.org (Ruth's Attic, Billy Graham Bookstore).

[18] Graham, *The Holy Spirit,* 171.

[19] 1 John 4:1.

where the Word of God forbids you. Never. There are no exceptions."[20]

The Holy Spirit is truly holy and should be treated with reverence. Care should be taken not to vex or grieve the Holy Spirit for then God can become an enemy (Isaiah 63:10; *see also*, Matthew 12:31-32; Mark 3:28-29). One should also be careful not to take or cite the Spirit of Truth or Holy Spirit's name in vain for He is an aspect of God (Exodus 20:7).

One of the easiest ways to test what one may believe to be a prompting of the Holy Spirit is to consider whether the prompting adds to, subtracts from, violates, or contradicts the Scriptures.[21] In fact, Charles Stanley has noted that "the Word of God is the weapon the Holy Spirit uses to expose and destroy the lies confronting the children of God."[22] A true prompting of the Holy Spirit will be consistent with the Scriptures and what we know of Jesus Christ and God the Father as revealed in both the Old and New Testaments. A true prompting should also be consistent with the teachings of the early church fathers. Legitimate promptings of the Holy Spirit should honor God and reflect well on the Christian faith. And lastly, an authentic prompting of the Holy Spirit should improve our ability to live according to the teachings of the Bible and bring us closer to living a Christlike life under the lordship of Jesus Christ.

The Spirit of Truth or Holy Spirit is one-third of the triune Godhead and as such cannot contradict God, Jesus Christ, or the Holy Scriptures which were themselves inspired by the Holy Spirit.[23] Had not previous generations of ministers and theologians understood this basic fact, the received canons of the traditional,

---

[20] Stanley, *The Spirit-Filled Life*, 237.

[21] DeYoung, *The Holy Spirit*, 22.

[22] Stanley, *The Spirit-Filled Life*, 108.

[23] Deuteronomy 4:2; 12:32; Joshua 1:7-8; Isaiah 40:8; Proverbs 13:13; 30:5-6; Psalm 119:160; Matthew 5:19; John 10:35; 1 Corinthians 4:6; Galatians 1:8-9; 2 Peter 1:20; Titus 1:9-11; Revelation 22:18-19; Stanley, *The Spirit-Filled Life*, 232, 235, 239.

orthodox Christian church would have descended into doctrinal chaos hundreds of years ago. Through the Holy Spirit, a part of Jesus still lives within the heart of every believer, giving them over time a more complete understanding of His message and helping them to live according to His teachings. In this way, the Holy Spirit does "guide us into all truth." Although the entire Bible was inspired by the Holy Spirit, a particularly good example of this inspiration is the Gospel of John, which goes far beyond biography to gives us valuable additional theological insights about Jesus and the nature of His mission.

The fruit of the Spirit of Truth or Holy Spirit is love, joy, peace, patience, kindness, goodness, faithfulness, gentleness, and self-control.[24] It brings us the insight, courage, and strength to be effective representatives of our Christian faith. The Spirit of Truth (Holy Spirit, Helper, or Counselor) also grants the believer a greater appreciation for the nature of what is good, right, and true in a more universal sense. It constantly pulls the believer away from the things of darkness toward the light.

Examples of conventional worldly wisdom abound in modern society, which has grown very confident of its ability to determine the great issues of life, death, right, and wrong. We are thus taught in our culture that everyone will get to heaven somehow. The Bible says exactly the opposite.[25] We are taught that it doesn't matter what we believe as long as we believe something. Again, the Bible says the opposite.[26] The real message of the Bible is that it matters very much what we believe. [27]

---

[24] Galatians 5:22-23.

[25] Matthew 13:41-42; 25:31-41; John 3:36; Carson, D. A. "Matthew." In *Matthew and Mark*. Vol. 9 of *Expositor's Bible Commentary*, rev. ed., edited by Tremper Longman III and David E. Garland, p. 192.

[26] Matthew 10:32-33; John 8:24; 14:6; Acts 4:12; 1 Timothy 2:5; 1 John 5:12; 2 John 1:7-11.

[27] 2 Timothy 4:1-4; Hebrews 9:27-28.

In contemporary society, the following statement is generally unpopular and is definitely not politically correct, but it is, nonetheless, true. If one is honest, the act of being a Christian involves believing that all other religions, philosophies, and creeds are wrong where they differ from the fundamental doctrines of the traditional, orthodox Christian faith.[28] While other religions and philosophies may have worthy attributes, one who professes to be a true Christian cannot believe all religions, philosophies, and creeds are equal and be intellectually or spiritually honest.[29]

Jesus stated, "I am the way, the truth, and the life. No one comes to the Father except through me" (John 14:6). To believe otherwise is to "die in your sins" (John 8:24). Peter boldly affirmed, "Nor is there salvation in any other, for there is no other name under heaven given among men by which we must be saved" (Acts 4:12; *See also*, 1 Timothy 2:5-6). As Jesus taught the Pharisee Nicodemus, "He who believes in Him (Jesus) is not judged; he who does not believe has been judged already, because he has not believed in the name of the only begotten Son of God" (John 3:18). Tradition states that each of the Apostles, with the possible exception of John, met violent deaths bearing witness to the fact that salvation came to mankind through Jesus Christ and no other.

We are taught that God is a God of love and, therefore, no one will go to hell. We are not frequently taught that God is also a God of justice and accountability as well as love.[30] The picture we are often given of God is frequently more like a father from a 1950s television sitcom than the actual God of the Bible. We are not taught that one of the messages of the Old Testament is that God is holy to a degree that it is almost impossible for the modern mind to grasp, and that violations of His law are invariably punished both on an individual and a national basis.

---

[28] Lewis, *Mere Christianity*, 35.

[29] G.K. Chesterton, *The Everlasting Man* (Radford, VA: Wilder Publications, LLC., 2008 [1925]), 128; *See also*, 1 Corinthians 8: 6.

[30] Nahum 1:2-3; John 3:36; John 5:28-29; Matthew 7:21-23; Matthew 13:36-43.

In the New Testament, God is manifest through Jesus Christ as a fatherly, caring God of love, which is true. We are not, however, often reminded that in the New Testament Jesus, though kind and caring, also exhibits righteous anger[31] and speaks of a final judgment, heaven, and hell.[32] Jesus clearly believed that both Satan and hell are definitely real and very much to be avoided. As a matter of fact, Jesus mentions hell more often than heaven due to His wish that we avoid hell at all costs. The parable of the wheat and the tares and the parable of the dragnet are specific warnings from Jesus that there will be a final judgment and grim punishment for those found wanting.[33]

Jesus also notes that not everyone who claims to be a Christian will be admitted into the kingdom of heaven.[34] These are important details worth studying in greater depth for any person of faith who takes eternity seriously. The other option is to decide based upon our own individual hubris and pride that the Scriptures, which have survived across the centuries, are simply wrong or that God does not exist. To do this, however, we must be willing to wager our eternal future on the correctness of our position. Regardless of the beliefs one ultimately embraces, we all end up believing something. For the Christian, the infinitely wiser course is to embrace the wisdom and truth of the Bible. The seventeenth-century French mathematician, physicist, and philosopher, Blaise Pascal, made exactly this argument when he advised that, considering the eternal scope of the gamble, it is always better to wager "without hesitation" that God exists.[35]

---

[31] Matthew 21:12-13; Mark 3:5.

[32] Matthew 13:40-42, 49-50; 18:8-9; 25:41-46; Mark 9:43-48; Luke 12:5; John 5:28-29; *See also*, Graham, *The Holy Spirit*, 277.

[33] Matthew 13:36-50.

[34] Matthew 7:21-23; Luke 13:24-28.

[35] John Hicks, *Philosophy of Religion*, ed. Elizabeth and Monroe Beardsley (Englewood Cliffs, N.J.: Prentice-Hall, Inc, 1963),64; Blaise Pascal, *Pensées*, tr. F. W.

For the sincere person of faith, there is no compelling reason to disbelieve the Scriptures or to begin rewriting them to suit our twenty-first-century culture. God intended the Bible to be a handbook containing the laws of life from which we are, ideally, never to deviate.[36] It was never intended to be merely a menu from which we were to select the entrees we felt like honoring and ignore the rest.[37] As we have already seen, the Bible we have today is essentially identical to the words of the earliest sources yet discovered. As already referenced, an extremely persuasive case has now been made that the entire New Testament was written within the living memory of the eyewitnesses (or people who had known them) of the events described. There is simply no compelling reason to believe that the Bible is anything less than what it purports to be, namely, an accurate account of God's fellowship with and direction for the human race.

The Holy Bible is in fact worthy of belief, and it is just as relevant today as it was thousands of years ago. In the final analysis, the most plausible reason for denying the Christian faith may be that its promise simply seems too good to be true. If, however, one dares to believe that God exists, that He cares, and that something wondrous and good can happen to mankind, then the Christian creed[38] offers more hope than any other in human

---

Trotter (London: J. M. Dent & Sons, and New York: E. P. Dutton & Company., Inc., 1932), No. 233, p. 67.

[36] Joshua 1:7-8; Matthew 5:17-19; Luke 16:17.

[37] Graham, *The Holy Spirit*, 40.

[38] The Nicene Creed is a succinct statement of the Christian faith dating from A.D. 325 which has the distinction of being recognized by Protestant, Anglican, Roman Catholic, and Eastern Orthodox churches. It states as follows: I believe in one God the Father Almighty, Maker of heaven and earth, and of all things visible and invisible. And I believe in one Lord, Jesus Christ, the only-begotten Son of God, born of the Father before all Ages, God of God, Light of Light, true God of true God; begotten, not made, of one substance with the Father, by whom all things were made, who for us and for our salvation came down from heaven. And He became flesh by the Holy Spirit of the Virgin Mary and was made man. He was also crucified for us, suffered under Pontius Pilate, and was buried. And on the

history. The life, death, resurrection, and promise of Jesus Christ constitute the crowning moments in the history of humanity and the greatest miracle of all time.

The main message of the New Testament is that, notwithstanding all of the disappointments in the Old Testament, God, in the New Testament, stretches forth His hand through Jesus Christ to offer eternal life to anyone who sincerely repents of their sins and has the faith to accept eternal life through Jesus. This promise is made possible by virtue of Jesus' atoning sacrifice for our sins upon the cross.[39] Jesus warns that those who reject Him (Jesus) as the Son of God[40] and, thereby, God's offer of eternal life through Jesus,[41] will be judged under the law.[42] Jesus grimly noted that "not the smallest letter or stroke" of that law shall pass away or be overlooked.[43] He also stated that the "Scripture cannot be broken" (John 10:35). Jesus went on to say, "Whoever then annuls one of the least of these commandments, and teaches others to do the same, shall be called least in the kingdom of heaven; but whoever keeps and teaches them, he shall be called great in the kingdom of heaven."[44]

---

third day He rose again in accordance with the Scriptures. He ascended into heaven and sits at the right hand of the Father. He will come again in glory to judge the living and the dead. And of his kingdom there will be no end. And I believe in the Holy Spirit, the Lord and Giver of life, who proceeds from the Father and Son, who together with the Father and the Son is adored and glorified, and who spoke through the prophets, and one holy Christian (the ancient texts use the word Catholic to mean universal here), and Apostolic Church. I confess one baptism for the forgiveness of sins. And I await the resurrection of the dead and the life of the world to come. Amen.

[39] Romans 3:23-25; 6:23.

[40] John 3: 18, 10:30, 14:6; Matthew 10:32-33.

[41] 1 John 5:11-12.

[42] The Ten Commandments, the Law of Moses, the Prophets, and the additional teachings of Jesus Christ.

[43] Matthew 5:17-18; Luke 16:17.

[44] Matthew 5:19.

Clearly, it was not Jesus' intent to back away from the great moral and ethical standards of the Old Testament. In fact, his standards for morality were considerably stricter than even those of the scribes and Pharisees as illustrated by his negative views on anger, adultery, and divorce.[45] Of like mind, the Apostle Paul also testified that he believed all things "written in the Law and the Prophets."[46] Billy Graham reminds us that "Jesus never once told us to doubt the difficult passages of the Old Testament Scriptures." Graham points out that "time after time Jesus (and the New Testament writers) quoted the Scriptures as authoritative and the very Word of God."[47]

The Old Testament is in fact the foundation upon which the New Testament is built. It is difficult to fully understand the grand cosmic wonder of New Testament salvation without being familiar with the truth and prophecy of the Old Testament from which it springs. Indeed, the Apostle Paul goes so far as to note that the Christian believer is a wild olive branch grafted onto the cultivated Jewish olive tree, because Christianity also draws life from the root of God's original covenantal promises to the Jewish patriarchs (Romans 11:17-18). Paul further notes that "if you belong to Christ, then you are Abraham's descendants, heirs according to the promise" (Galatians 3:29). William Barclay states that Paul was reminding the Christian that "there would have been no such thing as Christianity unless there had been Judaism first."[48] Paul thus warns the Christian to feel no arrogance against the Jew. New Testament scholar Michael G. Vanlaningham affirms that the fact

---

[45] Matthew 5: 20, 21-22, 27-28, 31-32, 19:4-9; Mark 10:2-12; *See also*, Carson, D. A. "Matthew." In *Matthew and Mark*. Vol. 9 of *The Expositor's Bible Commentary*, rev. ed., edited by Tremper Longman III and David E. Garland, pp. 177-179. (Grand Rapids: Zondervan, 2012).

[46] Acts 24:14.

[47] Graham, *The Holy Spirit*, 38-39.

[48] William Barclay, *The Letter to the Romans*, 177.

that the Christian believer benefits from the Abrahamic covenant makes anti-Semitism "ludicrous."[49]

For those who have not reviewed the Ten Commandments[50] lately, it will quickly become evident upon doing so that there is no one who has not violated one or more of them probably multiple times. No one is, therefore, good enough to approach a holy God based on the efficacy of their works.[51] All, including even David, Israel's greatest king, have fallen short of the glory of God.[52]

In essence, the promise of the New Testament is that those who sincerely repent[53] of their sins, and accept Jesus Christ as the son of God, believing that He died upon the cross for our transgressions and was raised from the dead, will bypass the judgment under the law and be accepted into the family of God. Once accepted into the family of God, one becomes a child of God receiving eternal life.[54] Those who trust in Jesus will thus receive mercy as a freely given gift rather than the justice reserved for everyone else. It is an enormously liberating and comforting proposition. It is, in fact, good news, which is what the word *gospel* means. As the Apostle Paul stated, "There is now no condemnation for those who are in Christ Jesus . . ."[55]

Billy Graham distinguishes between the confession or acknowledgment of one's sins and true repentance, which is a renunciation or conscious turning away from one's sins.[56] The

---

[49] Vanlaningham, Michael G., "Romans." *The Moody Bible Commentary*, edited by Michael Rydelnik and Michael Vanlaningham, 1763. (Chicago: Moody Publishers, 2014).

[50] Exodus 20:3-17.

[51] Galatians 2:16; Ephesians 2:8-9.

[52] Romans 3:23.

[53] Psalm 7:12; Matthew 3:2; Mark 1:15; Luke 17:3; Acts 3:19; Acts 17:30.

[54] John 5:24; 6:39-40; Romans 8:15-17.

[55] Romans 8:1.

[56] Graham, *The Holy Spirit*, 136.

sincerity of one's faith and repentance should be proven by a renunciation of one's prior sins and the performance of "deeds appropriate to repentance" as one makes the attempt to lead a Christlike life that conforms to the will of God.[57] We are to hear "the word in an honest and good heart, and hold it fast, and bear fruit with perseverance" (Luke 8:15). Jesus stated that the members of His family would be those "who hear the Word of God and do it" (Luke 8:21).

> Not everyone who says to Me, 'Lord, Lord,' will enter the kingdom of heaven, but he who does the will of My Father who is in heaven will enter. Many will say to Me on that day, 'Lord, Lord, did we not prophesy in Your name, and in your name cast out demons, and in Your name perform many miracles?' "And then I will declare to them, 'I never knew you; depart from Me you who practice lawlessness.'[58]

Jesus goes even further to state that "unless one is born again he cannot see the kingdom of God" (John 3:3). The Apostle Paul states that we are to "walk no longer just as the Gentiles also walk," but, in reference to our former manner of life, we are to "lay aside the old self" and "put on the new self, which is the likeness of God" (Ephesians 4:17-24). When Jesus healed the man who had been crippled for thirty-eight years and forgave the woman taken in adultery, he cautioned them both to "sin no more" (John 5:14; 8:11). God thus grants forgiveness as a free gift of grace through belief in Jesus Christ, but He is still Holy and will never approve evil or look with favor upon wickedness (Habakkuk 1:13; *See also*, Hebrews 6:4-8;10:26-31; Matthew 13:19-23). God specifically commanded Moses to tell the children of Israel: "You shall be holy, for I the Lord your God am holy" (Leviticus 19:2).

---

[57] Acts 26:20.

[58] Matthew 7:21-23.

Even devout, faithful, and well-intentioned Christians will continue to sin in various ways until taken to heaven because absolute perfection will never be achieved in this life. A cynical, entitled, deliberate, calculating, and willful pattern of ongoing sin is, however, a more serious matter (Hebrews 6:4-8;10:26-31). One of the great fallacies of our time is the belief that one can purport to accept Jesus with one's lips while clinging to an ungodly lifestyle of rebellion, pride, selfishness, addiction, drunkenness, violence, or sexual sin and hope to be saved.[59] The Apostle Paul was adamant that individuals who continue the sins of their pre-conversion lifestyles will not inherit the kingdom of God (1 Corinthians 6:9-11; Galatians 5:19-26; Ephesians 5:3-6; Romans 6:1-2; 11-16).[60] New Testament scholar William W. Klein notes that Paul is not implying "that those once transferred from darkness to light can revert back to darkness by their sinful behavior," but, rather, may be suggesting that "failure to live as children of the light" may indicate that they have never really been saved in the first place.[61] This takes us back to the sincerity of one's original faith and repentance. On this point, William Barclay reminds us that we "often confess God with our lips and deny him with our lives."[62] Paul is blunter when he refers to those who "profess to know God, but by their deeds deny Him, being detestable and disobedient and worthless for any good deed" (Titus 1:16).

---

[59] Matthew 7:19-27; Luke 13:25-28; Romans 6:1-6;15-23; 1 Corinthians 5:11-13; 6:9-11; Galatians 5:16-25; Ephesians 4:17-32; 5:1-17; Thessalonians 4:3-8; 1 John 2:3-7; *See also*, Lewis, *Mere Christianity*, 207; *See also*, Carson, D. A. "Matthew." In *Matthew and Mark*. Vol. 9 of *The Expositor's Bible Commentary*, 229-231; *See also*, William Barclay, *The Gospel of Luke*, rev. ed., 183-184; *See also*, Graham, *The Holy Spirit*, 107.

[60] *See also*, Robert A. J. Gagnon, *The Bible and Homosexual Practice, Texts and Hermeneutics* (Nashville: Abingdon Press, 2001), 338.

[61] Klein, William W. "Ephesians." In *Ephesians ⮂Philemon*. Vol. 12 of *The Expositor's Bible Commentary*, rev. ed., edited by Tremper Longman III and David E. Garland, p. 135. (Grand Rapids: Zondervan, 2012).

[62] William Barclay, *The Gospel of Matthew*, Vol. 1, rev. ed., 290.

The clear message of the New Testament is that the Christian is not to conform to the relaxed standards of contemporary society. The Apostle Paul commanded that the Christian "not be bound together with unbelievers," believing that it was impossible for a religion of light to be in partnership with lawlessness and darkness (2 Corinthians 6:14). When Christian values and morality differ from those of contemporary society, the Christian is not to conform with unbelievers, but rather to "come out from their midst and be separate" (2 Corinthians 6:17). Paul explained that he did not mean by this that the Christian is to withdraw physically from society, but rather that the Christian must stand firm in the teachings of Jesus Christ and the Bible without compromise (1 Corinthians 5:9-10).

Paul acknowledges that the church cannot determine the beliefs, ethics, values, and morality of society at large, but expects the church to maintain the purity of its own beliefs and thereby its opportunity to be a positive example. Paul lays out a clear expectation that the church is to make certain that the behavior of church members is consistent with the teachings of Jesus Christ and conforms to biblical ethical and moral standards (1 Corinthians 5:11-13; *See also*, Matthew18:15-17). For Paul, the ideal goal is to strive to "cleanse ourselves" from sins of the body and the spirit, "perfecting holiness in the fear of God" (2 Corinthians 7:1). Paul went on to note, with respect to the sins he had listed in 1 Corinthians 6:9-10, that some individuals belonging to the churches in Corinth and Colossae had once walked in such sins before putting them aside as part of their new life as Christians (1 Corinthians 6:11; Colossians 3:7-10).[63] Paul thus documented the fact that the Christian church has always been open to the diversity of anyone who accepts Jesus Christ, sincerely repents of their sins, and makes the attempt to lead a Christlike life.

---

[63] 1 Corinthians 6:9-10, "Or do you not know that the unrighteous will not inherit the kingdom of God? Do not be deceived; neither fornicators, nor idolaters, nor adulterers, nor effeminate, nor homosexuals, nor thieves, nor the covetous, nor drunkards, nor revilers, nor swindlers, will inherit the kingdom of God."

Many think that because they believe in one God they are saved, but the Bible states: "You do well. Even the demons believe—and tremble! But do you want to know, O foolish man, that faith without works is dead?" (James 2:19-20 NKJV). The faith by which the Christian is saved is to be authenticated or "perfected" by the example and works of his or her new life (James 2:17-19). In this manner, Christians become "ambassadors for Christ, as though God were making an appeal through us" (2 Corinthians 5:20). Thus, the appropriate role for the Christian is to be an ambassador from Christ's church to the world by example and deed, rather than an ambassador from the world to Christ's church. This is a critical distinction often ignored in modern times. The great nineteenth century minister Charles Haddon Spurgeon expressed this crucial point slightly differently when he stated: "We shall not adjust our Bible to the age; but before we have done with it, by God's grace, we shall adjust the age to the Bible." The Christian's aim should always be to adjust the times in which one lives to the Bible, rather than the Bible to the times in which one lives. God Himself commanded that we "learn not the way of the [heathen] nations" (Jeremiah 10:2). This takes us back to the Apostle Paul's often repeated command that we stand firm in the faith.[64]

Jesus means for his followers to change and make the attempt to follow His example (Matthew 5:48; Romans 12:1-2; 2 Corinthians 5:5-20).[65] When Jesus told his followers to "be perfect, as your heavenly Father is perfect," he was not kidding (Matthew 5:48). Jesus advised that anyone seeking to follow Him "calculate the cost" to see if one has the commitment to complete a process of transformation that will last for the rest of one's life and beyond.[66] During this process, every believer walks with Jesus through the power of the Holy Spirit. When we stumble, or fail (as everyone

---

[64] 1 Corinthians 15:2, 16:13; Galatians 5:1; Philippians 4:1; 1 Thessalonians 3:8; Titus 1:9.

[65] *See*, William Barclay, *The Letter to the Romans*, 184-186.

[66] Luke 14:28; Lewis, *Mere Christianity*, 202-205.

does) in our journey to live according the teachings of the Bible and fulfill Jesus' intent for our lives, He is always there to help us to our feet if we are sincere of heart (Matthew 18:21-35). In this sense, the only way one can fail in the Christian life is to give up and turn away from Jesus, because, as long as we are trying, He will never give up on us. He simply asks that we "come to our senses" (Luke 15:17), have faith, rise from our mat of earthly sin, and make the attempt to walk in His ways and teachings. He knows that we will not achieve perfection in this life, but He wants us to see this ongoing process of self-improvement as a worthy goal. He wants us to care enough to make the attempt. It is our willingness to take up His cross and attempt to lead a moral Christian life that is of critical importance. Jesus' attitude is beautifully illustrated in his parables of the lost sheep, the lost coin, and the prodigal son (Luke 15:4-32).

The Christian life is thus meant to be a process of sanctification as one constantly tries, with the help of the Holy Spirit or Spirit of Truth, to become more like Jesus (2 Peter 1:3-11; 2 Corinthians 3:7-18; 1 Thessalonians 4:3-8). C. S. Lewis goes so far as to say that this slow process of learning to become a child of God is "the whole of Christianity."[67] If individual Christians had not understood the need to be transformed by the morality of the Bible and the teachings of Jesus Christ from the beginning of our faith, today's world would differ very little from the ancient pagan world condemned by Jesus and the Apostles.

---

[67] Lewis, *Mere Christianity*, 195; 199.

Chapter 6: An Ancient Burden?

Our popular culture often creates the impression that the principles and teachings of Christianity are an ancient burden inconsistent with the realities of modern life. Our popular culture fails to convey an accurate grasp of either the God described in the Old Testament or of God's further revelation, through Jesus Christ, in the New Testament. The misinformation floating about as to what the Bible does and does not say goes to the heart of our collective ethical and moral consciousness, both on an individual and a national level. The Founding Fathers knew what the Scriptures stated, and this knowledge shaped their dreams for the country they were creating. Our current moral confusion is leading us far astray from those early dreams on many issues of grave consequence.

To illustrate the above, how many of us have read Jeremiah 32:35 wherein God says through Jeremiah, "They built the high places of Baal that are in the valley of Ben-hinnom to cause their sons and their daughters to pass through the fire to Molech, which I had not commanded them nor had it entered My mind that they should do this abomination, to cause Judah to sin"? God says through Ezekiel, "Moreover, you took your sons and daughters whom you had borne to Me and sacrificed them to idols to be devoured. Were your harlotries so small a matter? You slaughtered My children and offered them up to idols by causing them to pass through the fire."[1] Speaking of such practices, the Psalmist explains, "Thus they became unclean in their practices, and played the harlot in their deeds."[2]

When most people read the passages noted above, their initial thought will probably be that human sacrifice, at least, is not a sin our culture has to be particularly concerned about. For many, however, this sense of self-satisfaction will shortly thereafter be dimmed when they recall the issue of abortion. We may not be sacrificing our children to Molech, but it could be argued that we

---

[1] Ezekiel 16:20-21.

[2] Psalm 106:37-39.

are sacrificing them to expediency. Today, King Herod the Great of Judea still looms large in the popular imagination as both a tyrant and a butcher primarily due to his massacre of the infants as chronicled in Matthew 2:16. We think that such wicked behavior would never be tolerated in our own time, and yet, abortion is tolerated on an industrial scale. The Bible teaches that claims that we were misled or did not know will not avail us at the final reckoning.[3] T. S. Eliot wisely believed that "the World will constantly confuse the *right* with the expedient" unless the Church is resolute in its definition of what is *wrong*.[4] In fact, the resolute defense of the Christian faith and the absolute and timeless nature of its moral and ethical teachings is one of the primary functions of the Christian Church.

The modern secular critic often forgets that the cultural stability for which Western civilization is famous has always been rooted in the moral imperatives of its traditional, orthodox Judeo-Christian heritage. Judeo-Christian values, ethics, morality, and faith cannot be discarded without fatally compromising the peace, security, freedom, tolerance, and opportunity for which Western civilization is famous. A quick examination of those parts of the world that do not share Judeo-Christian values readily proves the truth of this premise.

Over and over in the Bible we see that God expects the Ten Commandments to be honored and that He absolutely will not tolerate pride, idolatry (the worship of other gods), human sacrifice, and sexual immorality or aberration.[5] Of these, the greatest sin may

---

[3] Proverbs 24:10-12.

[4] Eliot, *Christianity & Culture*, 76.

[5] The following citations are not meant to be all inclusive. *Pride*: Proverbs 16:18; Luke 18:10-14; Matthew 23:5-12; Mark 7:22; 1 John 2:16; Proverbs 21:4; James 5:6; Jeremiah 17:23; 19:15. *Idolatry*: Exodus 20:3-5; Exodus 32:7-10; Leviticus 19:4; Deuteronomy 27:15; 1 John 5:21; 1 Corinthians 5:11; 10:7,14. *Human Sacrifice*: Exodus 20:13; Leviticus 18:21; 20:2-5; Deuteronomy 12:31; 18:10; Jeremiah 32:35; Ezekiel 16:20-21. *Sexual Aberration*: Exodus 22:19; Leviticus 18:6-18; 18:22-24; 20:11-23; Deuteronomy 27:20-23; Genesis 2:24; Genesis 19:1-25; Matthew 5:17-19; Matthew 19:4-6; Romans 1:26-28; 1 Corinthians 6:9; 1 Timothy 1:10; *See also,*

be that of pride for it leads to the self-will that makes all other sin possible. As a matter of fact, pride could possibly constitute the sin against the Holy Spirit, which alone of all sins will not be forgiven.[6] Only pride and hubris have the capacity to so harden the human heart that one can no longer tell right from wrong. Only pride and hubris can embolden one to falsely claim that the Holy Spirit has led him or her to the knowledge that parts of the Holy Scriptures are wrong and need to be revised or discarded. A person possessed by excessive pride may eventually become incapable of repenting of sin because he or she gradually becomes incapable of recognizing it.

Once pride gains control of one's character and one begins to see one's self as truly important, as opposed to a servant, the virtues begin to fall away one by one in the interest of expediency. Those who violate life's appropriate timing,[7] ethical priorities, or the natural order of things will end up sadder for it in the end. This is almost a universal rule. Ultimately, no one truly gets away with anything in the long term.

Today, we make policy decisions on issues such as those above as though we do not know what the God of the Bible would think about such things, His view is irrelevant, or we do not care. Most attorneys will quickly tell you that ignorance of the law is no defense. While it is true that the law of God is not the law of our land, there is no doubt that in the beginning the law of God was the

---

Verbrugge, Verlyn D. "1 Corinthians." In *Romans-Galatians*. Vol. 11 of *The Expositor's Bible Commentary*, rev. ed., edited by Tremper Longman III and David E. Garland, pp.308-309, (Grand Rapids: Zondervan, 2012); *See also*, Köstenberger, Andreas. "1 Timothy." In *Ephesians-Philemon*. Vol. 12 of *The Expositor's Bible Commentary*, rev. ed., edited by Tremper Longman III and David E. Garland, pp.502-504, (Grand Rapids: Zondervan, 2012).; *See also*, Robert A. J. Gagnon, *The Bible and Homosexual Practice, Texts and Hermeneutics* (Nashville: Abingdon Press, 2001).

[6] Matthew 3:28-29.

[7] Ecclesiastes 3:1-8.

basis for the Common Law and its evolution into our own.[8] In his work, *A History of the English Speaking Peoples*, Winston Churchill traced the Judeo-Christian influence upon the English Common Law back to King Alfred's Book of Laws, or Dooms.[9] Sir William Blackstone, a devout Christian as well as a noted eighteenth-century jurist, reflected this view in his four-volume treatise on the Common Law entitled *Commentaries on the Laws of England*. This historic work was extremely influential upon our Founding Fathers and subsequent leaders throughout the nineteenth and early twentieth centuries.

Blackstone stated that man is "subject to the laws of his creator." The "will" of mankind's maker is called the "law of nature," wherein God "laid down certain immutable laws of human nature" which include the "laws of good and evil." The happiness of the individual is thus inextricably "interwoven" with the "laws of eternal justice." The law of nature, being "dictated by God Himself," is superior to any other obligation. To enable man, whose ability to discern and reason acutely has been corrupted, to understand more specifically those aspects of God's greater law of nature that applied directly to him, God was "pleased at sundry times and in divers manners" to clarify His expectations through "immediate and direct revelation" in the "revealed or divine" law which is "found only in the Holy Scriptures." This "revealed law" is to mankind "of infinitely more authority" than the larger body of natural law. In summary, therefore, all human laws depend upon the "law of nature and the law of revelation" and "no human laws should be suffered to contradict these."[10]

---

[8] Winston S. Churchill, *A History of the English Speaking Peoples, The Birth of Britain*, 4 vols. (New York: Dorset Press, 1990 [1956]), 1:120-122. Winston Churchill traced the influence of the Mosaic code and Christian principles upon the evolution of the English Common Law to King Alfred's Book of Laws or Dooms circa AD 893.

[9] Ibid.

[10] 1 W. Blackstone, *Commentaries*, Sec.2, "Of the Nature of Laws In General", 39-43.

Blackstone was born into the middle class and he was often in poor health. Success came slowly for him. He persevered and overcame all obstacles to be admitted to the Bar. He was, in many respects, a common man with a common man's practical understanding of the Common Law as a mechanism upon which the wheels of the English-speaking world turned. In the grand cosmic scheme of things, his intuitive understanding that all law evolving from the law of nature or the revealed law (as opposed to matters of a more "indifferent" character such as trade laws) is ultimately derived from God is theologically more mature and astute than the more secular view that tends to dominate in our own time.

The reference source most often cited in the documents of our Founding Fathers was the Bible, followed by the philosopher Charles Montesquieu, followed by William Blackstone, followed by John Locke.[11] If one has read even a little of Blackstone, his influence can easily be identified in documents like the Declaration of Independence. William Blackstone used the talents of intellect, organization, composition, and writing given to him by God to fulfill God's purpose for his life.

With respect to the law of God, on any given controversial issue, many will state that the Bible is not really saying what it appears, on its face, to be saying. There is, however, an old saying in the law that a "paper writing says what it says." It is not God's intent to shroud His laws and commandments in hidden truths or mystery.[12] When He tells us through the Scriptures what behaviors are godly and wise and which behaviors to avoid, that is what He means. He does not change His mind to suit the shifting sands and tides of our contemporary morality. A red flag is immediately raised when anyone tells a common man or woman that the Bible is not really saying what it plainly does say, or that it is actually saying something that it plainly does not say. In such instances, the

---

[11] David Barton, *America's Godly Heritage*, 3rd ed. (Aledo, TX: Wallbuilder Press, 2007), p. 23.

[12] Matthew 10:27.

notions of common sense and credibility by which we govern our lives are simply and obviously violated. We are not accustomed to accepting such sophistry in our workplace or business, so why would we accept it in our spiritual life when eternity is at stake?

These issues have been explored not in the expectation that the reader will necessarily accept all of the conclusions reached, but to pique the reader's interest in learning more about the contents of the Bible and forming his or her own informed opinion with respect to the eternal issues with which it deals. We live in a time of charlatans, demagogues, and false prophets. Many of the people in our culture to whom we have traditionally looked for moral or ethical guidance are now marching to the beat of the secularist, progressive drum with political and social agendas that have little to do with one's individual salvation. Such sources can no longer be granted the unquestioned trust given in simpler times. Sometimes those who have lost their way even hide behind walls upon which the cross itself is hung.

More than ever before, we need to familiarize ourselves with the Scriptures and reach our own conclusions. That is exactly what the common men and women did who crossed the Atlantic Ocean in small ships like the *Mayflower*—when such a voyage was tantamount to space exploration—to found this country on godly principles. In the end, we will each be held accountable for the decisions we make with respect to this life. That being the case, we should make those decisions based upon our own informed interpretations of the Scriptures rather than the hearsay and heresy of our popular culture. The Bible is truly the indispensable guide for those who take their lives and eternity seriously.

In conclusion, one of those little-known stories from the Old Testament is illustrative of the times in which it could be argued that we find ourselves today. After the death of King Solomon, the Kingdom of Israel was divided into Judah, which contained Jerusalem and the temple; and Israel, which eventually contained Samaria. Both kingdoms had an extremely checkered history after the division, suffered under many evil kings, and eventually lost their independence. In the latter days of the Kingdom of Judah, a good king came to the throne after two very bad kings. These bad kings had violated the Ten Commandments, introduced the idols of foreign gods into the temple built by Solomon, and allowed the temple to fall into disrepair. The good king's name was Josiah, and the Bible says that he did what was right in the sight of the Lord and walked in the ways of King David.[13]

King Josiah commanded that the House of the Lord, the temple, be repaired.[14] During the course of the repairs and the cleaning of the temple, the high priest Hilkiah discovered the long-lost book of the law of the Lord given through Moses. When the manuscript was read to good King Josiah and he saw how far his kingdom had strayed, he was filled with fear of God's wrath.[15] He immediately ordered the book to be read to all the people of Judah, and the inhabitants of Jerusalem great and small.[16] He dedicated the rest of his reign to spiritual as well as other reforms which averted Judah's conquest during his lifetime.[17]

King Josiah was a very wise king and his story illustrates a principle, often ignored by both individuals and modern leaders, which states that "the fear of the Lord is the beginning of wisdom."[18] King Josiah realized that the commandments of God and the great moral truths contained in them are not relative to the moral climate of a given generation, but eternal just as God is eternal and unchanging. He realized that a culture that loses sight of the moral compass by which its original course was plotted will not long prosper.

---

[13] 2 Kings 22:2.

[14] 2 Kings 22:4-5.

[15] 2 Kings 22:8-13.

[16] 2 Kings 23:1-2.

[17] 2 Kings 23:3.

[18] Proverbs 9:10.

Chapter 7: Four Great Secrets

People search for the secret to life, but it is actually bound up in more like four secrets. These secrets are not profound or difficult, but most of mankind manages to stumble at some point in their lives over one or more of them. These secrets escape us because they are hidden directly in front of our eyes. We are so conditioned to look at the forest of life that we forget to notice the trees. These almost obvious secrets hold the answers to (1) the purpose of life, (2) the nature of love and marriage, (3) patience and self-control, and (4) the selection of one's career or life mission.

Secret 1—Purpose

The first and foremost secret deals with the meaning of life itself. Why are we here? What is the purpose of life? So much of life seems futile and pointless; we ask ourselves if there is an overriding purpose. There is a purpose and it is such that virtually no experience in life is wasted. That purpose is that we are placed here to develop our faith and learn to love. Every value and every experience that contributes to making life worth living is to some degree predicated in terms of this emotion. Love of all emotions stands uniquely astride both worlds of the human experience for it contains elements of both the corporeal and the divine.

It is difficult to love that which we cannot see—the intangible. It is, therefore, difficult for many to love God. Yet, God has no intention of sharing eternity with individuals who do not know how to love Him or anyone else.[1] In the Bible, John states that "the one who does not love his brother whom he has seen, cannot love God whom he has not seen."[2] When Jesus was asked which commandment was the first of all, he answered:

---

[1] John 13:34-35.

[2] 1 John 4:20.

The foremost is, 'Hear, O Israel! The Lord our God is one Lord: And you shall love the Lord your God with all your heart, and with all your soul, and with all your mind, and with all your strength.' The second is this, 'You shall love your neighbor as yourself.' There is no other commandment greater than these.[3]

In Romans 13:10, Paul states, "Love does no wrong to a neighbor; therefore, love is the fulfillment of the law." This theme runs throughout the Bible. As C. S. Lewis noted, however, this kind of love can be difficult to achieve at times.[4] The ability, therefore, to love our wives, husbands, children, friends, and neighbors teaches us to love. This capacity to love brings us beyond a selfish preoccupation with ourselves and into the presence of something larger and more important than our own destiny.

Some people state that life is so full of misery, pain, and injustice that there can be no God and no meaning to life. In reality, the opposite is true. The evidence of God is all about us in the beautiful functionality of this essentially benevolent universe. The evidence of divine origin and purpose is further evident in our capacity for sublime emotions like love, honor, and self-sacrifice that unaccountably rise above the baser realities of this existence. With all of eternity hanging in the balance, if we can traverse a lifetime of tribulations and sorrow, and still meet God at the end with love and faith in our hearts, then we have passed the test of this existence.[5] If at the end, our hearts have been hardened and filled with bitterness or hatred, then we have learned nothing from our life and have failed the test. Ultimately, therefore, life is a

---

[3] Mark 12:29-31.

[4] Lewis, *Mere Christianity*, 131-132.

[5] 1 Corinthians 13:1-3.

process of learning to care about others more than ourselves—of learning to love.[6]

In summary, God is the Alpha and the Omega, the Beginning and the End.[7] God is also love.[8] In love we thus find the beginning and the end of all that is truly meaningful in this life and the next.

Secret 2—Love

For most of us, one of the most valuable experiences in life with respect to nurturing and maturing our ability to love is the institution of marriage. The socially sanctioned union between a man and a woman[9] has been viewed by virtually all societies since the dawn of time as an honorable, wholly natural, and desirable state. So, when we speak of love within the context of a man and a woman spending their entire lives together what are we talking about? What is this type of love?

In our culture, we have been vastly confused by movies, novels, and television as to the nature and definition of love. Our modern divorce rate can probably be attributed more to this cultural confusion as to the nature of love than any other single factor. The shocking and simple truth is that true love is not the heated, obsessive, romantic love we see portrayed everywhere about us. Unfortunately, romantic love is more grounded in illusion and hormones than in the true love born of a genuine commitment. As we all know, illusions frequently cannot survive the cold, harsh light of life's ongoing challenges. This fact is at the heart of romantic love's often transitory nature. Romantic love, ideally, should be a prelude to real or true love. When it is not, the results can be disastrous in terms of future happiness.

---

[6] 1 Corinthians 13:13; Philippians 2:2-4.

[7] Revelation 1:8.

[8] 1 John 4:7-9.

[9] Matthew 19:4-6.

If real love is not romantic love, then what is it? Although too young to fully grasp and accept it at the time, I was blessed to be given insight on this point while attending the Wake Forest University School of Law. At this time, North Carolina's foremost expert in Family Law was Robert E. Lee (not the general). Although then an old man, Lee was full of energy and accumulated wisdom. He still taught a full load of classes, which included the class in Family Law. One day during class discussion some probably immature comment on the part of a member of our class prompted Lee to expound on the nature of true love. Although approximately forty years have since transpired, his words are still a vivid memory:

> You young people today do not even know what real love is. Based on what you have seen in the movies and the media, you think love is rockets and fireworks exploding in the sky of passion. That is not the case. Real love is something of a quieter and gentler persuasion. Real or true love is simply eternal friendship between a man and a woman. The quest for love is a quest for someone with whom you can go through an entire life in mutual friendship and respect. Many people today divorce several times only to end up much poorer, with someone no better than their first spouse, simply because they did not understand the true nature of love.

Lee must have known something about the true nature of love, because he remained married to the same woman throughout his long life, and frequently punctuated his lectures with loving references to his wife, Louise, as "she who must be obeyed."

Finding lasting love is, therefore, all about finding someone whom one can really like and trust. It simply is not enough to love someone; one must be able to like them after the lights of youth and passion have faded. It involves finding a kindred spirit with whom you share a commonality of interests and desires. One of the joys of life is sharing the things that interest and delight you with your beloved. If one's companion in life does not share one's interests in the things that truly matter to one, then it makes for a very lonely and complicated life indeed. It is, therefore, possible to be married with children and yet be dying of loneliness. In such a case, one has a wife or husband, but no friend—no companion.

Most of my working life was spent in a community hospital where, ultimately, there were few permanent secrets. This circumstance afforded plenty of opportunities to observe the ebb and flow of human relationships. In this microcosm of ordinary life, it quickly became evident that the happiest and most idyllic marriages resulted from the marriage of true friends. One of the most happily married women in the hospital once stated that she had dated a lot of guys looking for passion, but something was always missing. One day it occurred to her to marry her best friend simply because they always had a good time together, shared the same interests, respected each other, and met each other's emotional needs. She said, "It suddenly occurred to me that there was no rule against marrying my best friend." She noted that "when our bodies and passion fade, we will still be friends, because our love is based upon the aspects of life that last."

It is probably true that more spouses leave their marriage for companionship rather than sex. Romantic love alone often fades within a few years or less. If, however, that love is planted in the rich soil of a true and caring friendship, based upon kindred spirits and mutual interests, it will flower into something beautiful that will last forever.

When most people look back across their lives, they may note that they have kept track of their friends, or at least mourn their loss, but how many individuals know what happened to the various people with whom they have had a purely romantic or sexual relationship? Love without companionship and friendship can lead to loneliness, self-pity, and creeping bitterness. This is the antithesis of what life is supposed to be about; i.e., learning to love and care about more than ourselves. So ideally, the purpose of marriage is to enhance or help us nurture our ability to love. That is the standard by which we should judge our relationships; do they promote love or threaten our ability to love? Do they make us better or bitter? Do our relationships lead us out of a fatal preoccupation with ourselves toward a greater loving of everyone? The ultimate objective is to eventually be capable of loving everyone, which is for most of us an admittedly daunting task.

Jesus makes the point just discussed clear, however, when he states:

> But I say to you, love your enemies and pray for those who persecute you, so that you may be sons of your Father who is in heaven; for He causes His sun to rise on the evil and the good and sends rain on the righteous and the unrighteous. For if you love those who love you, what reward do you have? Do not even the tax collectors do the same? If you greet only your brothers, what more are you doing than others? Do not even the Gentiles do the same? Therefore, you are to be perfect, as your heavenly Father is perfect.[10]

As noted above, this is no small or insignificant challenge. The Apostle Paul described love as follows:

> Love is patient, love is kind and is not jealous; love does not brag and is not arrogant, does not act unbecomingly; it does not seek its own, is not provoked, does not take into account a wrong suffered, does not rejoice in unrighteousness, but rejoices with the truth; bears all things, believes all things, hopes all things, endures all things.[11]

When one considers it, these words are a fairly good description of an ideal eternal friendship. Few purely romantic liaisons can rise to these ideals, but a marriage, if grounded in the give and take of these precepts, can last forever and lead us into a greater fellowship

---

[10] Matthew 5:44-48.

[11] 1 Corinthians 13:4-7.

with the rest of humanity. We are to take care and marry the right person for the right reasons, and then rejoice in the spouse of our youth all the days of our lives that we might be truly blessed.[12]

Secret 3—Patience

Life is like a gigantic picture puzzle. Each year we find a few more pieces to the puzzle. By the end of our lives, hopefully, we can look back upon a beautiful picture because, with patience and good fortune, we will have found most of the pieces. As we go through life, the things that are truly meant to be fall into place with comparative ease. A piece of the puzzle, that is a true fit, snaps into place with very little trouble. One knows that it is the correct piece from the manner in which it crisply snaps home. Things that are meant to be have an air of easy reality and a sense of permanence about them that mark them as appropriate bench marks in our lives. One generally knows when something is right.

Most of the time we also sense when something is wrong. Sometimes, we will pick up a piece of the puzzle which does not fit. Sometimes, we will want so desperately for it to fit that we are tempted to reach for our scissors and work on it until it does fit. One can in this manner whittle on a piece of life's puzzle until it does appear to fit into the designated vacant spot. As time goes by, however, we will find more of the correct pieces, and more and more of the picture will begin to emerge. When we eventually stand back to look at the picture of our lives, the piece of the puzzle that we trimmed to fit will often stick out like a sore thumb. The sad part is, that by the time we notice the mistake, the correct piece of the puzzle may be lost forever. In short, things that are meant to be usually cannot be stopped; they constitute part of our destiny or God's intent for our lives. Things that are not meant to be are not meant to be for a purpose. One who attempts to force such matters frequently does so at the peril of their future happiness.

---

[12] Proverbs 5:15-19.

Many things of great worth in life, such as getting a good education, are difficult and yet must be pursued at all costs. These are not the sort of things just referenced. Far from it, some of the most valuable achievements in life come only with perseverance and self-sacrifice. The cautionary words above are meant to convey simply that any attempt to manipulate or force events in a manner that circumvents life's natural process, constituting an obsessive effort to take an inappropriate shortcut, is not without great risk. God "acts in behalf of the one who waits for Him" (Isaiah 64:4; Psalm 37:7, 9, 34). The Bible lists the fruits of the Holy Spirit as love, joy, peace, patience, kindness, goodness, faithfulness, gentleness, and self-control.[13] If we lack the virtues of patience and self-control, we often find that we have forfeited the rest of the fruits along with any hope of enjoying the life God originally planned for us.

The modern world is a rabbit warren of beguiling, but often illusory shortcuts which constitute ever present temptations. Generally, such paths do not lead to happiness. The rules of life, God's law, human nature, economics, and cause-and-effect never change. This is a lesson as old as humanity itself, but it appears that each generation must discover it anew—usually only after great suffering.

God has a plan for each of us and we should pray for the wisdom to recognize God's will and purpose for our lives. Things pursued outside God's will bring neither happiness nor long life. On the other hand, if we "delight ourselves in the Lord, He will give us the desires of our heart."[14] In a world where timing is everything, we often forget that God's timing is always perfect— even if we do not always fully appreciate that fact as we move through life.

---

[13] Galatians 5:22-23.

[14] Psalm 37:4; Luke 12:31.

Secret 4 — Mission

With regard to one's career or mission in life, one should pick a profession that truly interests one. Most people who achieve preeminence in their field are doing things they enjoy. They will say things like, "It isn't work to me; I enjoy it." They are not pursuing a profession because it is hot and promises to pay well; they are simply pursuing or satisfying their interests. As both an attorney and a hospital executive, I have known many attorneys and physicians who went into their fields in the quest of profit only to become bitterly disillusioned and unhappy.

Depression, obsession, and burnout can rule one's life when one's job becomes a weary, heavy "Guinea-coast slavery of solitary command."[15] How many have walked the deck of despair with Melville's Captain Ahab[16] when the realization dawns that their career and life are not what they envisioned during those halcyon days of youth when the sun seemed always to shine upon the golden lands of the future? Even the great economist Adam Smith was moved to write: "The contempt of risk and the presumptuous hope of success are in no period of life more active than at the age at which young people chuse [sic] their professions. How little the fear of misfortune is then capable of balancing the hope of good luck. . . ."[17] Today, there are far too many individuals earning a living through vocations which they shame and dishonor, because they entered those professions for the wrong reasons and without sufficient thought. Just as there are physicians who have no love of people, and attorneys who have no love of justice, there are even

---

[15] Herman Melville, *Moby Dick* (New York: W.W. Norton & Company, Inc., 1967[1851]), 443.

[16] Captain Ahab was the captain of the whaling ship, Pequod, in Herman Melville's great novel of the sea, *Moby-Dick*. His vengeance driven obsessive quest to kill the great white sperm whale, Moby-Dick, blinded him to his obligations both as captain and as a man.

[17] Adam Smith, *The Wealth of Nations*, ed. Edwin Cannan (New York: Bantam Dell, 2003 [1776]), 151.

ministers who have no faith in or love for the God described in the Holy Scriptures and the truth He represents (John 5:42).

In many respects life is short, but, with respect to one's profession, it can be very long indeed if one is not interested in and fulfilled by what one does. Everyone on this planet has a gift for something and a natural talent or interest. For this reason, everyone should ask God to reveal His will for their life prior to selecting a career or life's work. One should then pray for the opportunity to pursue that path. In our modern world, however, many individuals frequently fail to seek God's guidance prior to selecting their occupations or careers. They often fail to consider where their true abilities lie, and pursue careers simply because they deem the entry requirements manageable and the prospects lucrative.

Happiness aside, the people with the courage to defy convention and pursue their true interests have at least the chance to be happy and truly outstanding in their field and perhaps even become a captain of history. There have traditionally always been jobs for those who are truly good at what they do.[18] A good friend of mine pursued his dream, against all of the odds, of becoming an interplanetary geologist. Yes, there are jobs today in that field, and he has had a life of adventure more fulfilling than anything he could have imagined while in high school, because he persevered in the pursuit of both his interests and his dreams.

With respect to one's career, as with marriage, one would do well to marry the profession or interest that one truly loves for the right reasons. Hitch your wagon to your abilities and dreams; then, follow the north star of your fondest desire. Pursue your natural interests and talents and make them one with your career. Our lives are our time and, in the United States of America, that time is still alive with endless possibilities. Seek the peace and the fulfillment of your heart's desires, and perhaps earthly success will follow if one

---

[18] Proverbs 22:29.

walks in the path of the Lord. "It is the blessing of the Lord that makes rich and He adds no sorrow to it."[19]

Know, however, that as we practice our calling, trade, profession, or career we stand upon a pedestal for all the world to see. One's sense of honor, or lack thereof, will inevitably be revealed at some point in one's professional life regardless of the path chosen. It is for this reason that the Church has always taught veneration and respect for one's calling or job. In fact, the great pastor Charles Stanley has noted in his book, *The Spirit-Filled Life*, that since Christians are servants of God, all work is to be considered part of that service.[20] The Christian is to consider God as his or her ultimate employer regardless of the company name on one's paycheck. The Christian brings discredit upon his or her faith when tested upon the fields of everyday life and found wanting in truth, honor, honesty, goodness, loyalty, or faith. Thus, those who call themselves Christians, while stating that they cannot afford the luxury of Christian values and principles in the workplace, are fatally misguided. Over the course of a lifetime, most individuals will be able to recall moments when they have failed to live up to the ideals of their faith, but this should stop no one from learning from one's mistakes and trying to make the future better than the past. If everyone did this, the world would be a far better place.

---

[19] Proverbs 10:22.

[20] Charles F. Stanley, *The Spirit-Filled Life* (Nashville, Tennessee: Nelson Books, 1995, 2014), 161.

Chapter 8: The Nature of Life

Ultimately, a Christian's cosmic view is fundamentally positive and optimistic without the pervading negativity and fatalism that characterizes many other faiths, creeds, and philosophies. This is true because our faith is grounded in love. As we have seen, the great purpose of this life is to develop our faith, learn to love, and build character. If one cannot love his fellow man here on earth, whom he has seen, how can he love God whom he has not seen?[1]

How we react to misfortune, therefore, has a lot to say about the type of person we are and the spiritual progress we have made. It is not that God constantly tests us with bad things to build our character, but perhaps that He places people of faith where they can do the most good. This is not necessarily where they will be the most comfortable or happy. Sometimes we pass through dark times because it has been left to us to fight for good in the world or to accomplish some greater end that may not be readily apparent to us.

This takes us to the other great purpose of life, which is to teach us that it is important to take a stand for the things that are good and right, and to oppose, or at least stand firm against,[2] darkness wherever we find it. The truth is not relative. God is eternal and everlasting. His commandments and laws do not change over time to accommodate the declining morals of a given generation. It is pride and hubris to think that a holy God makes mistakes or that we can or should rewrite the portions of the Bible with which we might disagree.[3] Just as there is darkness and light, there is, and always has been, good and evil.

The backdrop to our individual experiences is a vast cosmic struggle between good and evil, darkness and light, and God and

---

[1] 1 John 4:20.

[2] Ephesians 6:11-14.

[3] Proverbs 30:5-6; Matthew 5:18-19; Luke 16:17.

Satan that has unfolded across the eons. The Bible tells us that God won this struggle on the cross,[4] and that this will become evident to all in the end when evil and darkness are banished forever. What many do not realize is that this ongoing war has many far-flung battlefields in virtually every corner and community of the world. What many fail to see is that we are all soldiers on one side or the other. As we go to work, serve in the community, select ministers for our church, or cast our votes in political elections, we have more opportunities than we realize to either support the good, the right, and the true or to support that which we know in our hearts is not right. Although the original wording is in dispute, Edmund Burke is generally credited with the statement that "The only thing necessary for the triumph of evil is for good men to do nothing."[5] The Bible teaches that it is accounted a sin when one knows the right thing to do and fails to do it.[6]

We know that God is sovereign, and that the fate of Satan, as well as the outcome of the war between good and evil, was sealed from the moment Jesus uttered the words on the cross, "It is finished!"[7] One of the great mysteries is why God allows the struggle to continue when its end is no longer in doubt. It is probable that the war produces too many important possibilities for each of us on our individual spiritual journeys in this life. It forces us to choose which side we are on and whether to be children of light or of darkness. As we go through life, the goats often voluntarily separate themselves from the sheep, and perhaps this is part of God's plan.[8] The struggle also hopefully teaches us that sitting on life's moral and ethical fence, in an attempt to play it safe and offend no one, is ultimately a losing proposition from the spiritual perspective. The Bible teaches that those who choose this

---

[4] Hebrews 2:14-15; Revelation 12:11.

[5] Kirk, *Edmund Burke, A Genius Reconsidered,* 204.

[6] James 4:17.

[7] John 19:30; Hebrews 2:14-15.

[8] *See,* Matthew 25:32.

course become salt that has lost its taste, and therefore are fit only to be discarded.[9]

More ordinary people than one might realize have quietly and silently gone over to the other side in the cosmic struggle referenced above. One can see their negative impact throughout our modern culture. Other individuals, whose fate is not yet determined, are still not willing to take a stand for righteousness. Speaking of individuals that hang suspended between Christianity and unbelief, T. S. Eliot wrote, "Many people live on an unmarked frontier enveloped in dense fog; and those who dwell beyond it are more numerous in the dark waste of ignorance and indifference, than in the well-lighted desert of atheism."[10] Those individuals that are willing to give witness to the truth—to stand between the flickering candle of hope and the cold drafts of darkness—are frequently placed by God in situations that may be stressful and unpleasant simply because they can be trusted to take a stand for the good, the right, and the true.

While there is good in the world and it is worth defending wherever it may be threatened, the struggle and the circumstance can be very unpleasant in the short run. As we noted earlier, if one looks across the arc of history, good has ultimately always triumphed over pure evil in the long run. For example, slavery was vanquished in the Christian countries of the West, Hitler was defeated, and communism failed, but it took the sacrifices of many good people to accomplish these ends.

The decisions we make each day in the capacities in which we serve are important and do have consequences in the greater global sense. Just as we as individuals ultimately become the product of the ethical decisions we make or fail to make, so, too, is our nation shaped by those decisions. In truth, we each have a personal fiduciary responsibility for the fate of our faith, our nation, and the culture in which we live. Edmund Burke taught us that society is in

---

[9] Luke 14:34-35.

[10] Eliot, *Christianity & Culture*, 147.

fact a partnership or contract "between those who are living, those who are dead, and those who are yet to be born" because a society's goals can only be achieved over many generations.[11] Viewed in this light, each generation is both a trustee for those who have come before and a custodian for those who come after. Both are sacred trusts and neither should be betrayed lightly.

Many people assume that all bad things or evil things come from God as well as good things, or that He is somehow responsible for all misfortune simply because we believe that God has the power to control all things. Some believe, when something bad happens to them, that God has decided to punish them for some reason. This is clearly not always the case because Jesus indicated that God is the "vinedresser," and that every branch of His vine that bears fruit is pruned that it might bear even more fruit.[12] Yet, the Bible clearly contains instances of God's righteous and punishing anger, particularly in the Old Testament. It is also clear that God will sometimes discipline us in an attempt to get our attention when we have strayed from His path.[13] As a source of everyday misfortune, however, God's anger is probably not the culprit as often as many believe.[14]

The perspective of the New Testament is that many bad things come from Satan[15] and are part of the ongoing cosmic struggle between good and evil. An old adage cautions us that if one achieves a position from which it is possible to do great good, Satan will lash out and try to prevent it. This is one reason Satan is characterized as the Enemy because he opposes goodness and light.

---

[11] Edmund Burke, *Reflections on the Revolution in France,* ed. L.G. Mitchell (Oxford University Press, New York, 2009 [1790]), 96; *See,* Eliot, *Christianity & Culture,* 116.

[12] John 15:2.

[13] 1 Corinthians 11:32.

[14] Exodus 34:6; Lamentations 3:31-33;Jonah 4:2; John 9:1-3.

[15] John 13:2; Luke 13:16; 22:3; 1 Peter 5:8; Matthew 13:28, 39; 2 Corinthians 2:11; Ephesians 6: 11-13; 1 Thessalonians 2:18.

Adverse events are sometimes visited upon us in an attempt to weaken our faith and drive a wedge between us and God. God may permit this in order to strengthen us for His purposes.[16] Other misfortunes befall us due to our own bad decisions. God did give each of us free will. Bad choices, even when freely made, usually result in negative consequences. Biblical scholar D. A. Carson has noted that "in the biblical perspective, sin is the basic (if not always the immediate) cause of all other calamities."[17] The Bible notes, "The foolishness of man ruins his way, and his heart rages against the Lord."[18] Sometimes we receive mercy when we make bad choices, but many times we receive justice and that justice can be painful.

When presented with misfortune, many people do end up cursing God and therefore abandoning the light. As just noted, however, God is not to blame for everything negative that may befall us. Again, how we react to misfortune tells God a lot about who we are and where our spiritual allegiance really lies. It is easy to have faith and be a good example when life is going well. It is when misfortune rears its ugly head that we are presented with one of our best and strongest opportunities to be a good example and a positive witness for our faith—difficult though that might be at times.

How we react to the learning process, trials, and tribulations of this life does prepare us to take, as C. S. Lewis noted, our eventual place as eternal children of God.[19] We will spend eternity either in darkness or light. This being the case, it is important that we consciously make a decision to be sons and daughters of light[20] and

---

[16] Romans 5:3-5; Genesis 50:20.

[17] Carson, D. A. "Matthew." In *Matthew and Mark*. Vol. 9 of *The Expositor's Bible Commentary*, 101.

[18] Proverbs 19:3.

[19] Lewis, *Mere Christianity*, 92-93, 119,147.

[20] Matthew 5:14, Ephesians 5:8-9, 1 Thessalonians 5:5

to oppose or at least stand firm against the forces of darkness during this life. Jesus warned, "But whoever denies Me before men, I will also deny him before My Father who is in heaven."[21]

The conscious resolution to try to be good people does not necessarily always require us to be heroes. Sometimes all that is required is that we refuse to be corrupted. Sometimes we may be placed in a certain position or circumstance simply as caretakers to prevent someone else who is corrupt from achieving a position of power. Often the role God would have us play does not demand that we be brilliant, strong, or daring, but simply honorable, honest, and trustworthy.

Many of us have been in meetings when a simple courageous reminder to all of the truth or history of a certain situation turned the entire meeting back onto the correct path when someone was trying to inappropriately manipulate circumstances. Many have also witnessed situations when intelligent, good people who knew better remained silent and allowed negative events to transpire that should have been avoided. People in positions of trust and responsibility who remain silent in the face of injustice, dishonesty, or evil forget that silence betokens consent and therefore effectively casts their vote for injustice in whatever form it may take.[22] The Bible teaches that it is accounted a sin when one "knows the right thing to do and does not do it."[23]

We really have no way of accurately ascertaining the good that may ultimately flow from honest action that we ourselves regard as merely routine attempts to do the right thing.[24] When we throw a pebble of truth, goodness, or courage into the great pool of life, it is impossible to know the lives that may eventually reap a positive

---

[21] Matthew 10:33.

[22] Qui Tacet, Consentire Videtur: He who is silent is supposed to consent. The silence of a party implies his consent. Black's Law Dictionary 1414, 1554 (4th ed. rev. 1972).

[23] James 4:17.

[24] Matthew 25:34-46.

benefit from the benevolent ripples set in motion. Surprising though it may seem, it may just be that, in the grand scheme of things, our lives are not meant to be just about us. As we travel through life, we move through an often unseen realm of higher purpose that may or may not ultimately be revealed to us.

The fact that bad things happen does not, therefore, mean that God does not care about us. God does care very much and desires a personal relationship. God is not capricious as He is often portrayed. Jesus stated, "If you had known Me, you would have known My Father also."[25] He also said, "No one comes to the Father but through me."[26] God is, therefore, like Jesus, and He does want the best for us. He does care when bad things happen. Jesus spent much of his time healing the sick, feeding the hungry, and forgiving the penitent sinner. He cared very much for the afflictions of mankind.[27] In the end, he died a horrible death to ransom us from our sins and (through his resurrection) ensure the ultimate defeat of both evil and death.

God has a special purpose for everyone, but not everyone actively seeks to discover what that purpose might be. Each of us is born with some special talent, ability, or capacity.[28] This natural distribution of unique abilities, interests, and capabilities is no accident. This division of labor is in fact an important aspect of the intelligent design by which God created the world in which we live. It is a basic principle of economics that the division of labor creates greater efficiency, diversity, and ingenuity. When an individual has the freedom, opportunity, and initiative to identify and develop one's true interests and abilities, then everyone in society ultimately benefits. This is one reason why free societies tend to be happier

---

[25] John 14:7; 2 John 1:9.

[26] John 14:6.

[27] John 9:4-7.

[28] Romans 12:6-8; 1 Corinthians 12:4-11.

and more prosperous than those societies that seek to limit individual freedom of choice.[29]

Even though one might not be rich, brilliant, beautiful, or strong, it may yet be possible for such a person to set in motion events that will have a positive impact upon the world far greater than such a person can imagine. The Apostle Paul had an unimpressive appearance, only average public speaking ability,[30] and some sort of affliction,[31] but he used his gifts of superior intellect, literary composition, theological insight, endurance, administrative ability, and faith in a manner that changed the course of Western civilization. Some of the most famous and successful individuals in American history started out as very common and ordinary people; e.g., Benjamin Franklin and Abraham Lincoln. Notwithstanding the enormous potential for everyone's life, regardless of present circumstance, most people never seek God's guidance before making the major decisions of their lives. Most people only pray when they are in desperate need—moments of extremity. There has been no effort to develop a previous relationship with God.

Does God answer all prayers? The poor beggar who had been cured of blindness by Jesus reminded the Pharisees, "We know that God does not hear sinners; but if anyone is God-fearing and does His will, He hears him" (John 9:31). The beggar's words echo Psalm 34:9-20 which urges the believer to approach God with respect and clean hands, stating, "The eyes of the Lord are toward the righteous and His ears open to their cry" (*See also*, Psalm 24:3-5; Proverbs 15:29). This by no means implies that one must be free of sin before approaching God in prayer. As Jesus' parable of the Pharisee and the tax collector who went up to the temple to pray illustrates, God

---

[29] Harry C. Veryser, *It Didn't Have To Be This Way, Why Boom and Bust Is Unnecessary-and How the Austrian School of Economics Breaks the Cycle*, (Wilmington, Delaware: ISI Books, 2013), 148-153.

[30] 2 Corinthians 10:10.

[31] 2 Corinthians 12:7-9.

looks into the human heart in search of sincere repentance for one's sins and a sincere desire to turn from those sins and attempt to do better (Luke 18:9-14). Grace comes to those who "love our Lord Jesus Christ in sincerity" (Ephesians 6:24). The Apostle Paul's statement in Romans 8:28, upon which many rely, does state that "God causes all things to work together for good," but it goes on to add, "to those who love God and to those who are called according to his purpose." We often forget that the promises of the Bible are for those who believe in the God of the Bible. The many wonderful promises made by Jesus Christ are for those who accept Him as both the Son of God and the Savior whose atoning death washes away the sins of all believers. Thus cleansed, those who truly repent of their sins and accept Jesus are permitted to approach Holy God directly in prayer. This direct access to God through prayer is one of the great blessings of Christian life.

The Apostle Paul teaches that the essence of Christ Jesus is "not yes and no, but yes. For as many as are the promises of God, in Him they are yes. . . ."[32] We are told that "if we ask anything according to His will, He hears us. And if we know that He hears us in whatever we ask, we know that we have the requests which we have asked from Him."[33] When one has a genuine need for justice or God's help, Jesus asks that we continue to pray until, in the fullness of His timing, God responds (Luke 18:1-8). That being said, however, we know that, in His wisdom, God does not answer all prayers in the manner and timing we initially envision. He does, however, generally respond to a sincere effort on our part to discover His will and purpose for our lives.[34]

As to why all of our prayers are not answered promptly and in the manner we desire, it may be that it would not be in our long-term best interest to have all of our prayers answered verbatim. In an existence where timing is often everything, God's timing is

---

[32] 2 Corinthians 1:19-20.

[33] 1 John 5:14-15.

[34] Psalm 25:12-14; Psalm 32:8; Proverbs 3:5-6.

always perfect. It is when we step outside and ahead of God's timing that we frequently get into trouble.[35] It is also true that not all of our prayers are necessarily according to God's will, worthy, or wise. Indeed, it was the Apostle Paul's opinion that "we do not know how to pray as we should" and that the Holy Spirit "intercedes for us" with prayers in our behalf "according to the will of God."[36] One of the twelve disciples even asked Jesus to teach them how to pray.[37] The pattern prayer that Jesus gave to encourage them in their prayers has come to be called the Lord's Prayer.[38] Throughout the Gospels Jesus is depicted as constantly in prayer. As our ultimate Christian role model, the example of Jesus shows us the importance of prayer if we are to develop our relationship with God.

With respect to why bad things are at times allowed to happen, notwithstanding our prayers, we must conclude that we simply do not know everything and that there are mysteries concerning this existence that have not been revealed to us.[39] Sometimes events must play out in a certain way because we are part of a bigger drama that we cannot see. This is where one's faith is called into play. God's ways are not our ways,[40] and it is sometimes difficult to discern His purpose, but that higher purpose always exists.[41] We are assured that those "who love God and are called according to

---

[35] Psalm 37:34; Isaiah 40:31; 64:4.

[36] Romans 8: 26-27; *See,* William Barclay, *The Letter to the Romans,* 131-132.

[37] Luke 11:1.

[38] Matthew 6:7-15; Luke 11:2-5: "Our Father who is in heaven, Hallowed be Your name. Your kingdom come. Your will be done, on earth as it is in heaven. Give us this day our daily bread. And forgive us our debts, as we also have forgiven our debtors. And do not lead us into temptation, but deliver us from evil. For Yours is the kingdom and the power and the glory forever. Amen."

[39] Deuteronomy 29:29.

[40] Isaiah 55:8.

[41] Isaiah 55:9.

His purpose" will find that "God causes all things to work together for good."[42]

The greatest figures of the Bible are frequently those who dared to believe that God did care and was interested in having a personal relationship with them. King David, from earliest childhood, comes to mind in this respect. David continuously sought to refine his relationship with God, notwithstanding the dangers and difficulties that threatened him. God frequently responds to and rewards such faith. God used the hardships and suffering that befell men like Joseph son of Jacob, King David, and the Apostle Paul to temper them for His purpose, and to make them capable stewards of the responsibilities He would later bestow upon them.[43]

God is not too busy to take an active interest in the affairs of our personal lives. Those who jump to that conclusion usually do so because they hope that He is, in fact, too busy to notice everything they do. Sometimes one of the largest hurdles of faith that we face is simply daring to believe God cares about us, and sees each of us as unique and capable of fulfilling a special purpose. In the end, however, the fulfillment of His best promises is reserved for those who believe in Him and treat Him as a real entity Who is holy and worthy of respect, fear, and love.[44] God will pay a surprise visit to many of us at some point in our lives, often when we least expect it. Unlike the Pharisees and Sadducees of Jesus' time, we should each pray for the wisdom to recognize God's will when He comes upon us.

In this life, for those who believe in God, there is always hope for a better existence. In fact, the Bible states that the believer is "born again to a living hope" through Jesus Christ's conquest of death (1 Peter 1:3). Regardless of how bad things may get, those who believe have the hope and the promise of something better

---

[42] Romans 8:28.

[43] Romans 5:3-5; Genesis 50:20.

[44] Hebrews 11:6.

whether in this life or the next. The impact in our lives of the concept of hope is something we vastly underestimate. Hope is a special and wondrous thing. Think how colorless and depressing our lives would be without hope. This is, perhaps, the single most frightening aspect of hell for it is depicted as eternity without hope or dreams. Most of us are familiar with Dante's[45] vision of hell as a place where all those who enter must abandon all hope.[46] Eternity is a span of time virtually impossible to imagine. To lose the prospect of God's best reward for us in heaven and be sentenced, utterly without hope of reprieve, to a gray, dim, miserable realm (whatever its nature) is a frightening prospect that should not be entertained as glibly as many do in our secular society.

Hope contains the suspended essence of joy and all good things that we can anticipate and work toward both in this life and the next. Hope is in large part, though we may not realize it, predicated upon our belief in God and an ordered and ultimately benevolent universe. God gives us hope to sustain us through life's dark, difficult, and lonely times. It is a precious gift. The Apostle Paul experienced most of the discomforts[47] in the Roman world at one time or another during his long ministry. Yet, Paul could say, at a time when he knew that his martyrdom was probably approaching, "For I consider that the sufferings of this present time are not worthy to be compared with the glory that is to be revealed to us."[48] Just as in the case of Paul, there is a part of our hearts, no matter how buffeted, that knows that ultimately our hope will not be in vain.[49]

---

[45] Dante Alighieri 1265-1321: Perhaps the greatest Italian poet of the Middle Ages. His work *The Divine Comedy* referenced above is considered one of the World's great works of literature.

[46] Dante Alighieri, *The Divine Comedy*, [Canto III, line 9]

[47] 2 Corinthians 11:23-28.

[48] Romans 8:18.

[49] Romans 5:5; 8:38-39.

In summary, if we are earnest, we must make the effort to take ourselves more seriously than perhaps we have in recent decades. If we embrace the traditional Judeo-Christian wisdom and values upon which our civilization and nation were grounded, and make a commitment to stand up for those values as we live out our lives, then we will each take our place as part of something far greater than ourselves. By doing so we join the people of faith across the centuries who have labored before us to usher in a transcendent new age of love, joy, freedom, and light— where hatred, sorrow, totalitarianism, bigotry, and darkness are banished forever.

The Christian knows that, though this is a worthy goal, it will never entirely be accomplished in this world for this world is not, nor can it ever be, heaven. This realization and our fundamental love of liberty are what separate us from progressives, socialists, communists, and others who have lost their way. The values and wisdom enshrined in this nation's founding documents mark the United States, conceived as a shining city upon a hill,[50] as this present world's last best hope of attaining and preserving the lofty aspirations of the Founders of both our Judeo-Christian heritage and our nation—if we can but have a spiritual awakening that restores us to our original faith, values, and purpose.

---

[50] This phrase is a reference to Matthew 5:14 and was used in 1630 by John Winthrop, Governor of the Massachusetts Bay Colony, in a famous sermon entitled *A Model of Christian Charity*. It has since been used by politicians of both political parties such as John F. Kennedy and Ronald Reagan.

Chapter 9: The Values of Western Civilization

The Bible states that humanity was created in God's image.[1] There has been much speculation as to exactly what being created in God's image means. A strong case can be made that the fact that God gave us free will and an immortal soul is the essence of being created in God's image. God gave mankind the freedom to choose whether to follow Him or not. He did not desire slaves.[2] In fact, when the Hebrews became slaves in Egypt, God delivered them. Freedom is of God. The Apostle Paul tells us that ". . . the Lord is the Spirit, and where the Spirit of the Lord is, there is liberty."[3] He goes on to emphasize, "You were bought with a price; do not become slaves of men."[4] Our Founding Fathers recognized these truths when they were very careful to point out that our freedoms and rights were derived from God and not any government.[5] The government's only legitimate purpose is to protect the God-given rights of mankind. John F. Kennedy acknowledged this great fact when he stated in his inaugural address: "And yet the same revolutionary beliefs for which our forebears fought are still at issue around the globe—the belief that the rights of man come not from the generosity of the state but from the hand of God."[6]

Enslavement in all its forms is manifestly not of God. The greatest evils in human history have been perpetrated by authoritarian regimes such as those of Hitler, Stalin, and Mao Zedong. God created all men and women equal to be free,

---

[1] Genesis 1:26.

[2] Galatians 5:1.

[3] 2 Corinthians 3:17.

[4] 1 Corinthians 7:23.

[5] The Declaration of Independence, para. 3 (U.S. 1776)

[6] Kennedy, John F., Inaugural Address (January 20, 1961), John F. Kennedy Presidential Library and Museum, Accessed December 17, 2015.

industrious, and accountable. God created men and women to be capable of having a relationship with Him. He did not create man to be an oppressed dependent of the state or any other authoritarian organization, regime, or creed. As a matter of fact, when the ancient Israelites asked the prophet Samuel to select a king for them, God saw this development as a rejection of Him.[7] One of those interesting bits of forgotten Biblical wisdom occurs when God directs Samuel to respond to the people's desire for a king by describing the ways of the king that the people would have placed over them:

> This will be the procedure of the king who will reign over you: he will take your sons and place them for himself in his chariots and among his horsemen and they will run before his chariots. He will appoint for himself commanders of thousands and of fifties, and some to do his plowing and to reap his harvest and to make his weapons of war and equipment for his chariots. He will also take your daughters for perfumers and cooks and bakers. He will take the best of your fields and your vineyards and your olive groves and give them to his servants. He will take a tenth of your seed and of your vineyards and give to his officers and to his servants. He will also take your male servants and your female servants and your best young men and your donkeys and use them for his work. He will take a tenth of your flocks, and you yourselves will become his servants. Then you will cry out in that day because of your king whom you have chosen for yourselves, but the Lord will not answer you in that day.[8]

These words were a telling prophecy of the growth of big government and so has it been from ancient times. God was clearly

---

[7] 1 Samuel 8:7.

[8] 1 Samuel 8:11-18.

not an advocate of big government, and it has often been observed that even God asked for only one-tenth of a citizen's income. In the New Revised Standard Version of the Bible, Proverbs 29:4 states, "By justice a king gives stability to the land, but one who makes heavy exactions ruins it." It will be noted that most modern governments now take much more than one-tenth of a citizen's individual income and have become ever more insatiable in that regard. The fundamental human right to pass one's accumulated property on to one's heirs at death is now often abridged by high estate taxes even though the accumulation of that property has in most cases already been taxed during the deceased person's lifetime.[9]

The consequences of becoming dependent upon the government rather than God have even more insidious consequences than those described above. In his historic, classic work, *The Road To Serfdom*, F. A. Hayek warned that "even a strong historical tradition of political liberty" could not adequately protect a society against the power of "excessive government control" to alter the very character of a people, and ultimately undermine and destroy the spirit of liberty.[10] Hayek noted that the quest for too much security at the hand of government could threaten freedom itself, because "independence of mind or strength of character is rarely found among those who cannot be confident that they will make their own way by their own effort."[11]

Courageous presidents such as Grover Cleveland and Calvin Coolidge, who understood competitive capitalism, economics, the

---

[9] Edmund Burke stated that "the power of perpetuating our property in our families is one of the most valuable and interesting circumstances belonging to it, and that which tends the most to the perpetuation of society itself." When he listed the legitimate rights of man he included the "right to the fruits of one's industry" and the "right to the acquisitions of one's parents." Burke, *Reflections on the Revolution in France*, 51, 59.

[10] F.A. Hayek, *The Road To Serfdom*, ed. Bruce Caldwell (The University of Chicago Press, 2007 [1944]), 48.

[11] Ibid., 147.

principles of sound currency, and the virtues of small government and self-sufficiency, are today relegated to relative obscurity. These men put the long-term welfare of the nation ahead of their own political fortunes when they stood against insatiable progressive demands for higher taxes, larger government, and socialistic policies. Why are such heroes relatively unknown today? In her wonderful biography of Calvin Coolidge, Amity Shlaes reminds us simply that "Economic heroism is subtler than other forms of heroism, harder to appreciate."[12] In a time when individuals who are exempted from taxes are permitted to vote for politicians who promise them all manner of free things, fiscal restraint and economic responsibility are no longer perceived as positive political virtues.

In Egypt, the Israelites eventually became slaves and totally dependent upon the state for their needs such as food. After the people of Israel had been delivered into the wilderness, many desired to go back to slavery in Egypt where they had, though slaves, been cared for by their oppressors.[13] The Israelites had been so reduced by their servitude that they no longer knew how to care for themselves, and this caused them to fear their newfound freedom and even threaten to stone Moses for delivering them.[14] The Bible states that God had to rain bread (manna) from heaven, to keep the Hebrews from starving.[15] In a much later time, the concept of freedom had become so foreign to the men of Judah that they bound Samson, their hero and champion, and turned him over to their Philistine oppressors rather than engage the Philistines in battle (Judges 15:10-13).[16]

---

[12] Amity Shlaes, *Coolidge* (New York: Harper Perennial, 2013), 7.

[13] Exodus 16:3; 17:3.

[14] Exodus 17:4.

[15] Exodus 16:4.

[16] Samson did, however, escape this particular treachery, killing one thousand Philistines with the jawbone of a donkey in the process (Judges 15:14-20).

God kept the Israelites in the wilderness forty years until they once again became a self-sufficient people capable of taking back the Promised Land. It was apparently necessary that almost everyone who had known the debilitating and corrupting dependence of Egypt perish before the nation was once again strong and ready to enter the Promised Land. When the possibility of decisively crushing the Philistines in the time of the supernaturally endowed, herculean Samson had passed, the Israelites would battle the Philistines in one form or another into the reign of King Hezekiah.

One of the great strengths of Western civilization is that, traditionally, its people have been religious, hardy, adventurous, independent, self-sufficient, and accountable for their actions. This also pretty much describes the ancient Israelites prior to entering Egypt. Once these traits are lost to a nation or civilization as they were to the Israelites in the time of Moses, they do not return overnight and usually not without great suffering. Constant vigilance is required to maintain the characteristics necessary to win and defend liberty and independence. The old adage that the road to hell is often paved with good intentions could easily be applied to the constant attempts to expand government and make as many people as possible dependent upon it. The Apostle Paul desired that we "be dependent on no one."[17] The psalmist warned us not to "trust in princes" for in mortal man there "is no salvation."[18] The message of the Bible is that we are to lead God-centered lives.

Attempts to replace God with government have generally been the harbingers of tyranny and quiet misery for the individual. The words of Jesus extol freely given charity when appropriate, but not progressivism, socialism or other forms of oppression or authoritarian control.[19] In his parable of the talents, Jesus makes it

---

[17] 1 Thessalonians 4:12 (New Revised Standard Version).

[18] Psalm 146:3.

[19] Matthew 6:19-20; 22:21; Mark 12:43-44; 2 Corinthians 9-7.

clear that we will be held accountable as individuals for the use we have made of the gifts which God has given each of us.[20] The parable of the barren fig tree was Jesus' further gentle reminder that God expects each of us to be productive, and that God's patience is not without end.[21]

The concepts of individual worth, freedom, humanity, fairness, private property, voluntary self-discipline, accountability, and the rule of law distilled from the Bible became the cornerstone of Western civilization.[22] Indeed, Alexis De Tocqueville noted that Anglo-American civilization "is the result . . . of two quite distinct ingredients which anywhere else would have often ended in war but which Americans have succeeded somehow to meld together in wondrous harmony; namely the *spirit of religion* and the *spirit of liberty*."[23] These fundamental values evolved over time into ever greater protections for the freedom of the common man, woman, and child. Today, under the grand liberal (used in the nineteenth-century sense) tradition of our Judeo-Christian heritage and competitive free enterprise capitalism as they have evolved in the West, there are more rights for the common man, women, children, and the disadvantaged than at any other time in human history.

The Christian West stands an island of sanity in a greater world still mad with inequality, persecution, cruelty, terror, and oppression. That is simply a fact and one of the reasons so many people from other parts of the world wish to come to America. Those among us who revile Western civilization simply do not know what they are talking about. Our freedoms threaten tyranny in all its forms as it exists in other parts of the world. That is the reason so much of the world hates us and rejoices when we appear poised to go down the long-discredited path to socialism and other

---

[20] Matthew 25:15-30.

[21] Luke 13:6-9.

[22] *See*, Eliot, *Christianity & Culture*, 200.

[23] Alexis De Tocqueville, *Democracy in America and Two Essays on America*, trans. Gerald E. Bevan (New York: Penguin Group (USA) Inc., 2003[1835, 1840], 55.

historical follies. To stray from the Judeo-Christian principles and discipline upon which Western civilization has grounded itself over the past two thousand years is to stumble backwards into the abyss of human misery which has tormented mankind throughout much of its history. This age-old cycle of oppression, cruelty, and quiet desperation still endures in most of the rest of the world today.

Looking back across the centuries, Ayn Rand saw an ancient struggle between humanity's producers and the "moochers and looters" who schemed to take the fruits of the producers' labor without appropriate compensation. Although not a religious believer, Rand's analysis is consistent with the Bible which protects the right of property and condemns behavior such as extortion, theft, and plundering.[24] Rand believed that, prior to the rule of law, the recognition of private property rights, and the advent of capitalism, the average person and the exchange for his or her labor were basically controlled by the local ruler with the most weapons. In her work *Atlas Shrugged*, Rand deduced from this that money, as a medium of exchange, was not the root of all evil, but "the root of all good." At last the individual in the West could place a value upon his or her property and service, and sell it for a fairly determined price in a free market rather than having it extorted from him or her at the point of a sword, gun, or government edict.[25] In this, she was in agreement with F.A. Hayek who had stated in *The Road To Serfdom* that "money is one of the greatest instruments of freedom ever invented by man."[26] His study of history and, in particular, the influence of socialism upon Italy, Germany, and Russia had convinced Hayek that economic freedom combined with freedom of choice, the freedom to take risks, and personal

---

[24] Exodus 20:15, 17; Deuteronomy 5:19, 21; Proverbs 28:8; Ezekiel 22:12; Matthew 23:25; Luke 3:14; 1 Corinthians 6:10.

[25] Ayn Rand, *Atlas Shrugged* (New York: Plume, Penguin Group (USA) Inc., 1999), 410-415; *See also*, Ayn Rand, *Capitalism: The Unknown Ideal* (New York: Signet/The New American Library, Inc., 1967), 26-29, 47.

[26] Hayek, *The Road To Serfdom*, 125.

responsibility was the "prerequisite of any other freedom."[27] Famed Churchill scholar Larry P. Arnn notes that Winston Churchill opposed the relentless march of socialism throughout his long life because he found it dehumanizing and contrary to man's nature, producing inequality rather than equality, injustice rather than justice, and "grinding tyranny" rather than freedom.[28] Other than in the depths of World War II, Churchill refused to serve with Socialists and was vocally adamant in his total rejection of both the party and its creed.[29] Rand also knew whereof she spoke, because she had fled Bolshevik Russia.

Utopia is reserved for heaven. To paraphrase Voltaire, the quest for the perfect may sometimes threaten the possible. Those who denigrate Western civilization in their pursuit of some secular utopia through progressivism, socialism, the welfare state, communism, or some other totalitarian scheme should, perhaps, be more cautious in their dreams. As noted above, were it not for the humanistic principles derived from the Bible, the rule of law, private property rights, and competitive capitalism, most people in the West would still be covered in filth and digging potatoes in the field of whatever local tyrant had the most weapons. For much of human history, the life of man, as noted by Thomas Hobbes, has been "solitary, poor, nasty, brutish and short."[30] This weary doom was changed only by the evolution of Western civilization as it has slowly unfolded and flowered over the past two thousand years. Western Civilization may be far from perfect, but, with respect to freedom and opportunity for the common man, it is still the brightest lamppost on the long, often dark, often treacherous, corridor of human history.

---

[27] Ibid., 133.

[28] Larry P. Arnn, *Churchill's Trial* (Nashville: Nelson Books, 2015), 143, 150.

[29] Ibid.

[30] Thomas Hobbes, *The Leviathan*, chap. XIII (1651).

Most average men and women are at heart very practical, judicious, and wise. They would rather live in an imperfect world governed by Judeo-Christian concepts of faith, individual worth, morality, liberty, accountability, voluntary self-discipline, private property rights, and competitive free enterprise capitalism than a secular attempt at heaven on earth. History has taught those with the eyes to see that these secular heavens come at a heavy cost in terms of rights and freedoms lost to the individual. Such regimes bring with them a rule, regulation, or law to govern virtually every aspect of life. With very little practical accountability, this enormous body of regulation can be changed or expanded at the whim of the ruling elite.[31] We realize that, throughout history, the road to social hell and a totalitarian state has been paved with good intentions and the worthy cause of the day.

It may be true that, individually, we cannot control the course in which Western civilization slowly drifts, but the average person often has some small amount of authority with which to do some good in the world whether it is at work, in church, or on committees upon which we serve in the community or schools. We let society down when we accept, through political correctness, incursions or even assaults upon basic historical freedoms within the small spheres of life we can still control or influence. We let society down when we fail to consider the broader implications of such incursions to reduce the scope of freedom for everyone bit by bit.

Many brave individuals have died across the centuries to create and preserve this wonderful society in which we are free to worship God and live our lives peacefully as we choose. We are often far too quick to give up or fritter those freedoms away. In the final analysis, it falls to the vigilance of common men and women

---

[31] As a healthcare executive at a community hospital, I experienced this reality through chronically insufficient federal reimbursement, the mercurial nature of the ever expanding and changing Medicare Rules and Regulations, and the never-ending burden of unfunded mandates constantly issuing from the federal government.

to make certain that those hard-won freedoms are not given away piece by piece in the name of whatever worthy cause happens to be popular at the moment. If history has taught us anything, it is that the elimination of any freedom can always be rationalized. History has repeatedly shown that a government strong enough to take a citizen's property for redistribution or other governmental purposes is strong enough to kill or imprison those who object. Ultimately, the government's *gifts* are never free; what is given to one individual must be taken, in some form, from another. If the average individual were as assiduous at using the power in his or her possession for good, as the evil are to use theirs for mischief, the course of the world would be on a much brighter, higher, and incandescent arc.

Chapter 10: A Lamp Against the Darkness

There are few maladies more crippling to the human condition and spirit than ignorance. Unless redressed, it is a blight from which one never recovers. In many respects, ignorance, left untreated, is the wound that never heals. It chains individuals to the lower rungs of the economic ladder, eventually enslaves them to the government, and forever limits the horizons to which one's intellect can fruitfully wander. The "broad, sunlit uplands" of hope, insight, illumination, and spiritual enlightenment, like a paradise lost, remain largely out of reach. The state of ignorance leaves one defenseless prey to misinformation and bad advice.

Individuals, leaders, and nations make needless and often critical mistakes through ignorance simply because they have no comprehension of what they do not know. The famous adage that "those who do not know history are doomed to repeat it" is unfortunately all too true. The quest to read, to learn, to grow, and to expand one's knowledge and intellectual horizons should continue throughout one's life.[1] At a minimum, one should learn a trade or profession so that one can earn a decent living. A sound knowledge of one's faith and the history and basic documents upon which our individual liberty and the success of our nation rest constitutes nothing less than the seed corn of a fruitful and productive life. Unless one's intellect is thus plowed, planted, and enriched there can never be a harvest sufficient to fill the storehouses of one's future. In this, as in all other things, we reap what we sow.[2] It may not always be easy, but in the United States of America, and most countries of the West, almost anyone that really wants an education can get it.

It is a mistake to assume that true ignorance is the sole province of the poor or those not blessed with a college education. One can frequently find more wisdom, common sense, and a sounder grasp

---

[1] Proverbs 18:15.

[2] Galatians 6:7.

of concepts like the importance of religious faith, liberty, private property, and competitive free enterprise capitalism among average men and women than among many of those individuals considered part of the highly educated elite.[3]

Common sense, common experience, and the practical knowledge of how people really behave and how things truly function in the real world are generally critical to the examination of most of life's great questions. Yet, it is these vital elements that are frequently in short supply in the rarified regions of academia and the upper echelons of government. Alarmed at the sorts of individuals transforming the society of revolutionary France, Edmund Burke stated:

> [W]hen men are too much confined to professional and faculty habits, and, as it were, inveterate in the recurrent employment of that narrow circle, they are rather disabled than qualified for whatever depends on the knowledge of mankind, on experience in mixed affairs, on a comprehensive connected view of the various complicated external and internal interests which go to the formation of that multifarious thing called a state.[4]

Sometimes one can have a college degree but remain ignorant because one closes one's mind to reality and the demonstrated history of that which works to bring success and that which does not. In the work-a-day world of construction or commerce, once it is clear that something does not work, it is quickly discarded, because it is simply too expensive to retain. In politics failed policies, economic theories, and philosophies such as progressivism, socialism, Keynesian economics,[5] and big government are returned to over and over, "like a dog that returns

---

[3] 1 Corinthians 1:18-25; Matthew 11:25.

[4] Burke, *Reflections on the Revolution in France*, 44-45.

[5] Veryser, *It Didn't Have To Be This Way*, 102-103,131,254,258-259.

to its vomit ..."[6] A history of failure does not deter such waste because the bill is paid by the taxpayer.

While high school should ideally prepare one for college academically, today it is absolutely critical that parents provide essential spiritual, moral, and social guidance before sending their children off to the university. Parents dare not trust others to teach their children the difference between right and wrong, or the proper perspective from which to frame the great issues of life and faith.

My parents were of modest means. They could not guarantee that they would be able to meet the expenses of my education, but they expected me to go to college and promised all of the support they could give. What they lacked in financial resources, they more than made up in encouragement. They kept their word with respect to the level of assistance they could manage. Along the way, my emotional IQ and life experience were enriched immeasurably as I worked in a grocery store, construction, a university maintenance department, and various academic assistantships to meet the remainder of my educational expenses.

During that period, I knew of another young man who desperately wanted to go to college. His parents, however, were far less wise and visionary than mine. They told him that they could not afford to assist him with any of his college expenses, and actively discouraged him from even attempting to go to college. He drifted into construction for a number of years, but never really found his vocation in life. He never found the path to self-actualization, fulfillment, or happiness. His parents were not totally to blame for that outcome, of course, but had they been wiser, his life could have been directed down a far different path. Parenting is a very serious business. One should never encourage a loved one to settle for less than he or she is manifestly capable.

---

[6] Proverbs 26:11.

Given the responsibilities enumerated above, it is also well to be warned that there are dark forces running amok in our world seeking to undermine our faith, our nation, and our culture. These forces delight in the ignorance of our citizenry, and sow for us a bitter harvest of future disappointment among the innocent fields of our children. Ignorance makes us both malleable and gullible. It is the chief ally of those who would lead us away from God and into the wastelands of error and ruin. Education, and a basic knowledge as to what constitutes the truth and what does not, serves as a lamp against the darkness. Thomas Jefferson knew this and was consistently an advocate of education, stating both, "If a nation expects to be ignorant and free, in a state of civilization, it expects what never was and never will be,"[7] and "Enlighten the people generally and tyranny and oppressions both of body and mind will vanish like evil spirits at the dawn of day."[8] John Adams was of like mind, even adding to the constitution of Massachusetts, "Wisdom and knowledge, as well as virtue, diffused generally among the body of the people being necessary for the preservation of their rights and liberties; and as those depend on spreading the opportunities and advantages of education . . ."[9]

After seeing to our own education, there is no task more important than taking responsibility for the education of our children. In the Bible, Psalm 78:5-8 summarizes God's command that the ancient Israelites educate their children:

> For He established a testimony in Jacob and appointed a law in Israel, which He commanded our fathers that they should teach them to their children, that the generation to come might know, even the

---

[7] Letter from Thomas Jefferson to Charles Yancey (January 6, 1816), Ford, Paul Leicester, ed. *The Works of Thomas Jefferson in Twelve Volumes* (New York and London: G.P. Putnam's Sons,1904), Library of Congress Digital Collections

[8] Letter from Thomas Jefferson to Pierre S. Dupont de Nemours (April 24, 1816), Ibid.

[9] McCullough, *John Adams*, 223.

children yet to be born, that they may arise and tell them to their children, that they should put their confidence in God and not forget the works of God but keep His commandments, and not be like their fathers, a stubborn and rebellious generation, a generation that did not prepare its heart and whose spirit was not faithful to God.

Today many parents will simply say, "I told my children that I did not care what they believed as long as they believed something." The Bible, of course, teaches that it matters very much what we believe, and that believing the wrong things can have disastrous eternal consequences.[10] Parents also frequently say that they do not wish to unduly influence their children, but would rather allow their children to find their own path. When parents shirk their responsibility to mentor their children in this manner, they damage their children, their faith, and their nation. Rest assured that if parents do not wish to influence their children, there are plenty of other people who do wish to influence them and are happy to be given the opportunity to do so. When parents fail to pass on their accumulated life knowledge, faith, philosophy, and wisdom to their children, they create an intellectual vacuum in the lives of those children which liberal educators, venal politicians, and all sorts of other unsavory characters rush in to fill. T. S. Eliot voiced this concern when he stated that "by far the most important channel of transmission of culture remains the family: and when family life fails to play its part, we must expect culture to deteriorate."[11]

Proverbs 22:6 pleads that parents, "Train up a child in the way he should go, even when he is old he will not depart from it." This type of attention cannot wait until a child begins to concern one in high school, for by then the battle may be lost. The moral, ethical,

---

[10] John 12:48; 2 Corinthians 5:10; 6:14; 1 John 2:22-25; 5:12; 2 John 1:7-11; 2 Peter 2:1-9.

[11] Eliot, *Christianity & Culture*, 116.

and cultural education of our children must be undertaken from the very beginning of a child's development by the parents themselves. Our institutions and general culture can no longer be trusted with this important task. Francis Xavier, the founder of the Jesuit order, is reputed to have said, "Give me a child until he is seven and I will give you the man."

The principles of religious faith, morality, voluntary self-discipline, love of country, liberty, and competitive free enterprise capitalism should, therefore, be taught to children by the time they are seven or eight years of age. If parents will do this for their children, their faith, and their country, then, most likely, those children will be solid for life. If modern parents neglect this critical aspect of parental responsibility, they may not, in the end, be pleased with the concepts others will gladly pour into their children's minds. It is far easier to inject bad and unsound doctrines into a child's mind than it is to get them out once implanted. Alexis De Tocqueville noted that "each new generation forms a new nation."[12] If we fail to pass our Judeo-Christian values and the principles of liberty, discipline, and accountability on to our children, the nation they will form will no longer reflect these values.

The University of North Carolina (UNC) at Chapel Hill was, in the late 1960s and early 1970s, arguably, one of the finest, but also one of the most liberal universities in the South at a time when the anti-war and hippy culture was at its zenith. By the time I arrived on campus in the fall of 1969, my parents had done their best to help me understand who I was and instill within me the traditional values of our Judeo-Christian heritage, independence, liberty, and competitive free enterprise capitalism. It had not always been pleasant, and, in fact, it had at times been downright painful. My parents had taken their cultural and religious responsibility as parents quite seriously. For example, my parents insisted that we sit down as a family and watch each televised Billy Graham crusade.

---

[12] Alexis De Tocqueville, *Democracy in America*, 547, 348.

To this day, I am grateful for the spiritual insights and vision of Christianity bestowed by the Reverend Graham. In later years, I gained additional inspiration and insight from local ministers and the broadcasts of Dr. Charles F. Stanley.

By the time, I arrived at Carolina, I therefore knew I was a Christian due to the spiritual mentoring of my parents and the work of the Holy Spirit. As a result of the interest inspired by Billy Graham (and other earnest and godly ministers in southwestern Virginia and Piedmont, North Carolina, whom I heard with my parents), I had obtained a pretty good understanding of what was in the Bible, so the efforts of a lot of very liberal professors and other curious folks to punch holes in my faith were unsuccessful. I was actually encouraged in my faith at UNC, as were countless other students, by the lectures of Professor Bernard H. Boyd, who was a solid pillar of theological wisdom and learning in a sea of shifting theories and academic speculation. He was known by many at that time as the UNC professor of religion who actually believed.

Coupled with my work experience, I had also read enough history along with authors like George Orwell, Boris Pasternak, and Ayn Rand to have a fair idea of the philosophical dangers lurking in our modern world. The socialistic, hippy, anti-war drug culture had little allure for me. This was my one big chance to get a university education, and I knew that I had better make the most of it. Believe me; I was far from being all-wise and all-knowing. In many respects, I was an innocent. Such wisdom as I possessed at that time was due, in large part, to my parents, godly scout masters, and ministers of the traditional Christian faith who had each played their part in my life. I did, however, arrive on campus with a healthy dose of that practical skepticism for which the common man is famous.

As alluded to above, by the time I arrived at Carolina, I had worked in a grocery store, helped build bridges in the interstate highway system, and hiked the splendors of the National Boy Scout Ranch at Philmont. I had come to love the America of strength and upward mobility for everyone desiring to work for it. The radical changes advocated by the hippies and war protesters had no attraction for me. It was the original American dream that inflamed my imagination, and I was working very hard to attain it. I doubted that the reckless people advocating radical change and tumult had the life experience or the competence to make the assumptions and criticisms of which they were so supremely confident. To this day, I do not feel that these elements accurately prophesied the future so much as created a more limiting self-fulfilling prophecy than the United States might otherwise have enjoyed.

There was, during those times, a madness in the air that recalls to mind a quote from Herman Melville's book, *Moby-Dick*, "There is a wisdom that is woe, but there is a woe that is madness."[13] The Vietnam conflict had created an opportunity for those who had lost their way to open a Pandora's Box of societal madness, discord, and woe from which this country has never fully recovered.

It was during this period that I first learned how intolerant of all opposing points of view those who have lost their way can be. Often the principles of peace eluded the movement that bore the name. Had my parents grounded me less soundly, and had I allowed myself to be sucked into the drug culture of that time (my father would have killed me), my life might well have taken a far darker course. As it was, I ended up serving in the UNC Student Legislature for most of my time at Carolina, having many memorable adventures during those liberal times as part of the UNC *conservative coalition*.

The coalition was composed of an intrepid group of contrarian students who dared to be the voice of traditional American values in student politics during those turbulent times. I still have a picture of some of us on the steps of the United States Capitol that was taken when members of the UNC conservative coalition accompanied a veterans group to Washington, DC, at our own expense. The purpose of the visit was to actually protest (we wore

---

[13] Herman Melville, *Moby-Dick*, 355.

suits and ties) in support of our nation's Vietnam war effort and the sacrifices being made by our armed forces. This was not a popular act or one that was politically correct at the time or even now. There was little, if any, notice of the event in the network media. No one thanked us other than the veterans, who correctly saw the parallel between the current stand against communism and their stand against the evils of Fascism and Nazism in their day. The act of publically displaying respect both for our flag and the soldiers who were bravely honoring their obligation to that flag was simply the right thing to do.

Jesus once marveled that the people of His generation could not "discern the signs of the times."[14] He also warned that chaotic times would always breed false prophets who would use His name to lead the naïve into incorrect places.[15] The bad times in which we were fated to live had taught some of us the following invaluable lesson. Life, both as a Christian and as an individual, sometimes requires stepping back from the herd[16]and taking time for serious reflection when events present one with cosmic moments involving fundamental issues of right versus wrong.

It is time to stop in one's tracks and begin to think for one's self: (1) when the popular crowd begins to rush like lemmings to the sea in pursuit of a dubious proposition that seems too good to be true, defies conventional wisdom, or violates traditional values or the commandments of the Scriptures, (2) when popular magazine covers begin to suggest that "it is different this time," or (3) when pundits begin to wonder if the traditional rules or wisdom have been superseded by events and might no longer apply. As the events of the last two generations have frequently taught us, it is virtually never different this time, the rules of life never change, and the truth of God's Word is never superseded.

---

[14] Matthew 16:3.

[15] Matthew 24:23-26; Mark 13:21-22.

[16] Exodus 23:2.

Given the sudden collapse during my college years of much of the social, cultural, and moral order previously taken for granted, I consider myself fortunate to have made it through those volatile times without serious misadventure. The foresight of my parents, in instilling within me at an early age a basic understanding of the Christian faith and the values of where they hoped I would end up, rather than where we currently were, is largely responsible for this benign outcome. I also credit one of the tools my parents used in my upbringing—the Boy Scouts of America—but more of that later. Ultimately this reference to my years at Carolina during a period of national testing, protest, and unrest is more about the ability of Christ to lead believers through difficult times and into worthwhile service than it is about me. Notwithstanding the character of the times during my undergraduate years, I loved my time at Carolina and will always be grateful for the education, experiences, opportunities and friends that UNC-Chapel Hill made possible.

In summary, one should obtain the best education possible and resolve to continue the personal learning process throughout one's life. It is absolutely critical that we mandate that our children do likewise. Parents should make certain that they provide their children with a sound religious, moral, ethical, and historical foundation before sending them out into a world where the wolves are everywhere often disguised as sheep. In a world that grows increasingly dark and confused, God's word will be a lamp to our feet and a light to our path (Psalm 119:105). Ultimately, a life without a basic knowledge of the Bible, American history, Western thought, and competitive capitalism is a life robbed of the proper context by which to frame and inform one's moral, social, and political decisions.

Chapter 11: Rejecting the Devil's Etiquette

John Adams once stated, "Facts are stubborn things; and whatever may be our wishes, our inclinations, or the dictate of our passions, they cannot alter the state of the facts and evidence."[1] He would have been saddened by our brave new world of political correctness where nothing is as it seems or quite like we remember it. Just as a relentless surf can over time undermine the greatest of lighthouses by slowly removing the sand one grain at a time, political correctness is undermining our culture by removing bits of knowledge, history, and morality one grain at a time in a manner so subtle that it is hardly noticed. When the lighthouse finally topples, its light is extinguished and darkness rules. This has been the result throughout history when political correctness is permitted to dominate public discourse.

If it is true as Jesus stated that "[T]he truth will make you free,"[2] then it is logical to assume that the converse is also true in that the absence of truth can enslave one. Truth is an essential ingredient of a free society and helps to keep us all free. Sadly, truth is the first virtue to die at the hands of propaganda, and we must recognize that political correctness is nothing less than subliminal, liberal, secular propaganda ultimately backed by the coercive power of much of academia, the media, and the federal government. When there is a consistent practice of debasing the currency of the English language, and altering the truth or intimidating the truth into silence, we are all both threatened and weakened.

In the previous chapter, we noted that ignorance is an essential ally of those seeking to compromise, suppress or alter the truth. Where such ignorance is not readily found, it is today sown through the medium of political correctness. The ostensible original purpose of political correctness was to simply protect the sensitivities and feelings of groups thought to have been, in some

---

[1] McCullough, *John Adams*, 68.

[2] John 8:32.

way, disadvantaged or victimized. In practice, however, political correctness has always involved some element of untruth or distortion to the substituted language, history, or cultural memory. This alteration or distortion of the truth is unnecessary, because one can be polite while still being truthful. It is clear that political correctness involves motivations far less innocent than a mere desire to be sensitive or polite.

In a manner very much like George Orwell's depiction of "newspeak" in his chilling novel about the future, *1984*, political correctness seeks to slowly rob us of our proper understanding of both our historical past and our heritage of Judeo-Christian teachings, values, and morality.[3] When we omit or substitute another word, term, or phrase for the correct word, term, or phrase, or imply that a word, term, or phrase actually has a meaning different from that traditionally understood, then the result is generally either somewhat unclear, somewhat untrue, or seeks to obscure the original definition and significance of the term altogether.[4] For an example with which most people are familiar, when adherents of political correctness refuse to use terms like *terrorist* or *war against terror* or *radical Islam*, our allies are confused and our enemies emboldened.

In 1983 when Ronald Reagan publicly stated that "simpleminded appeasement or wishful thinking about our adversaries is folly," and that we could no longer "ignore the facts of history and the aggressive impulses of an evil empire," he was NOT being politically correct.[5] The entire world knew that Reagan clearly understood the international situation, and had the resolve to grapple with it. Reagan's lack of political correctness gave a

---

[3] George Orwell, *1984* (New York, New America Library, inc., 1961 [1949]), 246.

[4] For an excellent discussion of the pernicious effects of propaganda upon culture, language and society see Hayek, *The Road To Serfdom*, 171-180.

[5] Ronald Reagan, *An American Life* (New York: Simon And Schuster, 1990), 570.

much-needed impetus to a train of events that eventually toppled the Soviet empire.

Returning to the example of political correctness noted above, the attempts in recent history, by authority figures in our culture, to avoid terms like *terrorist* and phrases like *war on terror* or *radical Islam* create an appearance of confusion, weakness, or dangerous naiveté. Such impressions of weakness or incompetence can easily trigger a serious miscalculation on the part of our enemies, and cause our allies to fear association with us. While this is an example of political correctness on an international scale, this type of confusion can prove equally harmful to individuals in their personal relationships and religious faith.

In the same manner, political correctness can prove even more damaging to the stability of society and the culture upon which it rests. The substitution of cute or sanitized euphemisms for behavior traditionally deemed socially unacceptable, or the subtle denigration of behavior traditionally viewed as commendable, creates cultural confusion as to values, ethics, and morals.[6] Isaiah condemns something akin to political correctness in ancient Judah when he says:

> Woe to those who call evil good, and good evil; Who substitute darkness for light and light for darkness; Who substitute bitter for sweet and sweet for bitter! Woe to those who are wise in their own eyes and clever in their own sight![7]

From Isaiah, we therefore learn that political correctness is not unique to our time. It is rather a characteristic of any society that has become corrupt as a result of the decay of its basic values. Edmund Burke describes it at work in the atheistic regime of revolutionary France,[8] and we recall that political correctness was a

---

[6] Proverbs 17:15.

[7] Isaiah 5:20-21.

[8] Burke, *Reflections on the Revolution in France*, 111.

matter of life and death in the totalitarian societies of the twentieth century.

Political correctness seeks to corrupt and confuse a population as to the truth or true nature of whatever topic is currently its target. Its ambition is nothing less than to subtly pry us away from God, and the values upon which the unparalleled freedom and success of Western civilization rest.

We know that the ancient kingdom of Judah eventually drifted so far away from the vision, ethics, and morality of its religious heritage that its unique relationship with God was severely damaged. The political correctness of that time so confused and corrupted Judah's values, that the nation abandoned the true spirit of the Ten Commandments and the Law of Moses. God stated, through the prophet Jeremiah, during this time that "An appalling and horrible thing has happened in the land: the prophets prophesy falsely, and the priests rule on their own authority; and My people love it so!"[9] As a result, God withdrew His protection and gave the kingdom of Judah up to conquest and Babylonian captivity.

History teaches that the broad assumption within a culture or nation that God does not exist, or that He does not care, or that He will go along with anything desired by those seeking to manipulate the population, invariably leads to disaster; e.g., Israel, 722 BC; Judah, 586 BC; Judea (Judaea), AD 70; Revolutionary/Napoleonic France, 1815; Bolshevik Russia, 1917; Fascist Italy, 1943; and Nazi Germany, 1945.[10] The confusion and cultural decay resulting from

---

[9] Jeremiah 5:30-31.

[10] Israel was conquered by Assyria in 722 BC; Judah was conquered by Babylon in 586 BC; Jewish revolt in Judea was crushed by Rome resulting in the destruction of both Jerusalem and the Jewish Temple in AD 70; Napoleon's final defeat at Waterloo in 1815 symbolized the total defeat of France; the rise of the Bolsheviks to power in 1917 brought communism to Russia resulting in the murder of untold millions of Russians under leaders like Stalin; in 1943 Italy surrendered during WWII; the catastrophic WWII defeat of Nazi Germany in 1945.

rampant political correctness inevitably gives birth to dire consequences.

Political correctness was already rearing its head in the early 1970s when I was an undergraduate student, and I suffered as a result. Over the years, it has become a tyranny designed to intimidate and silence independent, non-politically correct, non-liberal, and non-secular thought and speech. This is true because, in more and more segments of our society, failure to write and speak in the liberal, politically correct "newspeak" comes at the price of lower academic grades, lost employment/advancement, or humiliation in the media. That such a subversive phenomenon should be allowed to threaten basic free speech in the United States would astonish our Founding Fathers.

The threat of political correctness has flowered slowly, unnoticed, and beneath the radar screen almost like poison ivy in one's back yard. It may have appeared harmless to some in the beginning, but, like poison ivy, it is in fact a poisonous thing and a thing to be avoided. Just as this nation's national symbol, the eagle, was brought to the brink of extinction by the insecticide DDT, free speech is threatened with a similar fate by political correctness. It is slowly turning our unwitting society into the equivalent of a re-education camp, such as those once used by totalitarian regimes to brainwash those not towing the party line. As a free society, we must recognize its threat, or we will awaken one day to a culture and nation that neither we nor the Founding Fathers would recognize. The subtle power of time and erroneous teaching to transform an entire culture in negative ways should never be doubted. Political correctness is much like a glacier. One cannot see it move from one moment to the next, and yet it does not stop its march until it has transformed the entire landscape in its path.

The Bible states that honoring the Sabbath (a day of rest and spiritual reflection) is extremely important to God, and yet that aspect of our faith has faded away in our culture . . . and we have accepted it. The Bible also states that marriage is to be honored and

Jesus speaks against divorce, but now divorce is almost as common as marriage . . . and we have accepted it. God is very clear in the Scriptures that He holds sexual morality of utmost importance, but in our society fornication, adultery, and now homosexuality have become commonplace and even glorified . . . and we have accepted it. God regards human sacrifice as anathema. In fact, few things make God angrier than child sacrifice, and yet abortion is now tolerated on an industrial scale . . . and we have accepted it. The turning away from behavior endorsed in the Scriptures to behavior specifically condemned was in each of these cases *politically correct*. The appetite for ungodly change on the part of those who have lost their way is never satisfied. The clergy who succumbed on each of the issues just noted, to maintain peace and good feeling in their time, now confront the demand for even more revisions to God's law.

In summary, we should be ladies and gentlemen. We should always endeavor to be polite and sensitive to the legitimate feelings of others. As Christians and Americans, we should, however, abhor political correctness, because it spreads secularism, confusion, distortion, untruth, and intimidation in its wake. It effectively silences, shuts down, and excludes the legitimate concerns, contributions, and wisdom of the ordinary people of daily life who arguably know our culture best. Political correctness presents a clear and present danger to the history and Judeo-Christian values upon which both our culture and our prosperity rest. By its nature, political correctness exemplifies and embodies the spirit of the Antichrist of which Christians were warned by the apostle John (1 John 4:1-6). In this sense one might characterize political correctness as the Devil's etiquette.

The best antidote to political correctness is simply the truth and the honest selection of the best word or phrase to articulate whatever issue is before us. In America and throughout the countries of the West, both our history and our news should be reported honestly, factually, and unaltered. The actual events of history should not be erased simply because we may disagree today with the decisions and moral choices of a different time, generation, or place. To erase or alter history is to deny future generations the opportunity to learn from the past. Historians, academics, and purveyors of the news betray the trust upon which their professions rest when facts are omitted, changed, or slanted to favor a particular ideology. Those who pray to the false god of government, and practice the false morality of political correctness, in the end have little patience or regard for the true God or true morality. This is the threat and the reality implicit in political correctness for both the individual and society.

Chapter 12: Of Guns, Capitalism, and Religion

Guns

In the previous chapter, the concern was expressed and explored that we are at risk of being slowly brainwashed and re-educated through the medium of political correctness as it subliminally immerses us in secular spin, and silences through intimidation opposing or alternate points of view. Things which most common men and women once accepted as articles of faith are now recast with a patina of suspicion and doubt including Christianity itself. In no three areas is this circumstance better illustrated than in our culture's changing views with respect to guns, capitalism, and religion.

Guns have long been demonized by those who have lost their way in our society, and would, no doubt, have been long since banned, had it not been for the tireless efforts of the National Rifle Association. Yet, it was not always so. Firearms have been with us from the earliest days of first settlement, and have become part of our national heritage representing self-reliance, accountability, independence, preservation, and defense. The firearm was simply one of many tools that our forefathers used to carve our nation out of the wilderness.

Our Founding Fathers, recognizing how important both firearms and a citizenry that knew how to use them had been to our struggle for independence, enshrined our right to bear arms in the Second Amendment to the Constitution of the United States. They realized that, throughout history, disarming the average citizen had been one of the first objectives of tyrants. Today, we watch accounts of evil regimes such as that of North Korea on the news, and wonder why its people do not overthrow such an abusive government. One reason is that the bad guys have all of the guns. It seems that even when the common man and woman have been disarmed, the bad guys always manage to keep their guns. Our

Founding Fathers intended for our freedom and independence to last, so they left the common man and woman armed.

Thomas Jefferson was perhaps the most sophisticated, erudite, and refined of all the Founding Fathers, and yet his biographer, Jon Meacham, notes that Jefferson owned guns, carried a gun when traveling, and felt that hunting was the best form of exercise. Meacham references a letter from Thomas Jefferson to Peter Minor, dated July 20, 1822, wherein Jefferson states in regard to Minor's son: "I presume he is a gun-man, as I am sure he ought to be, and every American who wishes to protect his farm from the ravages of quadrupeds and his country from those of biped invaders. I am a great friend to the manly and healthy exercises of the gun . . ."[1]

In his work, *The Book of the Sword*, originally published in 1884, Sir Richard Francis Burton, a British adventurer, explorer, and world traveler, made this interesting observation:

> But courtesy and punctiliousness, the politeness of man to man, and respect and deference of man to women—that Frauencultus, the very conception of knightly character—have to a great extent been 'improved off.' The latter condition of society, indeed, seems to survive only in the most cultivated classes of Europe; and, popularly amongst the citizens of the United States, a curious oasis of chivalry in a waste of bald utilitarianism—preserved not by the sword but by the revolver.[2]

While it may be that the day when the United States was an oasis of politeness and chivalry has long since passed, Burton seems to be saying that, in a society where common men and women are still permitted to defend themselves, a certain level of

---

[1] Jon Meacham, *Thomas Jefferson: The Art of Power* (New York: Random House Publishing Group, 2013), 287: Thomas Jefferson, http://www.monticello.org/site/research-and-collections/hunting (accessed February 7, 2015).

[2] Richard F. Burton, *The Book of the Sword* (New York: Dover Publications, Inc., 1987 [1884]), 20.

accountability is suddenly thrust upon those who would seek to disturb their peace—and that this is not altogether a bad thing. We tend to forget that Jesus did not say blessed are the peace lovers but rather, "Blessed are the peacemakers, for they shall be called sons of God."[3] The Apostle Paul commanded that Christians be at peace with all men "if possible."[4] The theologian William Barclay explained that there will be times when Christian politeness and civility must give way to Christian principle. Barclay understood what many today forget: "Christianity is not an easygoing tolerance which will accept anything and shut its eyes to everything. There may come a time when some battle has to be fought—and, when it does, Christians will not shirk it."[5]

King David, Israel's greatest king, was also a legendary warrior. The Bible states that when the Jews returned to Jerusalem from the Babylonian captivity every builder working to rebuild the city's walls "had his sword girded at his side as he built" (Nehemiah 4:18). When soldiers asked John the Baptist what they must do in order to be saved, he did not ask them to lay down their arms and leave the military. Instead, he asked that they refrain from accusing anyone falsely, or plundering, and that they be content with their wages.[6] Both Jesus and Peter had very positive interactions with Roman centurions.[7] In fact, whenever centurions are mentioned in the New Testament, it is with respect. Paul's life was actually saved by a Roman tribune[8] when he was mobbed in Jerusalem and later by the centurion named Julius during a ship wreck.[9] And lastly, we

---

[3] Matthew 5:9.

[4] Romans 12:18.

[5] William Barclay, *The Letter to the Romans*, 200.

[6] Luke 3:14.

[7] Matthew 8:5-13; Acts 10:1-48.

[8] Acts 21:31-32.

[9] Acts 27:42-43.

learn that at least two of Jesus' original disciples carried swords.[10] Apparently, one of them was Peter, for John tells us that it was Peter who cut off the ear of Malchus, the servant of the high priest.[11] Immediately, Jesus sternly commanded Peter to stop his attack.[12] Even in the heat of the moment, however, Jesus did not tell Peter to discard his sword, but simply to put it back "into the sheath."[13]

The Bible states that we are to exercise self-control,[14] and not to be prideful,[15] prone to anger,[16] hotheaded,[17] or quick to take offense.[18] It is absolutely clear that Jesus and His disciples were men of peace, and, in fact, Jesus rejected violence as a solution to the world's problems.[19] Proverbs teaches that those who seek gain through violence ambush their own lives (Proverbs 1:18-19). The fact that the Apostle Peter and at least one other disciple carried swords is probably only indicative of the fact that they simply understood that the best way to avoid having to confront violence is to appear strong and capable of dealing with it. The Bible teaches, "The Lord abhors the man of bloodshed and deceit" (Psalm 5:6). It is also equally clear that, although given many opportunities to condemn the military and weapons for self-defense, Jesus did not do so. He rose above easy, timeworn clichés to consistently condemn the evil in man that that would do harm in all its forms to others without justification or remorse.

---

[10] Luke 22: 38.

[11] John 18:10.

[12] Luke 22:51.

[13] John 18:11; Matthew 26:52.

[14] Proverbs 16:32; 25:28.

[15] Proverbs 8:13; 11:2; 16:18

[16] Proverbs 12:16; 14:17, 29; 19:11, 19.

[17] Proverbs 22:24.

[18] Matthew 5:39; Luke 6:29.

[19] Matthew 26:52; Luke 6:27-29.

There will always be wicked men and madmen who betray society's trust, and misuse their weapons of all types to do bad things. These sorts of individuals have always, in all times, been able to find ways to keep their weapons, even when the rest of society has been disarmed. In a world of terrorists and very bad men, good men should not be deprived of their means of self-defense. This is still common sense to the common man and woman, and they will always have a healthy distrust for any government that seeks to disarm them.

Capitalism

Today even well-educated people who should know better frequently condemn capitalism as though it is a bad word. It is not uncommon to hear misguided statements to the effect that capitalism has no heart, or that it is somehow unfair. While capitalism may not be perfect, it is in fact the fairest economic philosophy yet to evolve. Rather than question its fairness, it would be more accurate to comment on the fact that capitalism is blind. F. A. Hayek helped us to understand that this blindness is in fact a virtue.

Pure competitive capitalism derives its blindness from the nature of free market competition which is (or should be) blind. The very essence of true competition is that, ideally, it is blind to the extent that a third party cannot predict in advance who the economic winners or losers will be. It was in this context that F.A. Hayek reminded us that "to the ancients blindness was an attribute of their deity of justice."[20] One of the characteristics of a capitalistic society that makes it uniquely free is that wealth is distributed based upon ability, enterprise, ingenuity, hard work, good fortune, and the impersonal workings of the free marketplace. This is infinitely fairer than wealth distribution by individuals appointed by society to decide who gets what, based upon those individuals'

---

[20] Hayek, *The Road To Serfdom*, 134.

often arbitrary views of the relative merits or perceived value to society of the competing parties.[21]

The Bible does not teach coercive wealth redistribution because the Judeo-Christian God is a just God. As we have seen, God specifically forbids stealing, coveting the property of another, and murder in the Ten Commandments (Exodus 20:1-17; Deuteronomy 5:4-21). The government cannot give one person a *gift* without taking something from someone else. A government strong enough to seize the property of its citizens is strong enough to kill or imprison the citizens who object. Adam Smith helped us to understand that the true, elemental foundation for economics is individual self-interest, not government mandates or mathematical equations. Economic systems or theories that ignore the human element in functional economics are doomed to eventual failure. It is for this reason that wealth redistribution or confiscation is fundamentally unsound, as well unjust, because it ignores the economic realities of this existence, violates private property rights, stifles human ingenuity, and dehumanizes society as exemplified by Soviet Russia, East Germany, North Korea, and Communist China. It is unnatural because it is contrary to the nature of mankind which God fashioned to affirm freedom, hard work, initiative, achievement, and creativity. The fact that coercive wealth redistribution is fundamentally unnatural explains why it has never been successful in the real world whether it is called progressivism, socialism, communism, or some other name. Coercive wealth redistribution's first sin is its ruthless immorality, but its second sin is that it perniciously obscures the moral virtues of genuine compassion and true charity which are always individual, voluntary, and not compulsory.

Some condemn capitalism because they blame the economic theory for the sins of the bonus culture with which business has become infected in recent decades. When asked by the tax collectors and soldiers what they must do in order to be saved, John the

---

[21] Ibid.

Baptist directed the tax collectors to "Collect no more than what you have been ordered to." He said to the soldiers, "Do not take money from anyone by force, or accuse anyone falsely, and be content with your wages."[22] John is telling us to give an honest day's work and to be content with the salary to which we agreed when we accepted the job. It is true that there are occasionally exceptional circumstances that warrant a one-time bonus. Today, however, bonuses have almost become entitlements for aggressively performing the job the employee was hired to do in the first place.

In their quest for the quick wealth afforded by the often-excessive bonus, some in the business community do commit many sins against the future, their faith, and the spirit of the law—if not the letter. Boards, executives, and others often dangle the prospect of glittering annual bonuses before the eyes of employees to entice them to do things that perhaps the board or executive would prefer not to do themselves. The bonus culture of recent decades has become something of a cancer at the very heart of modern business. Individuals should ideally be content with their wages and perform their jobs to the best of their ability for the glory of God and the long-term best interest of their customers, employer, and nation. All too often the lure of an annual bonus is an irresistible incentive for behavior that is unacceptable or actually destructive. The modern bonus culture actively encourages ruthless behavior and short-term thinking for immediate gain which is often detrimental to the long-term welfare of the customer, employer, economy, and nation. It is, however, wrong to blame the economic theory of competitive capitalism for the excesses and abuses that sometimes flow from the bonus culture just described.

There are other people who condemn capitalism because they have been led to believe that big government solutions are a kinder and gentler alternative. As one who fought the long defeat, across more than two decades, to maintain the independence of an

---

[22] Luke 3: 12-14.

excellent community hospital in the face of federal regulatory, tax, and trade policies that robbed the community of its industrial base, provided chronically insufficient reimbursement for the federal Medicaid/Medicare programs, and constantly expanded, ever more onerous Medicare rules, regulations, and unfunded mandates, I can attest that one does not know the meaning of the word *heartless* until one is forced to deal with big government with respect to matters of survival.

Another misconception on the part of many seems to be that government solutions are less costly than private, free market solutions because of supposed economies of scale, or, perhaps, because the tax burden is generally borne by someone else. In her definitive account of the Great Depression entitled *The Forgotten Man*, Amity Shlaes recalls to mind the forgotten man made famous in an essay of that name by William Graham Sumner in 1883. For her, as for Sumner, the forgotten man is the average American who is never thought of—the taxpayer. The term *forgotten man* symbolizes the men and women who belong to no particular political constituency, work hard, try to survive without government assistance, and who long for genuine economic prosperity and the independence such prosperity represents. It is the forgotten man who actually pays for the big governmental programs, pork projects, and economic experiments.[23] The forgotten man or woman knows that such programs are not without ever escalating costs. These costs are manifest both in terms of higher taxes and the opportunity cost of funds that cannot be used for other purposes which might be more beneficial or yield a higher return.

We are also told that capitalism or free enterprise is somehow sinful and at odds with Christianity. Actually, the church has

---

[23] Amity Shlaes, *The Forgotten Man, A History of the Great Depression* (New York: Harper Perennial, 2008), 12, 13. 127-128; William Graham Sumner, *The Forgotten Man and Other Essays*, ed. Albert Galloway Keller (New Haven: Yale University Press, 1918), (accessed January 10, 2015), Online Library of Liberty. www.libertyfund.org.

traditionally been more interested in the effect of wealth upon those who possess it, and the use to which it is put, than in the wealth itself. The Apostle Paul never said that money is the root of all evil. Paul's actual words were: "For the love of money is the root of all sorts of evil, and some by longing for it have wandered away from the faith and pierced themselves many griefs."[24] Jesus stated that one cannot "serve God and wealth,"[25] but, yet, He also clearly understood and accepted the business world well enough to draw spiritual analogies from it in the parable of the talents and the parable of the workers in the vineyard.[26] As the oldest son, Jesus may well have been a small businessman, running the family carpenter business, after the death of Joseph, his presumed earthly father, until his siblings came of age.

When speaking of the rich young man who was so obviously attached to his great wealth, Jesus noted that "it is easier for a camel to go through the eye of a needle than for a rich man to enter the kingdom of God."[27] Yet, we know that, by the standards of their times, Abraham, Isaac, Jacob, Joseph of Arimathea, and Nicodemus were reputed to be wealthy, and they each receive favorable mention in the Bible. In fact, success, prosperity, and wealth are often (although not always) seen as signs of God's favor in the Scriptures (1 Chronicles 29:12; James 1:17). We learn in Deuteronomy 8:18 that we are to "remember the Lord our God, for it is He who gives us the power to make wealth. . . ." Biblical virtues such as honor, honesty, integrity, prudence, dependability, and accountability actually make those who practice them more effective businessmen and women. Proverbs 10:22 reminds us that "It is the blessing of the Lord that makes rich. And He adds no sorrow to it." The Bible is also clear, however, that "ill-gotten gains

---

[24] 1Timothy 6:10.

[25] Matthew 6:24.

[26] Matthew 25:14-30; Luke 19:11-27; Matthew 20:1-16.

[27] Matthew 19:24.

do not profit."[28] The answer to the apparent contradiction between Jesus' story of the rich young man and the treatment of wealth elsewhere in the Bible lies in the fact that, again, it is not the wealth itself that is condemned, but its powerful hold on the rich young man.[29] We forget that Jesus has the power to look into the human heart and perceive weakness, obsession, sin, and lusts of whatever nature.[30] Every human heart has a particular weakness that should not be there, and Jesus knows what it is. He will help us rout it out if we will but open the door to Him.

Wealth is synonymous with authority and power. Wealth, power, and authority can be used to do good or to do evil. It can also lead to vices such as pride, sloth, and avarice. As we have already seen, power in any form can quickly become intoxicating, and does have a tendency to corrupt those individuals susceptible to its allure. The power of wealth can, therefore, corrupt, but no more so than the power possessed by a politician, bureaucrat, university professor, or even the occasional minister who attempts to rewrite the portions of the Scriptures with which he or she might disagree.[31] The potential of wealth, power, and authority to corrupt and magnify the vices to which all humans are subject is, therefore, the essence of Jesus' warning. Nowhere in the Bible is a wealthy person, merchant, military officer, or ruler condemned who seeks to know God's will and sincerely tries to do what is right in the sight of the Lord.

Christianity demands that all men and women behave fairly and lawfully, and that no undue advantage be taken of our fellow man. Money is a medium of exchange, a valuable asset, and a useful tool—nothing more. It must never be allowed to compete

---

[28] Proverbs 10:2.

[29] *See*, Carson, D.A. "Matthew." In Matthew and Mark. Vol. 9 of *The Expositor's Bible Commentary*, rev. ed., edited by Tremper Longman III and David E. Garland, pp.211-212.

[30] John 2:24-25; Matthew 9:4; Luke 6:8; Acts 1:24; 1 Chronicles 28:9.

[31] Jeremiah 5:31.

with God or one's family for one's attention. Wealth and its pursuit have been an aspect of normal life throughout human history and are not, in and of themselves, bad things. It is the morality of that quest, and its potential impact upon one's faith, behavior, character, and ethics, that causes concern. We must remember to "seek first the kingdom of God and His righteousness" before the things of this world if we are to walk with God's blessings (Matthew 6:33).

A Christian should never become obsessed with any aspect of this world, whether it is wealth, sex, alcohol, power, or some other compulsive desire, to the point that one would utilize unethical or immoral means to obtain it. One must always guard against placing the acquisition of these temporary things above one's quest to lead a godly life consistent with the Scriptures. Thus, we are brought back to the point made earlier. When practiced within the law, competitive free enterprise capitalism in a free society is the fairest economic philosophy yet to evolve for the reasons already enumerated. Resolving economic issues freely and voluntarily, through honest competition and personal effort, is always preferable to solving them through the historical alternatives of intimidation, force, government fiat, or outright violence. Where capitalism and private property ownership are sown, liberty, independence, and freedom for the individual flower.[32] It is for this reason that capitalism is viewed with such suspicion by totalitarian regimes and those who have lost their way.

If wealth is obtained honestly, then the primary concern of the church is that one's wealth be used for good and not sloth, mischief, or evil. Christianity is, therefore, very much in favor of appropriate voluntary charity, but nowhere is the state or the church authorized to seize private property for the purpose of wealth redistribution. In fact, as already noted, God preserved the sanctity of private property in the Ten Commandments wherein He commands that

---

[32] *See,* Veryser, *It Didn't Have To Be This Way,* 167-168.

145

we neither steal nor even covet our neighbor's property.[33] It is very clear that the virtue of charity comes from its voluntary nature.[34] Christianity is at war with excess such as greed, theft, usury, and dissipation, but it has never been at war with free enterprise capitalism practiced justly and within the law.[35]

Those fortunate enough to accumulate extra wealth are deemed to have a moral obligation to voluntarily assist others, thereby gaining treasure in heaven. Jesus noted that the treasures of heaven are preferable to the wealth of this world, because the treasures one accumulates in heaven will never be stolen by thieves, or destroyed by moths, or rust.[36] Jesus condemned the Pharisees for acts like tithing and visible charity while ignoring justice and the love of God.[37] History has shown that competing socio-economic theories, such as various forms of progressivism, totalitarianism, socialism, and communism; have strewn more misery for the common man, and had far less to do with justice and the love of God than competitive free enterprise capitalism.

The sort of uninformed condemnation of capitalism alluded to above is, however, not surprising since criticism, both outright and implied, is literally ripe in both academia and the media. Yet, if we look back across history, when do we see the common man begin to rise out of the bondage of serfdom and slavery? It is with the advent of Judeo-Christian concepts of morality, ethics, and individual worth together with private property rights and free enterprise capitalism. When these concepts began to coalesce in Western Europe during the Middle Ages, sometime after the great plagues and particularly during the Reformation, we see a

---

[33] Exodus 20: 15, 17; Deuteronomy 5:19,21; Mark 10:19; Luke 12:15; 1 Corinthians 5:11-13; Ephesians 5:3,5; Hebrews 13:5.

[34] 2 Corinthians 9:6-9; Exodus 25:2; 35:5, 21, 29; Matthew 20:15; *See, Veryser, It Didn't Have To Be This Way,* 169.

[35] Matthew 25:14-30; Luke 19:11-27; 1Timothy 5:8; 2 Thessalonians 3:10.

[36] Psalm 112:7-9; Matthew 6:19-21; Luke 12:20-21, 33-34, 48.

[37] Luke 11:42.

flowering over the ensuing centuries of both rights and material comforts for the common man not seen in the previous history of the world. Take these five elements away, as they are in most of the rest of the world outside the West, and one still sees the common man in a state of quiet misery and semi-serfdom. Capitalism has done more to raise ordinary men and women out of the quasi-slavery that has characterized their lot throughout most of human history, than any other economic theory. This is simply a self-evident fact. While far from perfect, because this will never be a perfect world, no crimes have been committed in the name of capitalism to equal those of the atheist regimes of Stalin, Hitler, and Mao Zedong—all of whom practiced variations of socialism and sought to establish absolute control of their societies.[38] Millions have found the procrustean bed of socialism or communism to be far less comfortable than they had been led to believe.

Notwithstanding her highly controversial views on the subject of religion, Ayn Rand's eloquent defense of capitalism, in *Atlas Shrugged* and her other works, represented a breath of much needed fresh air on the subject as we noted earlier. Many of us were taught in school that the men who industrialized America and made it a world power were robber barons. Modern historians like Larry Schweikart and Michael Allen remind us, however, that J. P. Morgan saved the federal government from bankruptcy during the Panic of 1893, and that the prices of steel and oil products dropped consistently as Andrew Carnegie improved the steel industry and John D. Rockefeller improved the oil industry.[39] Schweikart even postulates that Rockefeller may have helped save the whale from extinction by lowering the price of kerosene.[40]

---

[38] *See*, Dinesh D'Souza, *What's So Great About Christianity* (Carol Stream, Illinois: Tyndale House Publishers, Inc., 2008), 218-219, 225.

[39] Larry Schweikart and Michael Allen, *A Patriot's History of the United States* (New York: Sentinel, Penguin Group (USA) Inc., 2007), 430-434.

[40] Ibid., 432.

Hundreds of millions of dollars were donated to charities and worthy causes by early capitalists like Carnegie and Rockefeller. In Winston-Salem, North Carolina, where I grew up, the old library building (now used for other purposes) made possible by Carnegie philanthropy still stands. Millions of Americans have enjoyed visiting historic Colonial Williamsburg, just one of the many dreams that Rockefeller philanthropy made possible. In Winston-Salem, North Carolina, money from the Z. Smith Reynolds Foundation made the relocation of Wake Forest University to Winston-Salem a reality, and the Kate B. Reynolds Charitable Trust continues to fund healthcare and many other worthy causes.

Another native of North Carolina, James Buchanan Duke, established The Duke Endowment in 1924, which to date has donated over $3.4 billion in grants to non-profit hospitals, educational institutions, and a variety of other religious and socially enlightened causes. As someone who spent much of his career in a non-profit community hospital, I will forever be grateful for the kindness, sympathy, and support consistently extended by The Duke Endowment to the non-profit hospitals of both North Carolina and South Carolina.

One strategy used by those who would lure mankind into error is to entice us to focus upon and become obsessed with those things which we do not have, rather than the many blessings that we do possess. This story is as old as the original temptation of Adam and Eve in the Garden of Eden when the serpent (Satan) successfully focused Adam and Eve's desire upon the one thing in the garden that God had forbidden them (Genesis 2:15-17; Genesis 3:1-24). In this tunnel vision mindset, nonproductive and destructive emotions like jealousy, greed, envy, and lust take root and flower. These emotions have more than once caused mankind to kill the goose that lays the golden egg, and take gigantic steps backward in its development and upward progress. The siren song of a slide way, a shortcut, or a free lunch has lured populations into developmental dead-ends more than once. A case in point is Russia's adoption of communism just as capitalism was beginning to transform its society in a positive manner. The relative status and standard of living of the common man in South Korea as opposed to North Korea, or West Germany as opposed to East Germany, have served as laboratory examples of the miracle of competitive capitalism as opposed to state control.

The positive course of private enterprise and competitive capitalism may not have always been obvious, tranquil, or pretty, but, over the course of time, it has steadily elevated the status and standard of living of the common man and woman beyond that of any competing economic theory. In fact, as Milton Friedman pointed out, both history and comparisons with parts of the world where it is lacking show that competitive capitalism actually results in less inequality than other economic systems or forms of social organization, with relative inequality declining more as competitive capitalism increases.[41] History also indicates that the introduction of competitive free enterprise capitalism has also been accompanied by a reduction in economic discrimination against various previously disadvantaged social, religious, and racial groups with discrimination being less where freedom of competition is the greatest.[42]

Notwithstanding the demonstrated verdict of history, there are still those who charge that capitalism does not work well enough today. It would perhaps benefit those individuals to remember that, for over one hundred years, in man's quixotic quest for the welfare state, the West has been slowly retreating from the free market principles[43] upon which competitive capitalism is based. The

---

[41] Milton Friedman, *Capitalism And Freedom*, (Chicago and London: The University of Chicago Press, 2002 [1962]), 169.

[42] Ibid., 108-109.print

[43] Harry C. Veryser lists the following prerequisites: individual liberty, limited government, free trade, economic freedom, rule of law, sacredness of contract, low taxation, sound specie-based currency, strong family structure, entrepreneurship, and pricing set by free markets. These principles were broadly and generally accepted from the end of the Napoleonic Wars in 1815 until the advent of WWI in 1914. Harry C. Veryser characterizes this period as the golden age of classical

principles questioned with suspicion and angst were and continue to be those which initially liberated the genius of man to elevate our status beyond the wildest dreams of our ancestors, and which gave the common man his first real chance to break free from the bonds of class and poverty.

Economic freedom can be suppressed by totalitarian leaders, oppressive economic theories such as socialism and communism or by excessive bureaucratic rules, regulations, and taxation policies. In 1835 Tocqueville wrote, "Despotism certainly brings ruin to men, more by preventing them from producing than by taking away the fruits of their labors; it dries up the source of wealth while it often respects wealth once acquired. On the other hand, freedom spawns a thousand times more goods than it destroys and, in nations where this is understood, the people's resources always grow more quickly than taxes."[44] Tocqueville clearly felt that the United States of 1831, the year of his visit, was a nation where this principle was understood for he wrote, "Not only do we see in the United States, as in all other countries, manufacturing and commercial classes, but also we see something which had never occurred previously, the whole community of men simultaneously engaged in production and commerce."[45]

Today, modern capitalism is often smothered beneath an enervating spider web of constantly increasing and ever more complex rules, regulations, laws, taxes, and penalties that punish both business and creative initiative. Tocqueville feared that a democratic society on the American model could easily fall prey to such restrictions on individual liberty. While one does not typically think of Tocqueville as a prophet, he wrote the following words almost two hundred years ago:

---

liberalism during which there was virtually no inflation, no world wars, an explosion of innovation, reduction in infant mortality, and a quadrupling of the standard of living. Veryser, *It Didn't Have To Be This Way*, 63-74, 186.

[44] Alexis De Tocqueville, *Democracy in America and Two Essays on America*, 243.

[45] Alexis De Tocqueville, *Democracy in America and Two Essays on America*, 524-25.

Thus, the ruling power, having taken each citizen one by one into its powerful grasp and having molded him to its own liking, spreads its arms over the whole of society, covering the surface of social life with a network of petty, complicated, detailed, and uniform rules through which even the most original minds and the most energetic of spirits cannot reach the light in order to rise above the crowd. It does not break men's wills but it does soften, bend, and control them; rarely does it force men to act but it constantly opposes what actions they perform; it does not destroy the start of anything but it stands in its way; it does not tyrannize but it inhibits, represses, drains, snuffs out, dulls so much effort that finally it reduces each nation to nothing more than a flock of timid and hardworking animals with the government as shepherd.[46]

The business climate in the United States, Britain, and Western Europe is far from being an ideal laboratory environment for the practice of pure competitive capitalism. To recall Ayn Rand's famous book, *Atlas Shrugged*, it would be small wonder if "Atlas" did finally decide to "Shrug." These days, the invisible hand[47] of which Adam Smith[48]spoke more often than not labors in handcuffs. It is a testament to competitive capitalism's efficacy, efficiency, and superiority over every other economic system that it has in fact survived. Few endeavors in the history of mankind have been as counterintuitive and ultimately unproductive as the misguided

---

[46] Alexis De Tocqueville, *Democracy in America and Two Essays on America*, 806.

[47] Adam Smith, *The Wealth of Nations*, ed. Edwin Cannan (New York: Bantam Dell, 2003 [1776]), 572.

[48] Adam Smith (1723-1790): Scottish philosopher and pioneer economist most famous for his highly influential work, *An Inquiry into the Nature and Causes of the Wealth of Nations*, published in 1776. Smith is considered by many to be the father of capitalism.

preoccupation of much of academia in the West with hobbling competitive free enterprise capitalism.

This period of increasing challenge for competitive capitalism also coincides with the continued decline of the Protestant asceticism or ethic to which Max Weber attributed, in large part, the original flowering of modern rational capitalism.[49] This Protestant ethic was characterized by pious faith and a belief that one's labor or calling in life was worthy of religious veneration. Indeed, the Apostle Paul had asked that we "walk worthy of the calling" to which we have been called and to do our "work heartily as for the Lord rather than for men."[50] One's calling demanded scrupulous honesty, morality, industry, accountability, frugality, discipline, and ultimately charity. Even today, Charles Stanley has written that "any division we may perceive between God's work and our jobs is a false one."[51] He goes on to note that "one reason so many Christians are not happy in their careers" is that they no longer "view their occupations as God's work."[52] As we have seen, the slow erosion of the biblical virtues described above undermines not only the capitalism upon which the economic success of our civilization rests, but every other pillar of an ordered, civilized, and disciplined society including democracy itself.

Can we say that capitalism, successful though it has been, has given us a perfect society, freedom from all want, and a utopia on earth? No, those things will always be reserved for heaven, but for the common man or woman who is willing to get an education and work hard; competitive free enterprise capitalism continues to be the goose with the best potential to lay the golden egg. In 1945, Winston Churchill summed up the choice before us best when he

---

[49] Max Weber, *The Protestant Ethic and the Spirit of Capitalism,* trans. Talcott Parsons (New York: Charles Scribner's Sons, 1958 [1920]), 27, 172, 176-177, 180.

[50] Ephesians 4:1; Colossians 3:23-24; *See also*, Stanley, *The Spirit-Filled Life,* 160-162.

[51] Stanley, *The Spirit-Filled Life,* 162.

[52] Stanley, *The Spirit-Filled Life,* 162.

stated, "The inherent vice of capitalism is the unequal sharing of blessings; the inherent virtue of socialism is the equal sharing of miseries."[53]

Having praised true competitive capitalism, it is only fair to cry shame to the politicians and captains of industry who have entered into unfair trade agreements and relationships with foreign countries. Such agreements and relationships often result in the loss of both American jobs and manufacturing capacity because those involved lacked the will and the discipline to demand reciprocity of access for American goods into the markets of those foreign countries on a basis fully equal to that granted to their goods in this country. President Reagan once noted that free trade should also be fair.[54] A treaty or contract is not worth the paper it is written upon if those involved lack the will to enforce it.

Economic globalism, at the expense of American values and legitimate national interests, has adversely impacted national defense, cost countless American jobs, blunted the economic progress of the American lower and middle classes, and undermined the Judeo-Christian culture upon which our unique society of individual worth and liberty depend. When masses of citizens are denied genuine economic prosperity and the security, self-confidence, pride, and independence that come with making a good life for one's family in the free market, the light of liberty and freedom will ultimately pale. This situation reflects not a problem with free enterprise, competitive capitalism, but a betrayal of it. It is a problem of will, discipline, ethics, intellectual acuity, strategic vision, and patriotism—not capitalism.

If the elimination of American manufacturing continues at its current pace, what will be the implications for future generations dependent upon nations that are not our friends for virtually every

---

[53] Churchill, Winston S., House of Commons Debate on Demobilization (October 22, 1945), vol. 414, cc 1704.

[54] Ronald Reagan, *An American Life* (New York: Simon And Schuster, 1990), 242.

article of daily living? What would be the implication for the future of America if we had to field our armed forces in a worldwide conflict similar to World War II for several years? We are told that America's future is in high-tech areas. There is, however, no assurance that the same countries that have siphoned away so much of our traditional manufacturing capacity will not also dominate the emerging high-tech/bio-tech industries. This is a particularly worrisome prospect if our current punitive trade, regulatory, and tax policies continue to place our own businesses and entrepreneurs at a competitive disadvantage. Thus far, it seems self-evident that our trade, regulatory, taxation, and energy policies have proven to be very shortsighted. Our actions to date raise the very real fear that this nation is selling its soul and its future security for a cheaper price on a flat-screen television.

Why do these matters concern us? They concern us because our Judeo-Christian heritage and our economic freedom are the foundational elements upon which all of our other freedoms rest. The human spirit, individualism, and liberty flower in an environment of Judeo-Christian values and accountability. The spirit of man sinks shackled and withered in those gray realms where these elements are absent. The plight of mankind throughout much of the rest of the world is a stark testament to this time-tested historical truth.

They concern us because, although far from perfect, the United States is still the world's last and greatest bastion of traditional, orthodox Judeo-Christian faith, morality, ethics, and hope. If its culture falls to the corrupt lethargy, heresy, neo-paganism, and atheism currently sweeping the world, the soft light of justice, limited government, accountability, individual freedom and self-worth, faith, hope, and charity born of, and sustained by, traditional Christianity will be extinguished in the West. While it is true that free enterprise competitive capitalism produces more wealth for all levels of society than any other economic system, perhaps its greatest, and often overlooked, byproduct is simply freedom and liberty.

154

Religion

From at least the time of the Mayflower Compact in 1620, which noted that the purpose of the settlers in coming to America was for "the glory of God and the advancement of the Christian faith," our society in the New World developed upon the foundation and principles of our Judeo-Christian heritage. Even today, according to the World Factbook section of the Central Intelligence Agency web site, at least 78.5 percent of our population is Christian and another 1.7 percent is Jewish.

Most of the Founding Fathers were openly and devoutly Christian which is reflected in their writings, speeches, and actions. In his book, *America's Godly Heritage*, David Barton traces the influence of Christianity upon the Founding Fathers through countless references to the original documents of the period. We learn that of the fifty-six Founding Fathers who signed the Declaration of Independence virtually all were members of traditional, orthodox Christian Churches, and "over half had received degrees from schools that today would be considered seminaries or Bible schools."[55] This influence is further affirmed by historians Larry Schweikart and Michael Allen who state that "any reading of the American Revolution from a purely secular viewpoint ignores a fundamentally Christian component of the Revolutionary ideology."[56]

In his book, *George Washington's Sacred Fire*, the Reverend Peter Lillback researches the original sources, which include George Washington's voluminous correspondence, the correspondence of those who knew him, the correspondence of those who knew those who had known him, and the historical record, to conclusively prove that George Washington was a devout eighteenth-century

---

[55] Barton, *America's Godly Heritage*, 8-9; *See also*, Schweikart and Allen, *A Patriot's History of the United States*, 71; Alexis De Tocqueville, Democracy in America, 346: In 1835 Tocqueville states in the footnote to this page that, "The greater part of education is entrusted to the clergy."

[56] Schweikart and Allen, *A Patriot's History of the United States*, 71, 97.

Anglican Christian with the same understanding of traditional Christianity that we know today. Washington was most definitely not a deist, as he has frequently been depicted by liberal revisionist historians since the first quarter of the twentieth century.[57] Lillback also gives valuable insight as to how Christianity was perceived and revered during the Founding era. John Adam's biographer, David McCullough, also notes that John Adams was a "devout Christian."[58]

Alexander Hamilton was one of the brightest intellectual lights in the star-filled firmament of the Founding Fathers. His biographer, Ron Chernow, states, "For Hamilton, religion formed the basis of all law and morality, and he thought the world would be a hellish place without it."[59] Like Edmund Burke, Hamilton was justly horrified by the bloody excesses of revolutionary France which was ruled by enlightenment atheism and the guillotine. He was raised as a Christian and continued devout as a young man "praying fiercely" while at King's College.[60] Although his faith appeared to moderate during the pressures of the Revolutionary War and the intense obligations of his subsequent political career, it seems that Hamilton's Christian faith flowered again in his last years. He was never a proponent of any specific denomination or regular church attendance, but appears to have always regarded himself as a Christian, as did his mentor, George Washington. Chernow notes that the materials of Hamilton's son, John Church Hamilton, present evidence of both theological and Bible study on Hamilton's part with specific quotes that indicate that, as a lawyer,

---

[57] Peter A. Lillback and Jerry Newcombe, *George Washington's Sacred Fire* (Bryn Mawr, Pennsylvania: Providence Forum Press, 2006), 714-716; *See also,* Jay A. Parry and Andrew M. Allison, *The Real George Washington* (National Center for Constitutional Studies, Seventh Printing, 2009), 604.

[58] David McCullough, *John Adams* (New York: Simon & Schuster Paperback, 2001), 19, 625.

[59] Ron Chernow, *Alexander Hamilton* (New York: Penguin Books, Penguin Group (USA) Inc., 2004), 659.

[60] Ibid.

Hamilton passed his "verdict" in favor of the authenticity of the Christian religion. Speaking of Christianity, Hamilton told his wife, "I have studied it and I can prove its truth as clearly as any proposition ever submitted to the mind of man."[61] The fact that Hamilton was a man of epic ability and glaring lapses has caused some historians to doubt the sincerity of his religious beliefs, but Chernow states that Hamilton's preoccupation with spiritual matters as he lay dying "eliminates all doubt about the sincerity of his late-flowering religious interests."[62]

While it was the Age of Enlightenment, the colonies had been settled by individuals deeply committed to the truth of the Scriptures and the integrity of their faith. That faith had been reenergized in the religious Great Awakening from roughly 1735-1750.[63] Religious perspective in the colonies was very different from that of France, and this, more than anything, probably accounts for the fact that the American Revolution was not stained by a reign of chaos and terror as was the case with the French Revolution. In his pamphlet entitled Information to Those Who Would Remove to America written in 1782, Benjamin Franklin noted: "To this it may be truly added, that serious religion, under its various denominations, is not only tolerated, but respected and practiced. Atheism is unknown there; infidelity rare and secret; so that persons may live to a great age in that country, without having their piety shocked by meeting with either an atheist or an infidel. And the Divine Being seems to have manifest his approbation of the mutual forbearance and kindness with which the different sects treat each other, by the remarkable prosperity with which He has been pleased to favor the whole country."[64]

---

[61] Ibid., 660.

[62] Ibid,.706.

[63] *See*, Jon Meacham, *Thomas Jefferson: The Art of Power* (New York: Random House Publishing Group, 2013), 113.

[64] See also, H. W. Brands, The First American, The Life and Times of Benjamin Franklin (New York: Anchor Books, A Division of Random House, Inc., 2002), 634.

The Founding Fathers saw the values and discipline distilled from the Ten Commandments and principles of the New Testament as critical to the development of an ordered society capable of appreciating and preserving the republican values of freedom and liberty.[65]They discerned that democracy was fundamentally based upon individualism and the love of personal liberty. They also understood the powerful positive effect upon the nation's citizens of government clearly grounded in Judeo-Christian moral and ethical principles. They were, for the most part, careful to display that positive example in their own words and deeds.[66] John Adams noted that "Avarice, ambition, revenge or gallantry would break the strongest cords of our Constitution, as a whale goes through a net. Our Constitution was made only for a moral and religious people. It is wholly inadequate to the government of any other."[67] In his Farewell Address, George Washington stated:

> Of all the dispositions and habits which lead to political prosperity, religion and morality are indispensible supports. In vain would that man claim the tribute of patriotism, who would labor to

---

[65] *See*, Alexis De Tocqueville, *Democracy in America*, 342: Writing in 1835 Tocqueville stated, "Religion, which never interferes directly in the government of Americans, should therefore be regarded as the first of their political institutions, for, if it does not give them the taste for liberty, it enables them to take unusual advantage of it. This is how the inhabitants of the United States themselves see their religious beliefs. I do not know whether all Americans put faith in their religion, for who can read into men's hearts? But I am sure that they believe it necessary for the maintenance of republican institutions. This is not an opinion peculiar to one class of citizens or to one party, but to a whole nation; it is found in every rank of society."

[66] *See*, Alexis De Tocqueville, *Democracy in America*, 341-342; *See also*, Schweikart and Allen, *A Patriot's History of the United States*, 123, 125.

[67] Letter to the Officers of the First Brigade of the Third Division of the Militia of Massachusetts, October 11, 1798, John Adams, vol. 9 (Letters and State Papers 1799-1810) [1854], ed. Charles Francis Adams. *Online Library of Liberty*. www.libertyfund.org. Accessed September 25, 2014. Some sources for this quote read "and licentiousness" rather than "or gallantry."

subvert these great pillars of human happiness, these firmest props of the duties of men and citizens. The mere politician, equally with the pious man, ought to respect and cherish them . . . And let us with caution indulge the supposition that morality can be maintained without religion. Whatever may be conceded to the influence of refined education . . . Reason and experience both forbid us to expect that national morality can prevail in exclusion of religious principle.[68]

In his Inaugural Address, John Adams noted that he felt it his duty to state that "if a veneration for the religion of a people who profess and call themselves Christians, and a fixed resolution to consider a decent respect for Christianity among the best recommendations for public service, can enable me in any degree to comply with your wishes, it shall be my strenuous endeavor. . . ."[69] Writing in 1835, Alexis De Tocqueville stated that "Americans so completely identify the spirit of Christianity with freedom in their minds that it is almost impossible to get them to conceive the one without the other; and this is not one of those sterile ideas bequeathed by the past to present nor one which seems to vegetate in the soul rather than to live."[70] On the eve of the Civil War, Abraham Lincoln stated in his Inaugural address his belief that "Intelligence, patriotism, Christianity, and a firm reliance on Him who has never yet forsaken this favored land, are still competent to adjust in the best way all our present difficulties."[71]

---

[68] George Washington, Farewell Address, September 17, 1796 (Library of Congress Digital Collections).

[69] John Adams, Inaugural Address, March 4, 1797 (Library of Congress Digital Collections).

[70] Alexis De Tocqueville, *Democracy in America*, 343.

[71] Abraham Lincoln, Inaugural Address, March 5, 1861 (Library of Congress Digital Collections).

President Harry S. Truman attributed our victories against Germany and Japan in World War II to God and established national days of prayer to commemorate the surrender of each.[72] In his address to the American people after the formal signing of the terms of surrender by Japan, President Truman again thanked God for victory against the "forces of tyranny" that sought to destroy God's civilization.[73]

The Constitution of North Carolina, my native state, still contains a reference to its Christian nature.[74] Clearly, if our nation was not grounded on overtly religious and Christian principles some of our greatest leaders were not aware of that fact. In fact, when Alexis De Tocqueville arrived in the United States in 1831 to begin his famous study of American democracy, he noted that "it was the religious atmosphere which first struck me."[75] Tocqueville stated that "Christianity has therefore maintained a strong sway over the American mind and—something I wish to note above all—it rules not only like a philosophy taken up after evaluation but like a religion believed without discussion."[76]

Thus, it was that the United States was pretty much universally accepted as a Christian nation with the moral and ethical values of the Bible reaffirmed in both our institutions and the education of our children (as can be readily identified in early text books like *The New England_Primer*) throughout the nineteenth and early twentieth

---

[72] Truman, Harry S., Broadcast to the American People Announcing the Surrender of Germany (May 8 1945), Public Papers of the Presidents: 27, Truman Library; Truman, Harry S., Proclamation 2660: Victory in the East—Day of Prayer (August 16, 1945), Public Papers of the Presidents: 105, Truman Library.

[73] Truman, Harry S., Radio Address to the American People After the Signing of the Terms of Unconditional Surrender by Japan (September 1, 1945), Public Papers of the Presidents: 122, Truman Library.

[74] N.C. Const., art. XI, §4.

[75] Alexis De Tocqueville, *Democracy in America*, 345.

[76] Alexis De Tocqueville, *Democracy in America*, 497.

centuries.[77] Noting that this preoccupation with the spiritual had existed in America from the time of first settlement and had influenced legislation such as that relating to public education from an early date, Tocqueville stated that "in America religion leads to wisdom; the observance of divine laws guides man to freedom."[78]

All of this suddenly began to change in 1947 when, starting with *Everson v. Board of Education*, 330 U.S. 1, 67 S. Ct. 504, 91 L. Ed.711 (1947), the Supreme Court began a legal trend that ignored, without significant comment, the reality of history, previous precedent, and the writings of the Founding Fathers on the subject of church and state. Although founded on a mistaken interpretation of the Constitution and history, this trend would eventually see the Ten Commandments removed from the courthouse walls, the manger scene off the public square, and all prayer, Bible reading, and religion out of the public schools. This was done in the name of *separation of church and state*, a phrase that does not appear in either the Constitution or the Bill of Rights. It was taken out of context from a letter written by Thomas Jefferson years after the Constitution and Bill of Rights had been adopted. In his concurring opinion in *Sherbert v. Verner*, 374 U.S. 398, 413-414, 83 S. Ct. 1790, 10 L. Ed. 2d 965 (1963) Justice Potter Stewart echoes this view when he states:

> I am convinced that no liberty is more essential to the continued vitality of the free society which our Constitution guarantees than is the religious liberty protected by the Free Exercise Clause explicit in the First Amendment and imbedded in the Fourteenth. And I regret that on occasion, and specifically in *Braunfeld v. Brown*, supra, the Court has shown what has seemed to me a distressing insensitivity to the appropriate demands of this constitutional guarantee. By contrast I think that the Court's

---

[77] *See,* Alexis De Tocqueville, *Democracy in America,* 496-497; *See also,* Barton, *America's Godly Heritage,* 17-19.

[78] Alex De Tocqueville, *Democracy in America,* 54.

approach to the Establishment Clause has on occasion, and specifically in *Engel, Schempp and Murray*, been not only insensitive, but positively wooden, and that the Court has accorded to the Establishment Clause a meaning which neither the words, the history, nor the intention of the authors of that specific constitutional provision even remotely suggests.

A close reading of the First Amendment and the writings of the Founding Fathers related to its proposal and adoption, seems to indicate that the amendment's purpose was to prevent the federal government from establishing a national church or denomination such as the Church of England, and to prevent the federal government from interfering with the public expression of religious preference by the citizenry. This view is reflected in the influential work *Commentaries on the Constitution of the United States*, published in 1833 by Associate Justice Joseph Story. Why is the opinion of Story of such interest? It is of great interest because Joseph Story was nominated to the United States Supreme Court by none other than James Madison, who is acknowledged as a principal author of the Constitution.

Story wrote that at the time the First Amendment was adopted it was, "probably the general, if not the universal sentiment in America . . . that Christianity ought to receive encouragement from the state, so far as it is not incompatible with the private rights of conscience and freedom of religious worship. An attempt to level all religions, and to make it a matter of state policy to hold all in utter indifference, would have created universal disapprobation, if not universal indignation."[79] Story goes on to state:

> The real object of the amendment was, not to countenance, much less to advance Mahometanism, or Judaism, or infidelity, by prostrating Christianity;

---

[79] Joseph Story, LL.D., *Commentaries on the Constitution of the United States with a Preliminary Review of The Constitutional History of the Colonies and States, Before The Adoption of the Constitution* [1833], 700. (Gale Making of the Modern Law Print Edition).

but to exclude all rivalry among the Christian sects, and to prevent any national ecclesiastical establishment, which should give to an hierarchy the exclusive patronage of the national government ... But this alone would have been an imperfect security, if it had not been followed up by a declaration of the right of free exercise of religion, and prohibition ... of all religious tests. Thus, the whole power over the subject of religion is left exclusively to the state governments ... and the Catholic and the Protestant, the Calvinist and the Arminian, the Jew and the Infidel, may sit down at the common table of the national councils, without any inquisitions into their faith, or mode of worship.[80]

Thus, on its face the language of the First Amendment, as well as Associate Justice Story's commentary, would appear to protect religious expression rather than promote the disestablishment of religion in the public life of the republic. Yet, since 1947 this is what has happened, leaving the morality of the Ten Commandments and the Bible to be reaffirmed only in the home and the church. In the name of political and/or ideological expediency, far too many Supreme Court justices have forgotten, in their analysis of the Constitution, that the actual intent and personal practices of the Framers are critical to a correct understanding of its meaning. Far too many Supreme Court justices have forgotten that basic and very fundamental bit of legal wisdom which states that "a paper writing says what it says."

One might ask why we care that tremendous power of the Bible to promote morality and ethical behavior in the population has been relegated to the home and the church. We care because the power of positive example is a potent force in the minds of children and the general public. When prayer, religion, and the Ten

---

[80] Ibid., 701-703.

Commandments are specifically excluded from public schools, it creates in some impressionable minds the specter that these concepts are at best no longer relevant in the modern world or at worse that they are flawed in some way. It places a distance between moral considerations and everyday life. It tends to promote the compartmentalization of morality and ethics in the minds of the population. There is a societal need for all citizens to reflect their moral and ethical scruples in everyday life, and not just see them as part of church service or home devotion. With the suppression of our Judeo-Christian heritage, we have hobbled one of our society's most potent and monolithic unifying cultural memories.

We also care because the value that Christianity places upon the fundamental worth of the individual makes democracy as we have known it possible. The renowned theologian, scholar, and teacher William Barclay went so far as to say, "If ever Christian principles are banished from political and economic life there is nothing left to keep at bay the totalitarian state where the individual is lost in the system, and exists, not for his own sake, but only for the sake of the system."[81] It is for this reason that, from the time of the Roman Empire, totalitarian regimes have sought to extinguish the light that Christianity represents. Alexis De Tocqueville wrote that "when a nation's religion is destroyed, doubt takes a grip upon the highest areas of intelligence, partially paralyzing all others," and creates a condition that both weakens the soul and "shapes citizens for slavery."[82] He noted that "if a man is without faith, he must serve someone and if he is free, he must believe."[83] T. S. Eliot was even more blunt when he wrote, "If you will not have God (and He is a jealous God) you should pay your respects to Hitler or Stalin."[84]

---

[81] William Barclay, *The Gospel of Luke*, rev. ed. (Philadelphia: The Westminster Press, 1975), 177-178.

[82] Alexis De Tocqueville, *Democracy in America,* 511-512.

[83] Ibid.

[84] Eliot, *Christianity & Culture,* 50.

It is becoming ever more awkward for individuals to affirm their Judeo-Christian beliefs in the activities of daily life. Good people now hesitate to even send out Christmas cards for fear of being politically incorrect. Even at the hospital where I formerly worked, there were some who, for reasons of political correctness, preferred to call our institutional Christmas tree a holiday tree. Fortunately, the common-sense wisdom of the common man was still alive in the hearts of the engineers who procured and decorated the tree. They were always quick to affirm that they were decorating a Christmas tree and wanted no part of a holiday tree.

It is also worth taking note of the tremendous power that the state has assumed over our lives since the 1930s. Schooling is now compulsory and many schools now have our nation's children for more of their waking hours than the children's parents. Justice Stewart emphasized these considerations in his dissent to *School District of Abington Township, Pennsylvania v. Schempp; Murray v. Curlett*, 374 U.S. 203,313, 83 S. Ct. 1560, 10 L. Ed.2d 844 (1963) in which the court banned Bible reading in public schools. Justice Stewart noted:

> It might also be argued that parents who want their children exposed to religious influences can adequately fulfill that wish off school property and outside school time. With all its surface persuasiveness, however, this argument seriously misconceives the basic constitutional justification for permitting the exercises (commencing school days with Bible reading) at issue in these cases. For a compulsory state education system so structures a child's life that if religious exercises are held to be an impermissible activity in schools, religion is placed at an artificial and state-created disadvantage. Viewed in this light, permission of such exercises for those who want them is necessary if the schools are truly to be neutral in the matter of religion. And a refusal to permit religious exercises thus is seen, not

as the realization of state neutrality, but rather as the establishment of a religion of secularism, or at the least, as government support of the beliefs of those who think that religious exercises should be conducted only in private.

The current cultural decline of virtually every aspect of American society and the societies of most Western countries, is testament to the fact that the state of affairs so feared by Justice Stewart has indeed occurred. The Supreme Court has led our governing institutions away from the religious neutrality that was intended to protect our right of religious expression, free of discrimination, into a heavy-handed preference for secularism. This secularism, despite the best efforts of churches and parents, has become so pervasive and overpowering that it has created a spiritual and moral vacuum in our society. This vacuum is being filled with variants of neo-paganism, agnosticism, atheism, and other characteristics inconsistent with a society founded upon moral principles designed to protect the integrity of the republic. The Founding Fathers including even Thomas Jefferson would have been appalled.

Since the legal trend discussed above, leading basically to the disestablishment of religion in America, was introduced by the Supreme Court in 1947 and subsequently expanded, presidents of both major political parties have occupied the White House and both national parties have controlled Congress at various times. To date, however, no president or political party has been willing to expend political capital to redress the miscarriage, of both history and the original intent of the authors of our Constitution, with respect to the Establishment Clause which these very liberal decisions represent.[85] Neither they nor subsequent Supreme Court Justices can legitimately claim ignorance, because, in his ringing dissent to *Wallace v. Jaffree*, 472 U.S.38, 91-114, 105 S. Ct. 2479, 86

---

[85] The Religious Freedom Restoration Act of 1993, passed with bipartisan support, relates only to the Free Exercise Clause and applies only to federal law.

L.Ed.2nd 29 (1985), Justice Rehnquist took it upon himself to trace the entire legislative and Constitutional history of the Establishment Clause. He also took this opportunity to dissect the court's prior erroneous use of Jefferson's "misleading metaphor" of the "wall of separation between church and state." Rehnquist made an extremely compelling case that the Supreme Court's decisions on this issue, in the thirty-eight years since its initial error in *Everson v. Board of Education*, had been based upon a mistaken understanding of constitutional history.

Justice Rehnquist noted that the "greatest injury of the 'wall' notion" was its "mischievous diversion of judges from the actual intentions of the drafters of the Bill of Rights."[86] He further stated that "no amount of repetition of historical errors in judicial opinions can make the errors true." For Rehnquist, as it should be for all of us, "the true meaning of the Establishment Clause can only be seen in its history." He argued that: "as drafters of our Bill of Rights, the Framers inscribed the principles that control today. Any deviation from their intentions frustrates the permanence of that Charter and will only lead to the type of unprincipled decision making that has plagued our Establishment Clause cases since *Everson*":

> The Framers intended the Establishment Clause to prohibit the designation of any church as a 'national' one. The Clause was also designed to stop the Federal Government from asserting a preference for one religious denomination or sect over others. Given the "incorporation" of the Establishment Clause as against the States via the Fourteenth Amendment in *Everson*, States are prohibited as well from establishing a religion or discriminating between sects. As its history abundantly shows, however, nothing in the Establishment Clause requires government to be strictly neutral between religion and irreligion, nor does that Clause prohibit

---

[86] *Wallace v. Jaffree*, 107

Congress or the States from pursuing legitimate secular ends through nondiscriminatory sectarian means.[87]

In conclusion, Justice Rehnquist observed, "George Washington himself at the request of the very Congress which had passed the Bill of Rights, proclaimed a day of 'public thanksgiving and prayer to be observed by acknowledging with grateful hearts the many and signal favors of Almighty God.' History must judge, whether it was the Father of his Country in 1789, or a majority of the Court today which has strayed from the meaning of the Establishment Clause."[88]

On a more positive note, in 2014 the U.S. Supreme Court case of *Town of Greece v. Galloway*[89] seems to shine a ray of sunlight upon the dismal judicial landscape represented by the cases just discussed. The Court reaffirmed the constitutionality of legislative prayer even at the municipal level as long as the prayers were not coercive or overtly sectarian in the sense of a pattern of using the prayer opportunity "to proselytize or advance any one, or to disparage any other, faith or belief."

The Court went on to note that the Establishment Clause must be interpreted "by reference to historical practices and understandings" and that any test of constitutionality "must acknowledge a practice that was accepted by the Framers and has withstood the critical scrutiny of time and political change." This implies that the Court is henceforth going to consider the actual intent and historical practice of the original Framers of the Constitution with respect to the Establishment Clause.

It also appears that the test for violation of the First Amendment is no longer whether an *endorsement* of religion is alleged, but

---

[87] *Wallace v. Jaffree*, 113.

[88] *Wallace v. Jaffree*, 113.

[89] *Town of Greece, New York v. Susan Galloway, et al*, No. 12-696 (U.S., May 5, 2014).

whether there is a charge of religious *coercion*. The court further noted that merely being offended does not equate with being coerced. The Court stated that it would be unwise to conclude "that only those religious words acceptable to the majority are permissible" in legislative prayers, because "the First Amendment is not a majority rule and government may not seek to define permissible categories of religious speech." It is the belief of the *Town of Greece v. Galloway* majority of the Court that "Government may not mandate a civic religion that stifles any but the most generic reference to the sacred any more than it may prescribe a religious orthodoxy."

There is much that is encouraging in *Town of Greece v. Galloway*. If future cases follow the train of reasoning exhibited by the court majority in this case, perhaps one day the Court will rebuild the wall that separates church and state in a manner that the original Framers of the Constitution would recognize and endorse.

With respect to the religious issues raised by these Establishment Clause Supreme Court cases, and, notwithstanding the irrefutable reference to the historical context and constitutional history of the Establishment Clause by Justices Stewart, Rehnquist, and the Court majority in *Town of Greece v. Galloway*, our political leaders to date, as noted earlier, have for the most part been content to be governed by the liberal judges who constituted the majority of the Supreme Court at the time cases like *Everson v. Board of Education* were decided. To date, there has apparently been no attempt to explore legislative or constitutional remedies which might exist to correct the miscarriage of history and precedent represented by these problematic decisions. The cases of this period represent a dark triumph of secular liberal ideology and error over both truth and history.

This very troublesome judicial trend was continued by the Supreme Court in 2015 with its decision on same-sex marriage in *Obergefell v. Hodges*. In this case the Supreme Court majority managed, within the pages of a single very political opinion, to undermine more than three thousand years of Judeo-Christian morality, the U. S. Constitution, the family, history, and the concept of popular self-government all in the name of the Fourteenth Amendment. F.A. Hayek once observed "if in the long run we are makers of our own fate, in the short run we are the captives of the ideas we have created."[90] The melancholy march of our culture into secularism or worse, fostered by the line of Supreme Court decisions just discussed, indicates that we are also apparently captives of our errors as well, even when we know them to be such.

To continue the analogy of governance by judges, there was a period in the Old Testament chronicled in the Book of Judges, after the deaths of Moses and Joshua, when the ancient Israelites were loosely governed by leaders called "judges" such as Gideon, Deborah, and Samson. This was a time of upheaval, tumult, spiritual confusion, and rebellion. Of this time, it was said that "everyone did what was right in his own eyes" (Judges 21:25) even though this violated God's teachings (Deuteronomy 12:8). Increasingly, this is where our society finds itself today. Many people are creating a vision of God that suits their own personal fancy. This vision often has little basis in either the Scriptures or objective fact, but it serves the purpose of permitting them to do whatever seems "right in their own eyes."[91]

In his work *Reflections on the Revolution in France*, Edmund Burke expressed his belief, in so many words, that once the moral constraints imposed by religion through centuries of faith, habit, manners, and custom are weakened, the demons of man's darker nature are released once more with the "terrors" of mere human

---

[90] Hayek, *The Road To Serfdom*, 58.

[91] When King Jehoshaphat instituted much needed reforms in ancient Judah, he strongly commanded his new judicial appointees to: "Consider what you are doing, for you do not judge for man but for the Lord who is with you when you render judgment. Now then let the fear of the Lord be upon you; be very careful what you do, for the Lord our God will have no part in unrighteousness . . ." (2 Chronicles 19:6-7).

law insufficient to contain them.[92] Burke would go on to state, "Men are qualified for civil liberty, in exact proportion to their disposition to put moral chains upon their own appetites. . . . Society cannot exist unless a controlling power upon will and appetite be placed somewhere, and the less of it there is within, the more there must be without."[93] It was Burke's belief that the atheistic rulers of revolutionary France sought to undermine the Christian church because they realized that those who fear God, fear nothing else. In Burke's view, the new revolutionary government intended that there be no "tribunal of conscience" independent of government authority, and that the citizens of France should stand in awe of no power higher than the new government.[94] Speaking of those times, Alexis De Tocqueville stated that "tyranny may be able to do without faith but freedom cannot."[95] He further noted that "Americans show in practice that they feel it necessary to instill morality into democracy by means of religion."[96]

Burke, one of the most famous politicians, philosophers, and intellectuals of eighteenth-century Britain, was an unrepentant Christian at a time when religious faith was often disparaged by the politically correct intellectual elite of Europe. Burke never allowed himself to be seduced by the sophistry of the reason and enlightenment proponents of his day, many of whom were atheists.[97] It could be argued that Burke's early and courageous condemnation of the excesses of the French Revolution, based in

---

[92] *See*, Burke, *Reflections on the Revolution in France*, 77-82, 86-87, 90-94, 99-103; *Letter To A Member Of The National Assembly 1791*, 289.

[93] Burke, *Reflections on the Revolution in France; Letter To A Member Of The National Assembly 1791*, 289.

[94] Burke, *Reflections on the Revolution in France; Letter To A Member Of The National Assembly 1791*, 276.

[95] Alexis De Tocqueville, *Democracy in America*, 344.

[96] Alexis De Tocqueville, *Democracy in America*, 630.

[97] Burke, *Reflections on the Revolution in France*, 90-93.

large part upon Christian principle which he refused to abandon, saved Great Britain from France's bloody fate.[98] Knowing the times to be evil, Burke had the courage to stand firm,[99] make the most of his time, and walk among the wise.[100] For this reason, Burke stands today an excellent example of the good that a single man of faith and principle can set in motion.

The Judeo-Christian moral compass, by which the course of our own republic was originally steered, was thrown overboard in large part due to the series of Supreme Court cases discussed above, and the ongoing ravages of political correctness. As a result, since these cases were decided, our ship of state has foundered in a sea of unwed pregnancies, sexually transmitted diseases, drug addictions, crime, divorces, and political corruption. The failure of our modern war on the illicit drug trade is alone sufficient to illustrate the truth of Burke's prophecy, that the "terrors" of mere human law would not, in the end, be sufficient to contain mankind's demons once humanity was freed of religious belief. The successful, disciplined, and ordered society founded on Judeo-Christian moral and ethical principles has been allowed to drift into chaos. Of these times the Apostle Paul prophesied:

> For the time will come when they will not endure sound doctrine; but wanting to have their ears tickled, they will accumulate for themselves teachers in accordance to their own desires, and will turn away their ears from the truth and will turn aside to myths.[101]

It is thus apparent, from the commentary of Associate Justice Joseph Story and others, that the society of self-reliance, liberty, and

---

[98] Russell Kirk, *Edmund Burke A Genius Reconsidered*, (Wilmington, Delaware: Intercollegiate Studies Institute, 1997), 216.

[99] Ephesians 6:13-14.

[100] Ephesians 5:15-16.

[101] 2 Timothy 4:3-4.

unique freedoms envisioned by the Founding Fathers, both assumed and was predicated upon a broad and continued acceptance of Judeo-Christian ideals, morality, ethics, and voluntary self-discipline, regardless of individual theological beliefs. Much like a fine automobile engine that is designed to operate within a given set of specifications, the United States and Western civilization were designed to run well within specifications derived from our Judeo-Christian heritage. When design tolerances are exceeded or discarded, a country or a civilization will begin to fail in much the same manner as an automobile engine, regardless of the care taken in its original construction.

Summary

In summary, one might ask what guns, capitalism, and religion have in common. As we have seen, a gun is not, in and of itself, a bad thing. In fact, in the hands of good people, guns have helped us defend our persons and our homes, carve our nation out of the wilderness, and preserve it in major world conflicts. Free enterprise competitive capitalism is also a good thing and one of history's great success stories. In those nations that have adopted it, capitalism has elevated more common men and women to prosperity than any other economic theory.

Those who would take God out of the public square, and then seek to replace Him with a rule, regulation, or law for every aspect of life, are attempting to legislate a morality, the basis for which, they have already removed. A gun or capitalism in the hands of an individual who no longer believes in God, a final judgment, or the possibility of heaven or hell can indeed be dangerous and heartless, but no more so than a godless, ever expanding, all powerful central government. The answer is not to ban guns or turn from the success of capitalism to the shared misery of socialism, as many of those who have lost their way would have us believe. Most common men and women know in their hearts that the real solution is to return the God of the Judeo-Christian tradition to His rightful and historical place in our society.

This is not a call for the establishment of a state religion, but merely an acknowledgment of the historical fact that the moral and ethical principles of our Judeo-Christian heritage constitute the pristine headwaters from which the freedoms and liberties all Americans enjoy flow. Anyone can come to the United States and practice any peaceful religion with the full protection of our laws as long as that person is loyal to the United States, causes no one harm, obeys our laws, and makes a good-faith effort to assimilate into our capitalistic culture. Everyone should, however, understand that the characteristics that make our society special derive from its Judeo-Christian heritage and a broad acceptance of Judeo-Christian values. Ideally, it should be clearly understood that our culture will continue to be governed by the Judeo-Christian rules, ethics, and morality that have produced the unparalleled success of Western civilization. Strip those values away and the attributes of peace, opportunity, security, individual worth, and freedom that make the United States and most countries of the West an attractive place to live will be lost as surely as they are already lost in most of the rest of the world.

Chapter 13: We Are Virtually Never Entitled

Since the 1930s, our nation has become so immersed in the culture of entitlement that, sadly, it now rarely occurs to even common men and women that we are virtually never truly entitled to anything beyond the freedoms and rights bestowed upon us by God, and protected in the documents of this nation's Founding Fathers. Under an almost never-ending barrage of social promises, we have forgotten that a sense of entitlement almost invariably leads to dependency, decay, and the decline and ruin of individuals, societies, and great nations. John the Baptist warned the people of Judea against the pride and hubris born of entitlement when he said:

> Therefore, bear fruits in keeping with repentance, and do not begin to say to yourselves, 'We have Abraham for our father,' for I say to you that from these stones God is able to raise up children to Abraham. Indeed the axe is already laid at the root of the trees; so every tree that does not bear good fruit is cut down and thrown into the fire.[1]

The Jewish leaders of that day did not heed John's warning and, within less than two generations, Jerusalem was utterly destroyed and the Jewish people scattered to the ends of the earth. In our time, we know that our own nation is buckling under the weight of the perhaps unintended, but foreseeable consequences of bloated entitlements. These entitlements were handed down to us by opportunistic politicians, union bosses, shortsighted executives, and others who, for their own immediate gain, sought to buy our votes or acquiescence without regard for the day of ultimate financial reckoning, that would no doubt come on someone else's watch.

An entitlement mentality also leads us into destructive error in other ways just as damning. Spouses who believe that they have

---

[1] Luke 3:8-9.

175

been neglected or wronged by their spouse often feel entitled to commit sins of their own such as adultery as a matter of right. Employees who feel that their salary is too low, or that they have been passed over for a promotion, or otherwise mistreated, often feel entitled to provide less than an honest day's work or to steal in other ways from their employers. Individuals who have been dealt some setback in life often feel that the government owes them a living simply because they are citizens of the United States. Increasingly, even those who are not citizens of the United States feel entitled to our largess.

There are few among us who have never suffered an injustice or inequity of some sort. Such is the nature of this existence. The fact that we may have been wronged in some manner in no way entitles us to do likewise. Two wrongs can never make a right. Someone else's perceived shortcoming never justifies sin on our part. God will judge others on the merits of their lives. He will judge each of us with respect to the merit of our own lives without regard to the sins of others against us. Proverbs 24:29 states, "Do not say, 'Thus I shall do to him as he has done to me; I will render to the man according to his work.'" Proverbs 20:22 states, "Do not say, 'I will repay evil'; Wait for the Lord, and He will save you." Jesus commanded, "Treat others the same way you want them to treat you."[2]

God created each of us with unique powers and abilities. Almost everyone, except perhaps the severely disabled (who have a legitimate claim upon society's charity), has the ability to make a positive impact upon the world. God clearly expects each of us to keep our faith,[3] and do our best with the cards life has dealt us without self-pity or recrimination. The Bible does not say that this will be easy, and in fact life was far from easy for the heroes of the Bible.[4] Although suffering great adversity, individuals such as

---

[2] Luke 6:31.

[3] 1 Corinthians 11:2; 15:2; 2 Thessalonians 2:15.

[4] 2 Timothy 3:12.

Moses, Joseph, David, Paul, and even Jesus triumphed through faith, principle, and perseverance.

Jesus illustrated this expectation with his parable of the talents.[5] In this parable, a wealthy man, leaving on a long journey, entrusts three of his slaves with a portion of his wealth to invest during his absence. Taking note of the relative abilities of each individual, he gave to the first five talents (a single talent was an enormous sum in those days), to the second he gave two talents, and to the third he entrusted one talent. After a significant period of time, the wealthy man returned and called his slaves into his presence for an accounting of the funds he had left in their care. The first slave had traded with his five talents and doubled them. The second had done likewise and doubled the two talents in his care. The third slave, however, had been so filled with fear and distrust of his master that he had dug a hole and hidden the money in the ground rather than risk losing it in trade.

Of the performance of the first two individuals, the wealthy man was extremely pleased and promised to give them more responsibility. He was not, however, pleased with the performance of the third slave. The wealthy man sternly remarked that, had the timid slave indeed been so fearful, he should have at least deposited the money in the bank, where it would have earned interest. He then took the one talent away from the third slave and gave it to the slave who had ten talents, saying:

> For to everyone who has, more shall be given, and he will have abundance; but from the one who does not have; even what he does have shall be taken away. Throw out the worthless slave into the outer darkness; in that place there will be weeping and gnashing of teeth.[6]

---

[5] Matthew 25:15-30; Luke 19:12-27.

[6] Matthew 25:29-30.

In discussing this point, the theologian, D. A. Carson points out that "to fail to do good and use what God has entrusted to us to use is grievous sin, which issues not only in the loss of neglected resource, but in rejection by the master. . . ."[7] It was Jesus' expectation that each of us use the abilities we have been given to be a light in the world. It was His desire that our individual lights shine before all men in order that they might see our good works and, thereby, glorify God.[8] The Apostle Paul stated that "if anyone does not provide for his own, and especially for those of his household, he has denied the faith and is worse than an unbeliever."[9] He also said, "If anyone is not willing to work, then he is not to eat, either."[10] We are to do our work in this world "heartily as for the Lord rather than for men" because "it is the Lord Christ" whom we serve.[11] The Apostle Paul's ideal Christian was a moral, industrious, trustworthy, responsible, and accountable member of society whose example reflected well upon the Christian faith. Even though he had a ministry that was both demanding and dangerous on multiple levels, Paul often supported himself by practicing his trade of tent making so that he would not be a burden upon those he was trying to lead to Christ.[12] The road to God's blessings lies not in assumptions of entitlement, sloth, and dependency, but in feelings of faith, trust, accountability, resolve, dedication, and discipline. These positive emotions or virtues take us ever onward and upward to our personal best. This is often the steeper and more strenuous path that leads to the sunlit meadows

---

[7] Carson, D. A. "Matthew." In *Matthew and Mark*. Vol. 9 of *Expositor's Bible Commentary*, rev. ed., edited by Tremper Longman III and David E. Garland, p.581. (Grand Rapids: Zondervan, 2012).

[8] Matthew 5:14-16.

[9] 1 Timothy 5:8.

[10] 2 Thessalonians 3:10.

[11] Colossians 3:23-24.

[12] Acts 18:3.

of fulfillment, peace, and self-respect. In the end, we will reap what we have sown in this life.[13]

The difference between this and previous generations is that our generation often seeks to normalize, ratify, and sanction our sins (as opposed to merely rationalizing them), saying simply that the Bible must be wrong. As we have noted, there are those who say that such prideful behavior may constitute the sin against the Holy Spirit which Jesus said was unforgivable.[14] If one has lost the ability to recognize that one has sinned, one is rendered incapable of repentance and asking for forgiveness. Nonetheless, our generation assumes that this nation continues to be entitled to the good fortune and success God bestowed upon earlier generations. We often fail to consider the possibility that those who came before us, although sinners themselves, may have been better people than we in terms of reverence for God's Word, religious faith, discipline, accountability, and the other biblical virtues. As noted above, the Jewish people made the same mistake in the time of Rome. They had also made such a mistake in the times of Assyria and Babylon.

Each generation will be judged upon its own moral and ethical journey.[15] Contrary to recent progressive interpretations, the Scriptures clearly indicate that salvation is individual rather than collective.[16] In fact, the verses attesting to the individual nature of salvation throughout the Bible are so numerous, it is difficult to comprehend how ideological beliefs such as social justice or collective salvation could have evolved. It is also true that entitlements earned by previous generations do not carry over.[17]

---

[13] Galatians 6:7.

[14] Matthew 12:31.

[15] Ezekiel 18:1-20; *see also*, Ezekiel 14:12-16; Proverbs 27:24.

[16] Acts 4:12; Revelation 22:12; Ezekiel 18:20; Matthew 7:21-28; 16:24-25; Acts 10:35; James1:23-25; Romans 2:6-10; 14:12; Mark 7:14; John 6:40,44-45,47; 2 Corinthians 5:10.

[17] William Barclay, *The Letter to the Romans*, rev. 3rd ed. (Louisville, Kentucky: Westminster John Knox Press, 2002), 171.

We must learn once again to forge our own paths with faith, independence, and self-reliance. The attempt should be made to avoid becoming ensnared by the policies, laws, rules, and regulations of the institutions, organizations, and governmental agencies that promise us a slide way to prosperity and salvation, while making us ever more dependent upon them and, thereby, slowly enslaving us.[18] In modern times, we often forget that God is extremely interested in what each of us will do individually with the life and gifts that He has given us. He will not, in the final reckoning, be particularly interested in what governmental agencies or others have done for us. From God's perspective, life's ultimate value is weighed in terms of what one has given to others rather than what one has gotten, hence it truly is "more blessed to give than to receive" (Acts 20:35).

Notwithstanding the vicissitudes of life, we are expected to seek the more difficult narrow path that leads to the high road[19] by which we are to travel through both good fortune and bad.[20] Traveling the high road in life is not unlike traveling the Blue Ridge Parkway. The Blue Ridge Parkway is one of America's most scenic highways, running the crest of the Blue Ridge Mountains for four hundred eighty-nine miles of unparalleled beauty. The Blue Ridge Parkway, like life's high road, can take some effort to reach, but once there the air is fresh, the views sublime, and, surprisingly, one often encounters few fellow travelers. Such is the reward of taking life's high road, which is often accessed by the more difficult, small, and narrow way.[21]

It is the kindness that flows upward from the love and charity of individual hearts that creates a good and godly society rather than the reverse. Curiously enough, famous words from Adam

---

[18] 1 Corinthians 7:23.

[19] Proverbs 15:24; Luke 13:24.

[20] Matthew 7:13-14.

[21] Matthew 7:14.

Smith's pen regarding economic theory seem to illustrate this spiritual truth as well. Smith notes that when an individual seeks his or her own self-interest, the individual is "led by an invisible hand to promote an end" which was no part of the individual's original intention.[22] Smith goes on to state that the fact that society has had no part in this is not necessarily a bad thing. Smith states: "By pursuing his own interest he [the individual] frequently promotes that of society more effectively than when he really intends to promote it. I have never known much good done by those who affect to trade for the public good."[23]

Thus, when millions of Christians, individually, and through the outreach of gospel-believing churches and ministries, attempt to lead Christlike lives consistent with the ethical and moral teachings of the Bible, society is transformed in countless positive ways never envisioned by the individual who is often simply trying to lead an honest, honorable, and decent life consistent with his or her faith. Since the time of Jesus there have always been those who do violence to the kingdom of heaven by seeking to redefine the terms of salvation, force God's hand, or enter the kingdom by means other than those sanctioned by God (Matthew 11:12). The doorway into God's kingdom is through Jesus Christ and its lock is opened by faith not works (Ephesians 2:8-9). The true Christian does good works not to earn eternal life, but to honor God in gratitude for salvation, which has already been granted through faith in Jesus. Christians do good through their desire to do unto others as they would have done to themselves, to glorify God, to leave the world better than they found it, and to store up rewards in heaven.

The moral character of society is elevated much more thoroughly and effectively by these individual, voluntary acts of common Christian decency and charity than by government attempts to legislate morality and regulate behavior through laws and regulations justified and rooted in socialistic, if not Marxist,

---

[22] Adam Smith, *The Wealth of Nations*, 572.

[23] Ibid.

non-biblical notions of liberation theology, collective salvation, or social justice. The heart of true justice is often pierced when it is forgotten that Judeo-Christian morality demands that the quest to do a good thing must also be a quest to do the right thing. In order that justice be not perverted, God has demanded since ancient times that our neighbor be judged fairly, showing neither partiality to the poor nor favoritism to the mighty (Leviticus 19:15). The failure to recognize this simple moral truth has often wreaked havoc in the countries of the West. There have always been and there will always be extremes of wealth and poverty in this world, regardless of the philosophical, economic, or religious beliefs of those temporarily in power. There is, however, no one so poor that they cannot extend the hand of charity to help someone, in some manner, at some point in their lives, thereby affirming their humanity.

This spark of love, self-sacrifice, kindness, and compassion, so at variance with the baser aspects of this existence, is one characteristic, along with faith in Jesus Christ, that marks the believer as a child of God. As noted earlier, one of the main lessons we are to learn from the trials and tribulations of this life is the meaning of love, and the virtue of caring for others more than ourselves. The narrow path that leads to the high road, of life as God intended, is paved not with assumptions of entitlement and selfish taking, but with individual acts of compassion, service, and giving.[24] The Apostle Paul urged that we labor "that we might have something to give those who have need" (Ephesians 4:28). One of the most popular, beguiling, and unscriptural misconceptions of modern times is that one can buy one's way into the kingdom of heaven by giving away other people's money.

Those societies and governments that seek to meet all physical needs of a dependent population, and thus relieve the individual of responsibility for compassion, love, kindness, and charity toward the rest of humanity, frequently seek to distance their citizens from

---

[24] Matthew 20:26-28.

God in other ways as well. The Supreme Court cases previously discussed indicate that this process is already well underway in our country, as evidenced by our government's increasing preference for secularism over the Judeo-Christian values from which our founding society evolved. Some might even argue that the ultimate goal of the entitlement culture is to elevate the state by attempting to make God irrelevant. This cannot, however, change the fact that the salvation extended by God in the New Testament through belief in Jesus Christ is not collective, but individual. True salvation requires a direct and personal relationship with God. This great truth was hated by the establishment in the time of the original apostles and it remains so today.

Chapter 14: Understanding Evil

We live in a time when many wish to deny that evil, as a distinct and utterly malevolent force, truly exists. The uncompromising eye of history and human experience, however, clearly reveals this perspective to be naïve and prone to dire if not fatal consequences. In His pattern prayer, known as The Lord's Prayer, Jesus even suggests that we pray to be "delivered from evil" (Matthew 6:13). It is, therefore, of great importance that we learn to identify evil and understand it to the extent that such understanding is possible.

The first step in understanding evil involves the recognition that those who are evil are far more confusing, sinister, and subtle than those who are merely bad. We have all done bad things at one time or another. Most of the people who break society's laws for personal gain or immediate pleasure are bad, at least at that moment, but generally they do not sink to the level of being evil. Early in my career while practicing law, I had occasion to represent criminal clients, some of whom I had to visit in jail. While, admittedly, I was never called upon to defend a murderer or pedophile, some of my clients did at times frighten me. Never, however, did I encounter a criminal client who struck me as evil. M. Scott Peck, M.D., the author of *People of the Lie*, made the same observation with respect to his work as a psychiatrist with inmates.[1]

The crimes the evil person commits are often against the human spirit itself. These crimes are committed without mercy or conscience, frequently beyond the dimension of the written law. Often pathological in nature, these acts of spiritual lawlessness and cruelty are usually committed in the quest for some type of unwholesome authority or control over a person, group, organization, or nation rather than material gain, although material gain can sometimes be a welcome byproduct of such actions. This unwholesome control can be achieved through confusion,

---

[1] M. Scott Peck, M.D., *People of The Lie: The Hope For Healing Human Evil* (New York: Touchstone, Simon & Schuster, Inc., 1983), 69.

manipulation, intimidation, fear, terror, or methodologies even more unsavory.

Sadly, even churches are not immune from the influence of the evil ones, both in the pulpit and otherwise, due to naivety, scriptural ignorance, and failures of appropriate oversight on the part of some congregations and denominations. The Bible repeatedly admonishes us to stand and hold firm[2] to the teachings of our faith. Yet, today there is scarcely a Christian denomination in the world, whether Protestant or Catholic, that does not have powerful advocates of parley, compromise, and appeasement with the dark forces that seek to undermine the truth of the Scriptures and the ancient doctrines of the traditional, orthodox Christian church.

The serpent has long been a symbol for Satan and the evil he represents. So it is that, like a serpent, one will often encounter evil lurking in places where one would have least expected to find it. This chapter is meant merely to alert the reader to the fact that there is something far worse than mere badness loose in the world. For an authoritative and more scientifically complete study of evil, the reader is referred to the excellent groundbreaking book previously mentioned, *People of the Lie: The Hope for Healing Human Evil*, written by M. Scott Peck, M.D.[3]

It is a dangerous precedent to ignore evil or attempt to rationalize it away. Society is not to blame for all inappropriate behavior. In fact, initially evil, as well as virtue, generally begins with the individual. Each individual has free will and must choose the path to evil or virtue. True evil is never thrust upon one. It is often the result of a series of poor choices or decisions made under the influence of misfortune or deception. Over time all of us are slowly transformed by the decisions and choices we have made on

---

[2] 1 Corinthians 15:2; 16:13; Galatians 5:1; Ephesians 6:13-14; Philippians 4:1; 1 Thessalonians 3:8; Hebrews 4:14; Revelation 3:3, 11.

[3] Peck, *People of the Lie: The Hope For Healing Human Evil* (New York: Touchstone, Simon & Schuster, Inc, 1983).

our journey through life. These decisions lead us toward darkness or light. One must open the door to the path he or she will follow, whether it is for good or evil. There are, no doubt, many circumstances of pain, woe, or extremity that can predispose some to choose the darker path, but such environmental factors are not always evident. Part of the mystery of evil is that many times those who choose the evil path appear to have had many social advantageous. Other people who have endured horrible circumstances go on to found loving families and lead virtuous lives. The life of Alexander Hamilton is a famous case on point.

Hamilton was born illegitimate on the Caribbean island of Nevis where he was abandoned by his father and orphaned by his mother with every step of his childhood haunted by "failed, broken, embittered people" whose "short lives had been shadowed by a stupefying sequence of bankruptcies, marital separations, deaths, scandals, and disinheritance."[4] Yet, Hamilton passed through this "abominable" childhood to become both a Revolutionary War hero and the most eminent of George Washington's Revolutionary War aides. He was a Founding Father of the United States, an influential proponent and booster of the U.S. Constitution, the first Secretary of the Treasury for the United States, and was apparently beloved by his eight children.[5]

Evil individuals, such as the perpetrator of the Fort Hood massacre, Nidal Malik Hasan, commit monstrous acts (thirteen individuals killed and more than 30 wounded), and yet some wish to make excuses for him or ask what society might have done to drive him to such acts. This angst notwithstanding the fact that Hasan had enjoyed a middle/working-class childhood in the United States, joined the United States Army, received military promotions, and had acquired a medical degree becoming a psychiatrist. It has become almost politically incorrect to notice or

---

[4] Ron Chernow, *Alexander Hamilton* (New York: Penguin Books, Penguin Group (USA) Inc., 2004), 26.

[5] Ibid., 165, 205, 246-266, 288, 500.

acknowledge evil, because recognition imposes a moral obligation to oppose it. Had Hasan's supervisors not been shackled by fears and apprehensions imposed by political correctness, Hasan might have been dealt with before becoming a mass murderer. To that extent, it might be argued that Hasan's victims were as much victims of political correctness as victims of Hasan. This is a graphic example of the protection political correctness affords those who would abuse their freedom and ignore civilized society's most fundamental social, ethical, and moral norms.

At least in the beginning, evil is usually concerned about its own preservation to some degree, so during this period it can be uncertain of itself and even somewhat timid. A display of resolute authority and appropriate intervention can sometimes stop or limit evil in its early stages, though perhaps not alter its predisposition. In today's world, there are plenty of easy places for evil to flourish, so it has little reason to linger where good people are solidly committed to the genuine welfare of the individual, group, organization, or nation in question. Why attempt to rob a house with a security system on a street where plenty of other houses remain unprotected? So, it is that evil also will generally take the path of least resistance. If left unchallenged, however, the evil eventually reside, supremely confident, in the Cyclopean-walled fortress of their selfish egos with the gates securely shut to any emissary of light, pity, or remorse from without.

When evil is ignored it is thus empowered and gains self-confidence, thereafter growing ever more potent. There is an old adage that states that one cannot dance with the Devil without getting burned. Those who feed evil in the hope of avoiding being eaten themselves inevitably discover to their horror that the appetite of those who are truly evil is impossible to satisfy. This is one of life's most important and most often ignored lessons. Almost invariably, those who ignore, permit, or collaborate with evil end up becoming its hostages to the ultimate ruin of all (e.g., the Jerry Sandusky child abuse scandal at Pennsylvania State University which finally came fully to light in 2012). Such enabling individuals usually have no part in creating, issuing, or promoting the schemes of the evil ones. By their inaction or acquiescence, coupled with the skill of the evil person, they allow themselves to be woven into the fabric of the evil person's falsehoods where, from the hindsight of history, they can almost always be clearly identified.

The classic example, which always comes to mind, of the scenario just described is, of course, Neville Chamberlain, Britain's prime minister during the years 1937 through 1940 just prior to World War II. Chamberlain was, by most accounts, not a bad man and, in fact, had a long, distinguished career as a civil servant and statesman. Winston Churchill even gave the eulogy at his funeral. In an earlier time, eerily similar to the years prior to World War II, Great Britain had once stood virtually alone against the might of revolutionary France. From that time, Edmund Burke had left a grim warning for future statesmen fated to confront comparable threats: "There is no safety for honest men, but by believing all possible evil of evil men, and by acting with promptitude, decision, and steadiness on that belief."[6] It was a warning that Chamberlain failed to heed. In the end, permitting his desire for peace at all costs to blind him to the reality at hand, Chamberlain allowed himself to be woven into the fabric of a tapestry which became Hitler's story. Created on the looms of hell with threads of shame, this tapestry would be destined to hang forever on the blood-splattered wall of history's greatest evils.

In retrospect, most of the individuals who ignored, enabled, or otherwise permitted Hitler's rise to unchallenged power prior to World War II can now be clearly identified, frozen in time, and woven into that grim tapestry of blindness, appeasement, failed hope, and ultimate horror. It could have been their time and their story, but they permitted Hitler to make the story his to the ruin of their reputations and the near ruin of the world itself. They would not be the first or the last to underestimate that intelligence,

---

[6] Burke, *Reflections on the Revolution in France,* Appendix: Letter to a Member of the National Assembly [1791], p. 256.

peculiar to the truly evil, that fails to recognize the moral laws that normally govern humanity. In Winston Churchill, on the other hand, we see what happens when a good man of courage decides to stand against evil, seize the historical moment, and make the story his.

It was of such transitional moments in the history of the world, nations, organizations, and individuals that Jesus said, "For if they do these things when the tree is green, what will happen when it is dry?"[7] Jesus' warning was not heeded in his time nor is it being heeded in ours, which bears a marked similarity to the decade prior to World War II, as forces today strive to introduce nuclear weapons into the tinderbox of the Middle East. As has often been the case in critical times, the book of human history remains unopened and its lessons unlearned. As will be discussed later, in confrontations with evil, central players such as Chamberlain often seem to be enveloped in a fog of confusion that obscures the true nature of the threat, its implications, and even logic itself. This stultifying confusion is often the red hourglass marker of an encounter with true evil. It was everywhere apparent in the fatal series of miscalculations that led to World War II. It is a curious historical fact that Winston Churchill, the British politician who understood Hitler best and saw him most clearly, was never in the same room with him—they never met face to face.[8] Lamenting the failure of Great Britain and Europe to react appropriately to Hitler's rearmament of Germany and growing international aggression, Winston Churchill effectively described the phenomenon just discussed before the British House of Commons in 1935:

> When the situation was manageable it was neglected, and now that it is thoroughly out of hand we apply too late the remedies which then might have effected a cure. There is nothing new in the

---

[7] Luke 23:31.

[8] Roy Jenkins, *Churchill A Biography* (New York: Plume, Penguin Putnam Inc., 2002), 469.

story. It is as old as the Sibylline Books. It falls into that long, dismal catalogue of the fruitlessness of experience and the confirmed unteachability of mankind. Want of foresight, unwillingness to act when action would be simple and effective, lack of clear thinking, confusion of counsel until the emergency comes, until self-preservation strikes its jarring gong—these are the features which constitute the endless repetition of history.[9]

Even when the great evil of a given period in time is finally defeated, as was Nazism in World War II, a remnant of evil always remains in a new form to challenge the next generation. This point is illustrated by the fact that the Nazi/Fascist threat was immediately followed by the great communist threat which has now been followed by the threat of Islamic terrorism. These are all different forms of evil, but they share in common an implacable, aggressive opposition to liberty, Judeo-Christian morality, Christianity, and the concept of the fundamental worth of the individual.

There seems little doubt that when the bombing of the United States destroyer, the USS *Cole*, was not followed by a response that was deemed decisive, Osama bin Laden was emboldened to unleash the attacks of September 11, 2001. It is a truism that when good people remain silent in the face of evil, fatal miscalculations often ensue which enable evil's power to blossom. The examples just described have dealt with evil on an international scale. In all probability, at least as much, if not more, misery has been caused by evil people on an individual or organizational basis in the commonplace venues of ordinary life. This type of oppression occurs largely beneath society's radar screen.

In the Bible, it is said that both sin and death were introduced into the world by Satan, the ultimate author of evil. Satan is

---

[9] Winston S. Churchill, http://www.winstonchurchill.org/resources/speeches/ 1930-1938-the-wilderness/air-parity-lost (accessed February 19, 2015).

depicted as the ancient whisperer of our darker moments whose temptations and advice, while many times superficially appealing, attractive, and even beguiling, always violate or corrupt some aspect of God's law or plan for one's life. His counsels, the antithesis of God's will, generally involve some aspect of the following: disobedience to God's Word, pride,[10] entitlement, envy, anger, injustice,[11] selfishness, vengeance[12], hatred, subjugation, and ultimately death. Satan sows hatred, falsehood, confusion, chaos, darkness and death in contrast to God who radiates love, truth, enlightenment, order, light and life for those with the faith to accept them.

When the evil are in power, those who have lost their way have their day. The road is indeed broad and the gate wide that leads to Satan's kingdom of destruction.[13] Throughout history, Satan's chief temptation for mankind has been the easier path of the slide way promising the proverbial free lunch and the immediate gratification of that which one most desires. Without considering the long-term eternal consequences, many in hope of some short-term gain or power take life's darker path.

Of Satan, Jesus states:

> [H]e was a murderer from the beginning, and does not stand in the truth because there is no truth in him. Whenever he speaks a lie, he speaks from his own nature, for he is a liar and the father of lies.[14]

The evil are so wrapped up in falsehood, both to delude themselves and others, that M. Scott Peck calls them the "people of the lie" in his book.[15] The evil justify the wicked and condemn the

---

[10] Proverbs 16:5; 8:13; 11:2.

[11] Proverbs 28:5.

[12] Proverbs 20:22; 24:29.

[13] Matthew 7:13-20.

[14] John 8:44.

[15] Peck, *People of the Lie*, 66.

righteous for they are by nature wicked themselves.[16] To such individuals, evil is good and good is evil; darkness is light and light is darkness; bitter is sweet and sweet is bitter, for they are supremely wise in their own eyes and clever in their own sight.[17] The universe of ethics, morality, and traditional concepts of commendable behavior is thus turned upon its head, "for the law of the Lord of hosts is rejected and the word of the Holy one of Israel despised."[18]

Ultimately, although often seductive in the short run, there is no long-term future or logic in the manipulations of those who are evil. Great, however, is the confusion and error the evil ones sow and incalculable the suffering and harm caused. The mesmerizing confusion engendered in their victims is in fact often a distinguishing characteristic of encounters with an evil individual.[19] Evil people create a beguiling fog and, under its influence, the feet of those not rooted firmly in reality and the truth of the Scriptures are frequently led astray from the path leading to life as God intended. The evil have thus littered history with the ruin of individuals, families, businesses, and nations who fell captive to their pernicious influence. Those who doubt this have only to recall the flaming Gotterdammerung[20] brought upon Germany by Hitler's leadership in World War II or the similar fate experienced by France under Napoleon.

As Jesus Christ has been identified with light and eternal life, Satan has been identified with darkness and death. Today, many no longer believe that Satan exists. Even a cursory reading of the New

---

[16] Proverbs 17:15; Romans 1:32.

[17] Isaiah 5:20-22.

[18] Isaiah 5:24.

[19] Peck, *People of the Lie*, 66; *See also*, 2 Thessalonians 2:11.

[20] Götterdämmerung: Most common original reference was to the fiery finale to Richard Wagner's *The Ring of the Nibelung* opera series entitled "Twilight of the Gods." Now often used as a reference to any apocalypse or catastrophic collapse of a society or political regime.

Testament, however, leaves no doubt that Jesus believed in the existence of Satan and that he was the Enemy of everything wholesome and good. So, it is that those who are truly evil are, like Satan, enemies of life, light, and goodness.[21] While the best-known examples of modern evil may be individuals such as Hitler, Stalin, Mao, and bin Laden, generally evil is a thing that is not flamboyant and may appear quite common, ordinary, or even attractive to the casual observer. When speaking of a type of Pharisee who overtly appeared very pious and religious and whom He knew to be evil, Jesus described them thus:

> They tie up heavy burdens and lay them on men's shoulders, but they themselves are unwilling to move them with so much as a finger.[22]

> [F]or you are like whitewashed tombs which on the outside appear beautiful, but inside they are full of dead men's bones and all uncleanness.[23]

Of the evil individuals who use the mantle of religious piety to mask their hardened hearts, Jesus said:

> Not everyone who says to Me, 'Lord, Lord,' will enter the kingdom of heaven, but he who does the will of My Father who is in heaven will enter. Many will say to Me on that day, 'Lord, Lord, did we not prophesy in Your name, and in Your name cast out demons, and in Your name perform many miracles?' And then I will declare to them, 'I never knew you; Depart from Me, you who practice lawlessness.'[24]

As mentioned earlier, many evil individuals are primarily interested in some sort of pathological control or power over

---

[21] John 3:20.

[22] Matthew 23:4.

[23] Matthew 23:27.

[24] Matthew 7:21-23; Luke 13:25-28.

something such as an individual, an organization, a nation, or even a church. In this they are reminiscent of the Ringwraiths, the Nazgûl, described by J. R. R. Tolkien in his works *The Silmarillion* and *The Lord of the Rings.* These creatures had once been men of authority and power until their humanity was devoured by their lust for the even greater power of the ring, and they became servants of the Enemy.[25]

The tragedy of the evil ones is that they are often in a position to use the power given to them by God to accomplish their own redemption by having a positive godly impact over the life of the individual, institution, or nation that has fallen under their control. Redemption in this sense should not be confused with salvation since salvation is a free gift to those who have accepted Jesus as their Savior. God does, however, give each of us a number of opportunities to be fruitful and make our lives count for something by using our lives as instruments of positive, benevolent, and godly impact upon others and the world about us.[26] Those who take advantage of these God-given opportunities for service earn rewards for themselves in heaven[27] and help make the world a better place. Like Tolkien's Ringwraiths, the evil ones throw this eternal prospect away in their thirst for immediate earthly power. Whether great or small, the power possessed by the evil individual is ultimately perverted and twisted to a purpose inimical to the

---

[25] J. R. R. Tolkien, *The Silmarillion*, 2nd ed. (Boston: Houghton Mifflin Company, 2001), 289. J.R.R. Tolkien, *The Fellowship of the Ring: Being the First Part of the Lord of the Rings*, (Boston: Houghton Mifflin Company, 2003), 50.

[26] Luke 13:6-9.

[27] Romans 2:6-10; 1 Corinthians 3:11-15; See also, Carson, D. A. "Matthew." In Matthew and Mark. Vol. 9 of Expositor's Bible Commentary, rev. ed., p. 316: In discussing Matthew 11:20-30, Carson notes that the third point being made by Jesus is "that punishment on the day of judgment takes into account opportunity. There are degrees of felicity in paradise and degrees of torment in hell (12:41; 23:13; cf. Lk 12:47-48), a point Paul well understood (Ro 1:20-2:16). The implications for Western, English-speaking Christendom today are sobering."

welfare of the person, entity, or nation which has fallen prey to its domination.

The evil ones, cloaked in whatever authority, position, or power they have achieved, can therefore appear very ordinary, respectable, charismatic, and even religious. Perhaps alluding to Satan's temptation of Jesus in the wilderness,[28] Shakespeare noted that "the devil can cite Scripture for his purpose."[29] Jesus did not exaggerate when He warned of ravenous wolves disguised in sheep's clothing.[30] It is not those who hear the Word [31] or those who can eloquently recite the Word that are good, but rather those who actually strive to live by the Word and do the will of God.[32] The Apostle Paul also warns of the deceptive nature of the evil ones when he states: "No wonder, for even Satan disguises himself as an angel of light. Therefore, it is not surprising if his servants also disguise themselves as servants of righteousness, whose end will be according to their deeds."[33]

This discussion of evil is both timely and relevant. Since it is no longer politically correct to notice evil, evil now finds it easier to hide in plain sight. For many reasons people today find their lives so stressful that they no longer wish to volunteer for civic duties or even to become a leader at work. They simply do not want the extra responsibility. Since one characteristic of some evil individuals is that they seek to control or dominate others, they may be more apt to volunteer or seek promotion than the average individual with no hidden agenda.

Today's leaders have become desperate for volunteers for civic organizations, churches, and other committees, boards, and

---

[28] Matthew 4:6.

[29] William Shakespeare, *The Merchant of Venice*, I, iii, 99.

[30] Matthew 7:15.

[31] Romans 2:13; James 1:22.

[32] Matthew 7:21.

[33] 2 Corinthians 11:14-15.

management roles. This fact may, therefore, lead some leaders to innocently welcome into their midst individuals whose drive overpowers others, and leads to an unhealthy domination of the group with which they have been placed. The drive of an evil person is more than healthy ambition or enthusiasm and masks a pathological need to control others in a way that is not in the best interest of the individual, organization, or nation involved. This unhealthy counterproductive control must be distinguished from the appropriate role of authority in directing, managing, or governing.

The vast majority of people who serve in various capacities with civic organizations, churches, and other avenues of public service or who seek promotions at work are just good hard-working people trying to do a charitable deed, and leave the world a little better than they found it. They have little stomach for disputes or for standing up to one who is bent on imposing his or her will upon others, and who may or may not be a psychological bully. For this reason, an evil person can often exert influence far beyond that warranted by the power he or she actually possesses. In fact, this unfortunate circumstance may partly explain how many organizations, foundations, and trusts, originally founded by men and women who feared God and believed in traditional Judeo-Christian values and capitalism, have ended up controlled by individuals who share none of these beliefs.

Evil almost always begins with an individual or a tiny, highly vocal, and very persistent minority trying to force its malevolent will upon a majority that is often timid, blind, and lethargic. A small infection, unnoticed, and left untreated can infect the entire body. And so, families, organizations, nations, and even civilizations have fallen across the ages of history leaving the silent majority to wonder how such ruin came to pass. We are thus brought back to the aphorism which states that "all that is necessary for the triumph of evil is that good men do nothing."

When we speak of the evil ones, we are not talking about individuals who are merely bad leaders, or ordinary folks who may engage in poor judgment or occasionally be overpowering. Most of us may be guilty of such behavior from time to time. The evil are individuals where, in human resource terms, there is a *pattern and trend* of a willingness to do things ordinary people will not do, and a repeated tendency to engage in behavior that seems to suck the life, light, and joy out of those they can control or dominate. Evil, then, is often more than a failure, crime, or terrible act. It is an ongoing *pattern and trend* of unwholesome domination and destructive behavior from which even most criminals would shrink. Many people have done very bad deeds and then repented, found Jesus, and been saved. This potential and ever-present hope for salvation and transformation is one of the miracles of the Christian faith. The truly evil person does not turn however. The truly evil person presses onward into the darkness in supreme self-confidence. He or she feels no remorse and accepts no blame because no need for repentance or salvation is felt.

Since the appearance of those who are evil is often so ordinary and respectable, their presence or nature can often best be detected by their reflection in the faces of those under their thumb. This may be what is alluded to in Proverbs 27:19 where we find the following words, "As in water face reflects face, so the heart of man reflects man." In the case of interaction with evil, this reflection is often the broken look of hopeless despair. The evil individual destroys self-confidence, kills dreams, crushes hope, and injures souls. They leave a debris field in their wake of chaos, despair, and misery. They bring darkness into their sphere of influence that can literally drive some to suicide. The evil individual can devastate a family, wreck a department or organization, and destroy a nation. They are recognized by their works:

> So every good tree bears good fruit, but the bad tree
> bears bad fruit. A good tree cannot produce bad
> fruit, nor can a bad tree produce good fruit. Every

tree that does not bear good fruit is cut down and thrown into the fire.[34]

The Bible likens evil individuals to "wandering stars, for whom the black darkness has been reserved forever."[35] It could thus be argued that when a soul loses its way, like a burned-out star, it implodes inward upon itself into darkness creating a psychological black hole that literally sucks all light, life, joy, and energy out of everything within its gravitational field. There is ultimately no darkness more profound or chilling than that of a soul that has forsaken the light for its own selfish path.[36] This is the ancient evil that still walks among us in our modern world often undetected.

When faced with the truly evil, M. Scott Peck advises us to get away from them if we can unless we are very strong and professionally trained for dealing with such individuals.[37] This is sage advice for those in a position to take it. The Bible does not command us to preemptively attack evil, but it does ask that we resist and stand firm against it.[38] Sometimes, however, one may be so constrained by circumstances, fiduciary responsibility to an employer, or loyalty or love for the victims of such an individual that one feels retreat is not an option. That is a noble sentiment, but often one of self-sacrifice.

Proverbs 25:26 says that a righteous man who gives way before the wicked is like a "trampled spring and a polluted well." The Apostle Paul urges us to "walk as children of Light for the fruit of the Light consists in all goodness and righteousness and truth."[39] It is such courage in the face of evil that originally led the United States and Great Britain to stand firm against the evil of Islamic

---

[34] Matthew 7: 17-19.

[35] Jude 1:13.

[36] Proverbs 4:18-19.

[37] Peck, *People of the Lie,* 65.

[38] Ephesians 6:13-14; 1 Corinthians 16:13; Galatians 5:1.

[39] Ephesians 5:8-9.

terrorism[40] in an otherwise timid world. If all else fails and one is forced to stand against the darkness, Jesus states:

> I say to you, My friends, do not be afraid of those who kill the body and after that have no more that they can do. But I will warn you whom to fear: fear the One who after He has killed, has authority to cast into hell; yes, I tell you, fear Him![41]

Know, however, that if you choose to confront the truly evil, you proceed at your own risk. Evil people are dangerous and if they feel threatened they will try to hurt you. At least in the countries of the West, most of these people have a vague recollection that they cannot overtly commit murder, rape someone, or burn a village without exposing themselves, but beyond these basic concessions to the prevailing law, the needle on their moral compass pretty much spins in any direction expediency takes it. God will always bless the efforts in this world or the next of those who sincerely seek His purpose, but you cannot always count on anyone else coming to your rescue if you find yourself overpowered in a confrontation with someone who is truly evil.

Even the Apostle Paul would write, at a time when he knew his life was drawing to a close:

> At my first defense no one supported me, but all deserted me; may it not be counted against them. But the Lord stood with me and strengthened me, so that through me the proclamation might be fully accomplished, and that all the Gentiles might hear; and I was rescued out of the lion's mouth.[42]

---

[40] For those interested in exploring this subject further, William Federer places Islamic terrorism within the historical context of the religious, political, and military system we know as Islam in the following book: *What Every American Needs To Know About The Qur'an-A History of Islam & The United States* (St. Louis: Amerisearch, Inc., 2011).

[41] Luke 12:4-5.

[42] 2 Timothy 4:16-17.

Just as in Paul's time, we have seen that many people in our modern, politically correct world prefer not to acknowledge evil; they are just not up for confrontations of principle that seek to right the cosmic scales of truth and justice.[43] Many will remember this not uncommon shortcoming of our fellow man graphically depicted in the classic film *High Noon* starring Gary Cooper and Grace Kelly.[44]

Notwithstanding the cautionary note above, we must remember that the freedoms we enjoy today were won by those who often paid a heavy price for resisting the evil of their day. Even though there will always be those who justify the wicked and condemn those who oppose them, there are some battles worth fighting regardless of the outcome.[45] We are not always responsible for the timing or the field upon which we may be called to stand up for what is right. We are, however, responsible for how we conduct ourselves in that hour. In the final reckoning, one's quest to help the downtrodden and uphold the truth will not go unnoticed by God:

> And we know that God causes all things to work together for good to those who love God, to those who are called according to His purpose.[46]

It may simply be that sometimes our fate calls upon us to enter the arena of faith to do our small part, during our brief moment, to ensure that that the truth and the light do not perish from the earth during our time. Such are the *Quo Vadis* moments of one's life referring to the legend regarding the Apostle Peter's escape from the city of Rome during Nero's persecutions of the Christians. As Peter was hurrying away from Rome down the Appian Way, he was suddenly startled to see Jesus coming from the opposite

---

[43] Proverbs 24:10-12.

[44] Stanley Kramer (Producer), Fred Zinneman (Director), *High Noon*, United Artists (1952).

[45] Proverbs 17:15.

[46] Romans 8:28.

direction. Peter asks, *"Quo Vadis?"* (Where are you going?) Legend says that Jesus replied, "If you are leaving our flock in Rome, I must take your place and be crucified again." Thereupon, Peter immediately returned to Rome, where he inspired the early church throughout the persecutions and was ultimately himself crucified by Nero.

The Christian church in Rome survived, and we remember Peter's faith and leadership to this day. We sometimes forget that Peter was only a fisherman—a common man—but he had heart, courage, commitment, and faith. He helped usher in a new age of salvation, hope, and light for the world. For those who would like to know more of this beautiful legend, I refer them to Henryk Sienkiewicz's historical novel, *Quo Vadis: A Narrative of the Time of Nero,*[47] and the movie, entitled *Quo Vadis,* filmed in 1951 starring Robert Taylor and Deborah Kerr.[48]

For those unfortunate enough to be faced with a *Quo Vadis* moment, there is a temptation to think that the story is about them or the victims of the individual or individuals that precipitated that dark and fateful confrontation. That would be a prideful mistake, however. One may, indeed, be fated to play a role or even make a great sacrifice at such times, as a servant of one's faith, in the hope of keeping the truth and the light from being extinguished. In a broader cosmic sense, however, the story really being played out or chronicled is the melancholy history of the evil individuals as they persist in their sad fall from grace while continuing to spurn the opportunities that God has given them for both salvation and redemption.

Since the story before us at such times may not be our own, we may, in the short term, be frustrated in our hope for justice or vindication. As previously noted, as long as we are players on this

---

[47] Henryk Sienkiewicz, *Quo Vadis: A Narrative of the Time of Nero* (Washington, DC: Gateway Editions, Regnery Publishing, Inc., 1998 [1896]), 653-655.

[48] Sam Zimbalist (Producer), Mervyn LeRoy (Director), *Quo Vadis,* Metro-Goldwyn-Mayer (1951).

earthy stage, there is the possibility that we may sometimes be overpowered by evil when others cannot see the truth or fear to assist us. Even then, however, we must have faith that God's higher unseen purpose is being accomplished in a dimension beyond our view.[49] Even though we may not always see it at first, the Light will always shine forth into the darkness for the darkness can neither comprehend it nor overpower it.[50]

At such times, we cannot allow anger or bitterness or hatred to gain a foothold in our heart. Neither Jesus nor His disciples had an easy time of it in this world. Notwithstanding the hardship, pain, and suffering they endured, they never allowed adversity to compromise their capacity for love and forgiveness. They never forgot that they were servants of God seeking to work God's will on a plane of higher purpose. Mentally, we must turn those who have hurt or harmed us over to God to deal with in His own time and according to His own wisdom, justice, and purpose. Unless we do this, bitterness, hatred, and self-pity are the corrosive fingerprints that the evil leave behind upon our souls.

---

[49] Romans 8:28.

[50] John 1:5.

Chapter 15: A Good First Impression

Over the past fifty years we have become a nation of immodest scruffiness. We wear our sloppiness, poor grooming, and oblivious dishevelment with a sense of almost defiant entitlement in a broader world that increasingly looks upon us with declining respect if not bemused contempt. The gate is indeed "wide and the way broad that leads" to sartorial disgrace in today's America.

John T. Molloy's books, *Dress For Success, New Woman's Dress For Success*, and *Live For Success*,[1] are three most illuminating and very practical books for anyone desirous of putting their best foot forward. These books should be required reading at every business, seminary, and professional school in America. One of Molloy's most important observations is that, since most people do not personally know you, your appearance becomes reality.[2] He notes, "People who look successful and well-educated receive preferential treatment in almost all of their social or business encounters."[3] Another of his observations is that, while fashions may change somewhat from year to year, the most important principles of appropriate dress and grooming are relatively timeless and change very slowly.

One's appearance is the only information most people have when they initially form an opinion of us. This may or may not be

---

[1] John T. Molloy, *New Dress For Success* (New York: Warner Books, Inc., 1988), 3,14-15,29,41,369; John T. Molly, *New Woman's Dress For Success* (New York: Warner Books, Inc., 1996); John T. Molloy, *Live For Success* (New York: William Morrow And Company, Inc., 1981), 21-25, 33.

[2] Molloy, *New Dress For Success*, 29: "We all wear uniforms and our uniforms are clear and distinct signs of class. We react to them accordingly. In almost any situation where two men meet, one man's clothing is saying to the other man: "I am more important than you are, please show respect"; or "I am your equal and expect to be treated as such"; or "I am not your equal and I do not expect to be treated as such."*See also*, Sirach 19:29-30. *Sirach*, also known as Ecclesiasticus, is a Hebrew treatise on wisdom located in the Apocrypha.

[3] Molloy, *New Dress For Success*, 3.

fair, but it is fact. If one looks like a lazy, uneducated slob then that is the picture projected on to the impressionable mental screens of the general public. Most people really do tend to assume that if one looks like a duck and walks like a duck, then the chances are that, nine times out of ten, one is a duck. For generations those who conduct interviews for advancement have regarded one's grooming, dress, and comportment to be the outward reflection of the discipline and order of one's mind.

There is virtually no limit to how bad anyone can look if they let themselves go. What many people have forgotten is that an important aspect of realizing the best our society has to offer is maintaining a relatively strict sense of personal propriety, self-discipline, and grooming standards. Appropriate grooming, which includes how we dress, how our hair is cut or styled, whether we are cleanly shaven (yes, this rule applies to both men and women), and how we carry ourselves, sends a message to the world as to our level of education, self-discipline, responsibility, authority, and even our perceived trustworthiness.[4] Good grooming does after all require discipline, judgment, time management, self-respect, and effort. These are, in fact, the daily rituals of a civilized and ordered life marked by respect for one's self and others. Virtually everyone has fallen short with respect to these precepts at one time or another, but such lapses should be the exception rather than the rule.

In our society one is free to display one's self to the public in virtually any manner one chooses, but, with very few exceptions, our society reserves its best rewards for those who respect relatively orthodox grooming standards. A casual walk through any mall or down any street in America reveals the degree to which this fundamental tenet of the common wisdom has fallen into disregard. When I worked as a carpenter's helper building bridges as a college student, the carpenters arrived for work each day, on a

---

[4] Sirach (also known as Ecclesiasticus) 19:29-30, a Hebrew treatise on wisdom located in the Apocrypha.

construction site closed to the public, better groomed than many today who can be found in malls or other much more public places.

Far too many confused or self-absorbed individuals are boldly exploring the outer limits of how far they can allow their appearance to decay as though no one else is there to notice. If one has ever viewed old news reels of people in the audiences of movie theaters or attending public events, it quickly becomes apparent that there was a time when most Americans tried very hard to put their best foot forward in public. Most individuals back then instinctively knew what John T. Molloy attempted to teach us, which is that we only get one chance to make a good first impression.

To a surprising degree much of the rest of the world still understands the truth of the principle just discussed. My wife and I had the opportunity to visit Chile several times a few years ago. We were always impressed by the fact that virtually everyone, regardless of economic status, tried to make the most of their appearance and display themselves to their best advantage (the same was generally true in Great Britain as well). This fact was driven home when we chanced to visit a supermarket in Santiago. We were nicely appointed in conservative casual apparel, or so we thought. Although Chile is a very safe country, we were a little self-conscious on that visit since it was just after the terrorist event of September 11, 2001. One of our party suddenly made the observation that we could easily be identified as Americans, because we were the only people in the store who looked like slobs. We then noticed that most of the housewives had dressed up to visit the market and actually looked almost like the mothers from the old 1950s sitcoms. I even noticed a butcher putting on a tie as he left the store for home. In respects such as these, Chile was reminiscent of the United States when it still retained more of its original discipline, values, and traditional common wisdom than is perhaps the case today.

It was during the twilight days of the more traditional time referenced above, while I was still small enough to sit on my father's lap, that the following conversation took place. We were seated in my grandmother's kitchen after breakfast when one of my uncles walked into the adjacent bathroom, leaving the door open. He intently scrutinized his face in the mirror for a few moments and then walked out. My father looked down at me and asked if I knew what my uncle had been doing. When I indicated that I did not, my father stated: "He was checking to see if he needed to shave today. When you get old enough to shave, I do not want to ever see you doing that. If you have lived another day, you will always need to shave."

I never forgot that conversation, and, over the years, I have rarely missed a day of shaving even when ill, rafting the Colorado, or otherwise out of my normal routine. Even though my father worked in construction at the time of that conversation, he was training me for where he hoped I would one day end up. He realized that a commitment to good hygiene and conservative grooming telegraphs a message to the world that one has respect both for one's self and others, a certain degree of discipline, positive world-affirming values, and a desire to make the most of one's attributes.

In short, for those who wish to experience society's best, unless one is a rock star, it is virtually never a good idea to partake of body piercing, or tattoos (Leviticus 19:28), or walk about displaying one's underwear. Unless a man is a pirate, buccaneer, or Elizabethan courtier, it is still generally a mistake in America for any man, who aspires to present himself to his best advantage, to wear a ponytail or an earring. Male ponytails simply have too many negative or confusing associations to be considered appropriate in a business or semi-formal environment where one wants to reaffirm respectability. Most common men and women do not have time to remember or sort out the various rules for what wearing an earring in one ear, or the other, or both ears symbolizes for a man. So, when a male is observed wearing an earring, regardless of where it is placed, he runs the risk of being judged guilty of poor judgment at the very least.

The bottom line is that the individuals in a position to dispense society's perks and largess in fields like healthcare, Wall Street, and corporate America are simply less apt to reward someone, regardless of their intellect or ability, who appears as though he or she has just stepped out of the jungles of Borneo—with no disrespect intended to the tribesmen of Borneo. As the Apostle Paul noted, just because something is lawful does not mean it is profitable.[5]

For the reasons noted above, it is best to avoid the dress-down day trap. The rules for appropriate dress in most professions are fairly well defined, but the rules for casual dress are a slippery slope filled with pitfalls for the gullible and the unwary. Most people have no idea what the term *business casual* means. Those who are ambitious and hope to advance should never dress down at their place of employment. Why would an individual, who makes a good professional impression four days out of the week, want to show up for work on the fifth day looking as though they are going to put up hay or camp out under a bridge? It does not make sense. Yet, many individuals think that dress-down day is meant to be a license to come to work dressed in this manner. This is true notwithstanding rules for dress-down day that have usually been previously established and communicated by the employer. Everyone involved with dress-down day also tends to forget that the public, which awards its business to the company for which one may work, generally has an expectation that workers appear businesslike and professional.

On a more serious note, while not specifically speaking about grooming, Jesus tells us that we are the light of the world, and that we are to allow our light to shine before men in such a way that they might see our good works and glorify God.[6] Jesus goes on to urge us to "be perfect," as our Father who is in heaven is perfect.[7]

---

[5] 1 Corinthians 6:12.

[6] Matthew 5:14-16.

[7] Matthew 5:48.

Indeed, the care that the Roman soldiers took to preserve Jesus' tunic in one piece at his crucifixion is some indication that Jesus dressed as well as His circumstances permitted.[8] As Christians, our witness is compromised when we appear in public before unbelievers looking less than our best. We are in fact human billboards. Our appearance, our behavior, and our example are each advertisements for our Christian faith.

Today, many individuals even attend church in attire that is far too casual or even inappropriate. They assume God will be so happy to see them in church that He will not care how they are dressed. They forget that God is utterly holy and is not only worthy of respect, but demands it.[9] God does not require a suit from someone too poor to own one, but He does expect that we present ourselves in His house with the best attire and grooming that our circumstances will permit. This is not only simple discipline on our part, but a showing of basic respect to the God who has given us every aspect of life. We are representatives and ambassadors both for our faith and our God, so the manner in which we present ourselves to the world does reflect upon both.

In the same vein, the Apostle Paul asks, "Do you not know that your body is a temple of the Holy Spirit within you, which you have from God, and that you are not your own?"[10] The message of the Bible is that we should make a sincere effort to be good role models for our faith both in our actions and our appearance. If we would be reluctant to burn a red light in the fixture on the front porch of our home, why would we disrespect our personal appearance in a similar manner? This is basic wisdom that was well understood in the early days of both the church and our nation.

---

[8] John 19:23-25.

[9] Malachi 1:6.

[10] 1 Corinthians 6:19.

Chapter 16: Scouting the Trail to Heaven

Most people are happiest and most at peace when nature is a prominent and natural part of their lives. Much has been written, across several different disciplines, about the fact that not that much time has elapsed, in evolutionary terms, since mankind left his hunter-gatherer origins to begin farming and become domesticated. Biologically and emotionally, our souls indwell essentially the same bodies possessed by our primitive ancestors thousands of years ago. Yet, over this relatively brief span of time, we have constructed a very intricate artificial world of our own making—a world in which we are largely aliens living lives which are, for the most part, foreign to our natures and divorced from many of our psychological and spiritual needs. Technology has largely freed modern man from moment to moment extremities of need and peril, but it has also often led to a weakening of the transcendent spiritual purpose that gives life meaning.

Our modern lives often seem to be dull, routine, and without higher purpose. Our spirits rarely soar because our indoor existence often fails to yield experiences that might give our spirits wings. Man is an essentially pastoral creature. He has, however, succeeded in constructing an incredibly complex and materialistic society which has, in many respects, left his body behind and rendered it something of an anachronism. This has created a spiritual imbalance in our lives which only religious faith and periodic infusions of nature can allay. This is the source of that haunting nostalgia that defies repression and forbids contentment, while continually urging us to get outside into the sunlight and perhaps even go exploring. In the Bible, many of those who seriously sought God, such as John the Baptist, did so in the wilderness where God's creation was least tarnished. The Christian never worships nature, but the cathedral of God's creation is an excellent place to worship Him.

Civilization can be enormously distracting from the spiritual perspective, causing us to put aside or ignore issues that go to the root cause of our existence until it is too late. Nature leads man away from a preoccupation with the mundane and into the presence of something greater than himself. In this manner, nature can help us see life in its proper perspective, thereby attaining a better vision of both our relationship to God and the truths that will ultimately matter. When faced with the wonder of God's creation, spiritual issues are far more difficult to ignore than when one is seated in front of a television or computer. It is for this reason that we need to leave our computer screens and get outside as often as possible. Great adventures may be rare events, but most of us can spend some time in the sun each day doing something we enjoy whether it be walking or mowing the yard.

In nature, which is vastly more complicated than even our own technology driven civilization, those, with eyes to see and ears to hear, can still sense the presence and the brilliance of our Creator.[1] When one is outside "light is sown like seed for the righteous and gladness for the upright in heart."[2] It is not difficult to see why the warmth of the sun and the feel of the wind are still a better balm for the human heart than many antidepressants. The most difficult and physically demanding job that I ever had was *decking the spans* when I worked building bridges during college. Due, however, to its closeness to the elements and a certain degree of danger and adventure, this job was also one of my most memorable, spiritually fulfilling, and liberating.

My journey toward the spiritual insights discussed above began on a fateful day in the early 1960s when my father loaded me into our aging 1955 Chevrolet Bel Air automobile and drove me to a local church where he enrolled me in the Boy Scouts of America. I did not know it then, but he had delivered me to the headwaters of a stream destined to course throughout the years of my life, upon which I would eventually travel to some of my most memorable

---

[1] The Christian knows that God does not reside in any aspect of nature for as nature's Creator He presides over it just as He presides over us. When one actively experiences the beauty, intelligence, symmetry, and wonder of God's creation, however, it is easy to imagine that one is hiking a trail previously traveled by God.

[2] Psalm 97:11.

and thrilling adventures. The living waters of this stream filled me with the spirit of adventure and a love of nature, the wilderness, and life itself.

Given the times and the size of our family, there were many demands upon my father's slender resources. Nonetheless, and probably at more sacrifice than I then realized, he bought the uniforms and camping equipment needed for my participation in the Scouting program. Then, each week, after driving me to my Scout meeting or the drop-off point for the monthly camping trip, he did a truly remarkable thing. He drove away, leaving me to negotiate the Scouting experience on my own and savor my first true taste of freedom. He pressured me to become an Eagle Scout (which was eventually achieved in the fullness of time), and he wished me success. He realized, however, that one of Scouting's virtues was that it taught its lessons under the watchful eye of the Scout Master and his assistants largely without the presence of parents who have a tendency to hover like vigilant angels, ever ready to fight their child's battles.

In those days, the lessons taught were God, country, character, honor, courage, love of justice and liberty, accountability, self-reliance, and initiative. The *Boy Scout Handbook* of that time was clear that, "Not only as individuals, but as a nation, too, we are committed to live and work in harmony with God and with His plan."[3] In those relatively innocent times, it occurred to no one to doubt the solemn nature of the obligation required in both the Scout Oath and the Scout Law to be "morally straight," and reverence both God and country.[4] The *Boy Scout Handbook* further reminded us that "Our country was built upon a trust in God."[5]

---

[3] William Hillcourt, *Boy Scout Handbook*, 7th ed. (New Brunswick: Boy Scouts of America, 1965), 51. The Handbook also tells the young Scout, "You are reverent as you serve God in your everyday actions and are faithful in your religious obligations as taught you by your parents and spiritual leaders."

[4] Ibid., 36-37, 38-39.

[5] Ibid., 36.

While the Boy Scouts have always been nondenominational, all who value our Judeo-Christian heritage can learn from the Scouting motto, "Be Prepared." The young scout learns very early to think ahead and place in his or her backpack everything he or she thinks might be needed on the upcoming hike or camping trip. Just so, every human being is hiking into eternity as the days of life pass. On this journey, there are many times when the sun does not shine and the trail is not clearly marked. As in the case of the young outdoorsman, everyone's backpack should include a flashlight and a compass to ensure that the correct path is not lost. The Bible is both light and compass for those who walk in the Judeo-Christian faith (2 Timothy 3:16-17).

When a child is on a camping trip one hundred miles from home without one's parents, it focuses one's young mind like a laser on learning to get along with others, planning, and self-reliance. If you have ever been in the high end of the middle of nowhere without a can opener, or hiking in a rain or hail storm without rain gear, or suffering through the deep dark of a cold winter's night without an appropriate sleeping bag, then you have had the importance of thinking ahead and anticipating the unexpected—planning—forever seared into your consciousness. It is surprising how many people never learn this basic skill which is embodied in the Boy Scout motto, "Be Prepared." Thanks to the predilection for planning instilled within me by the Boy Scouts, I have rarely been greatly bewildered, surprised, or bluffed whether hiking the never-timbered wilderness of Linville Gorge, rafting the Colorado River, walking amongst the ancient statues of Easter Island, or negotiating the politics of the boardroom. This is not, however, to say that it is possible to escape periodic disappointment entirely; even the Boy Scouts cannot completely insulate one from that.

Scouting gave me the foundational skills with which to face virtually all of life's challenges. The successes and positive achievements of my life owe as much to Scouting as to the university training which I later received. One of my uncles, who served in World War II, always credited the fact that his best friend in the service had been a Boy Scout with saving his life on more than one occasion. My uncle noted that, regardless of the nature of any situation that might suddenly be thrust upon them, his friend, the former Boy Scout, always seemed to know enough to enable them to survive. That is high praise, indeed, for the type of training one gets in the Boy Scouts.

Scouting also instilled within me a love of nature, the wilderness, and adventure that has never left me. The concept of the pastoral and the wilderness—the next horizon—was forever engraved upon my imagination. My love of the wilderness and the experiences it engendered became the platform from which my love of freedom, independence, individualism, and liberty was launched. In exactly this manner, the wilderness experience had earlier driven the love of freedom, independence, individualism, and liberty into the hearts and souls of many of the men who would risk everything to found the United States of America. The awesome reality of the vast wilderness, from which America had to wrest its destiny, has over the course of generations ground itself into the most intrinsic psychological depths of the American consciousness. It is one of the sources for our abiding faith in God, our fondness for exploring the next frontier, and our unique self-reliant exuberance.

As a young eleven-year-old boy, I passed through the doorway that separated everything that I had previously known and into the animating almost mystical presence of the wilderness on my very first camping trip. This took place on the Raven Knob Boy Scout Reservation in the mountains of northwestern North Carolina in early February. At this time of year in the mountains, it can be fiercely cold even in the South. On this trip, due to the fact that it was winter, we slept in three-sided cabins with one wall open to the elements called Adirondacks. One of my friends had knocked over a bottle of soft drink during the night, and I will always remember noticing the next morning that the escaping soda had frozen in an arc from the bottle to the concrete floor. The night had been very cold indeed, and I had thus learned the lesson of the insufficient sleeping bag on the first night of my first camping trip. Life's lessons can come very quickly in Scouting. The next day, however, was very sunny and pleasant notwithstanding the cold.

One of the great things about a winter camping trip to a place like Raven Knob is that, though it was a very large wilderness area (currently approximately 3,000 acres) and a premiere camping destination, my troop was the only troop camping there that weekend. It was a fantastic time for campfires, camaraderie, and exploration. The Scout Master and his assistants were content for the most part to stay near the campfire, so we eleven-year-olds had the run of hundreds of acres virtually unsupervised except for that provided by our older patrol leaders. I could not have been more excited if cloned dinosaurs had roamed the forests.

And, let me hasten to add that this lack of smothering supervision was not a bad thing. Those were the days when boys were expected to be men. It was a different time when everyone did not get a trophy, safety gear like bike helmets was unheard of, and children were much more rough and ready than they are permitted to be today. Campfires were routine because we actually still cooked over our campfires in those days. Virtually all of my young scouting friends had hatchets and hunting knives or even army surplus machetes or bayonets. Yet, I never witnessed a serious injury, involving such basic camping gear, or a fire caused by campfires in my years of scouting. This was due to the fact that we were given appropriate training from our first day and held accountable by our peers as well as our leaders. Due, no doubt, to the influence of our highly litigious society, Scouting is even safer today than it was when I was a boy.

It was not uncommon in those days for parents to tell the Scout Master that he was expected to discipline their child if necessary. Just that prospect meant that Scout Masters rarely had to take such measures. There was a look in the eyes of the Scout Master that most did not want to test. The specter of a trip to a hospital Emergency Department or being blamed for a forest fire was a genuinely horrifying prospect for all of us. We all bought into the notion that the opportunities and freedom that came with Scouting carried with them responsibility. And, every Sunday morning on every camping trip, most Scout Masters conducted religious devotions which all campers were expected to attend. Each evening, after supper during summer camp at Raven Knob, religious services called *vespers* were also held in a rustic pavilion by a beautiful small lake for all wishing to attend.

My first full day of camping at Raven Knob was thus a busy and exciting time. Cooking over open fires and advancement classes in subjects like first aid, fire safety, and totemanship[6] took the first half of the day, so it was early afternoon before several of my buddies and I could embark on our much-anticipated hike to the twin cliff faces at the top of the mountain which gave Raven Knob its name. Today, during the summer months the trees have grown so tall that they largely obscure the knob(s). At that time, however, the Knob loomed large and was an irresistible destination for our first hike.

We hiked around the marshy upper end of the lake and crossed the stream that fed the lake noting evidence of beaver everywhere. We found the trailhead to the Knob on the other side of the lake roughly across from the Order of the Arrow arena. As we embarked upon the trail, we entered the quiet sanctuary of ancient trees at the base of the mountain and heard the peaceful sound of a small stream trickling past us through moss covered stones. Due to the pine trees, rhododendrons, and mountain laurel there was still a surprising amount of dense greenery even though we hiked in winter. The silence of the winter forest had a magical intensity that was almost palpable. In my youthful inexperience, it was a unique moment of adventure, anticipation, mystery, and enchantment.

In those days, the trail ascended almost straight up the mountain to the knob(s), so it became quite steep relatively quickly and rapidly developed into a strenuous climb. When we were near the top of the mountain, at a place where the trail was particularly steep, we paused, almost leaning against the side of mountain, to catch our breath before making the final push for the top. As I

---

[6] Now apparently called *Totin'chip,* but still involving instruction in the proper handling of pocket knife, ax, and saw.

turned to survey the scene before me, the horizon stretched out seemingly forever until it eventually faded into the purplish haze of the Blue Ridge Mountains. The mountain upon which I stood seemed to fall away from my feet. I was thus permitted to look over the tops of the trees below as they marched downward to the lake which sparkled and shimmered in the brilliant afternoon light. The cold wind was in my hair and the sun was shining. I was healthy, young, and free from all care at that moment.

The exhilaration, freedom, and wild beauty of that almost transcendental moment gave wings to my spirit for the first time and allowed it to soar high and free across the broad vista stretching out in all directions. In an instant of revelation, it suddenly came to me that "this must be what heaven is like." Across all of the trials, disappointments, and successes of my long and eventful life; the impact of that moment has never left me. Heaven became real for me that day, and my vision of it was fixed not as a city of gold, but as an unspoiled garden wilderness. I understood why the psalmist stated that God "walks upon the wings of the wind."[7] As the wind rustled through the trees they did seem at that instant to sing for joy at being part of God's creation.

> Then all the trees will sing for joy before the Lord, for He is coming to judge the earth. He will judge the world in righteousness and the peoples in His faithfulness.[8]

In my mind, it seems almost fitting that, just as the current chapter of the human adventure began in the Garden of Eden, perhaps the next chapter will also find the redeemed, as Children of God, inhabiting a more perfect garden where "the sound of the Lord God walking in the garden in the cool of the day . . ." will be heard once again.[9]

---

[7] Psalm 104:3.

[8] Psalm 96:12-13.

[9] Genesis 3:8.

Anytime an individual, organization, or nation becomes capable of doing great good and projecting, pursuant to God's will, a godly example into the world, Satan will many times lash out and attempt to blunt, prevent, compromise or discredit that good. Like many organizations and even many churches in our modern secular society, the Boy Scouts of America is currently under assault from within and without by those who would force it to compromise its allegiance to the traditional values and wisdom of its long and successful history. There are, however, still many godly leaders, alumni, churches, and organizations struggling to preserve the soul of Scouting for future generations of young people. These grassroots leaders, in communities across our land, still work powerful deeds of courage, example, leadership, and faith. These leaders realize that, from its inception, while respecting all religions, the success of the Boy Scouts of America, and Scouting in most other Western countries, was built upon a firm foundation of Judeo-Christian ethics, morality, self-discipline, and accountability. Hopefully, the courageous efforts of these leaders will be successful, and this venerable and much beloved youth organization will not pass silently from God's grace and into the night.

Chapter 17: The Peace of Innocent Faith

Few people have perfect, idyllic childhoods. Most everyone can recall periods of want, injustice, misunderstanding, hurt, or worse in their early years. In today's complex world, it is virtually impossible for one's parents to shelter their children from all disappointment, hurt, or adversity. Even the best of parents, under the best of circumstances, are but ordinary people filled with all of the fears, vulnerabilities, failings, hopes, and aspirations as the rest of us. Yet, many former children blame their parents into adulthood for all of the things that went awry in their childhoods. Some individuals even use a disappointing childhood as an excuse or justification for failure throughout their adult lives.

A less than perfect childhood does not entitle anyone to deliver less than their best during their adult lives. As we have discussed earlier, God expects us to use the power of faith and the Holy Spirit to rise above our circumstances in the manner of the disciples and particularly the Apostle Paul. For them life embodied a sense of duty and faith that empowered them to live out their lives in a continuous attempt to do their best regardless of circumstances. God has given everyone special gifts and He expects us to use them. Many people who have had childhoods that could legitimately be viewed as pretty horrible have gone on, with faith and perseverance, to utilize their gifts to forge successful careers and found loving families. There is little excuse for permitting childhood disappointments, which litter the memories of most human beings, to blight one's chances for adult fulfillment and happiness.

Let us imagine what life could be like had we not suffered the "slings and arrows"[1] of childhood disappointments and the innumerable small injuries and phobias ensuing from them which plague so many individuals across the rest of their years. Those that do come through childhood without such wounds are life's

---

[1] William Shakespeare, *Hamlet*, III, 1, 58.

optimists, but most people do not travel into adulthood without carrying some heavy baggage from their early years in the dark trunk of their subconscious and otherwise. Blessed are those who can face life as innocents, taking each day as it comes, without conjuring up the shadows of a thousand different misadventures which might or might not ever occur.

Ideally, life should have an air of easy reality about it, flowing naturally like a spiritual river down through one's years.[2] Those things in life that truly are the most important should be treated as such. A partial list of those things that are often placed on the back burner of modern life might look something like the following: faith, love, honor, truth, justice, family, friends, the passing of the seasons, the wind in one's hair, the rain upon one's cheek, the sun upon one's brow, and the reassuring rhythms of peaceful sleep as one's spouse lies safely at one's side in the darkness of the night. Trouble and joy are both part of the natural order of things, and neither is meant to dominate the other. We should live life with thanksgiving for our joys and blessings while taking what the day brings us at face value without undue dread of the morrow, which may take them from us.

> So do not worry about tomorrow; for tomorrow will care for itself. Each day has enough trouble of its own.[3]

One should be able to live amongst life's joys and tribulations with a sense of equilibrium and balance. Admittedly, in today's stressful modern world, the quest for such balance can be a significant life challenge for many. We should, however, be able to live life free of excessive worry for the morrow, depression, anxiety, fear, and the cowardice that such emotions can sometimes engender. These negative emotions are the moths of our existence nibbling away at the very fabric of our souls. We are to have faith in

---

[2] John 7:38.

[3] Matthew 6:34.

God and a belief that the fundamental nature of existence is benevolent. Although we will undoubtedly suffer misfortune and eventually die, good always triumphs over evil, and life does have a meaningful purpose leading ultimately to an existence better than this one for those who believe. We are meant to live as the following words teach us:

> For this reason I say, do not worry about your life, as to what you will eat; nor for your body, as to what you will put on. For life is more than food, and the body more than clothing. Consider the ravens, for they neither sow nor reap; they have no storeroom nor barn, and yet God feeds then; how much more valuable you are than the birds! And which of you by worrying can add a single hour to his life's span?[4]

We are to have faith that God knows the things that we need to survive in this world. If we seek the things God values, He will add to those the earthly things we need.[5] When God offered to grant King Solomon a wish, King Solomon asked for "an understanding heart to judge Your people to discern between good and evil" (1 Kings 3:5-9). Since King Solomon was seeking the things God valued, God granted him riches and honor in addition to the wisdom of a wise and discerning heart (1 Kings 3:10-13). God also offered King Solomon a long life: "If you walk in My ways, keeping My statutes and commandments as your father David walked. . . ."

Today, it is fashionable to take social issues off the table of public discourse. In this we forget that the term *social issue* is but a euphemism for those subjects and behaviors that matter to God. These rapidly disappearing moral values constitute the glue making all of our other freedoms possible. Western civilization's Judeo-Christian values, morality, ethics, and voluntary discipline hold together the tenuous fabric of personal freedom, individual

---

[4] Luke 12:22-25.

[5] Luke 12:30-31.

worth, private property rights, freedom of religion, and economic freedom in which our privileged lives are draped. Simply put, without Judeo-Christian values, morality, ethics, discipline, and accountability, Western civilization's culture of unprecedented individual liberty begins to fray around the edges and then dissolve. In dismissing social issues, and by implication the morality, accountability, and discipline in which they are bound, modern mankind often fails to seek or honor the things God values such as wisdom and obedience. Yet, we continue to expect God to grant us the safety, health, and success we seek both as individuals and as a nation.

We saw in an earlier chapter that the ultimate purpose of this existence is that we learn to love. The antithesis of love is hate. As love is of heaven, so too is hate of the world. Too much care of the things of this world leads to stress, disappointment, bitterness, and despair which are the harbingers of hatred. If stress, disappointment, bitterness, and despair are the harbingers of hatred, then worry for the morrow, depression, anxiety, fear, and cowardice are its stepchildren. As we have seen, the test of this existence is that at its end our hearts are filled with love and faith rather than bitterness and hate. Given the nature of the world in which we live today, passing this test can be a significant challenge. When nourished with love and faith, however, one's heart can rise above circumstance and grow big enough to encompass the universe and transcend eternity. When subjugated to hatred and bitterness, the human heart withers and falls into darkness.

In summary, we were meant to accept the blessing of life and experience it with the innocent faith that young children enjoy prior to the temptations and disappointments of later life.

> Truly I say to you, whoever does not receive the kingdom of God like a child will not enter it at all.[6]

---

[6] Luke 18:17; Matthew 18:3.

To accept life as a child is tantamount to accepting life with the innocent faith that, no matter what ill may from time to time befall us, life is fundamentally good, and good will ultimately prevail over adversity and evil. This existence is good. Too much worry, however, about the things of this world and issues which we do not have the power to change can ultimately destroy us. While evil and adversity do exist in the world, and they touch each of us at one time or another, we are not meant to fearfully exist in their dark shadows. We are meant to enjoy life, to experience it fully, and to live life abundantly.[7] The experience of life teaches us that this is not always easy, but it is a wise goal and one worthy of our aspiration. The attainment of this goal can bring peace, joy, and contentment while at the same time adding years to one's life span.

---

[7] John 10:10.

Chapter 18: Debts of Honor

In these times of economic uncertainty, global unrest, and cultural decline, it is easy to get so caught up in the day-to-day struggle to make a living that we allow it to blind us to priorities of far more immediate consequence to our long-term happiness. Those who would reach their golden years with satisfaction, contentment, and peace must never lose sight of the ongoing need to nurture their relationships with God, their families, and their true friends. If properly cultivated, these relationships will flower and be a comfort in times of storm. The years pass quickly and cannot be recalled. Relationships left untended wither and fade.

The symbiotic social compact that once existed between employees and their employers has sadly fallen victim to the diverse forces that have conspired to undermine the security of the American workplace. Loyalty, honor, basic honesty, and trustworthiness are frequently sacrificed on the altar of expediency by both management and labor. There is plenty of blame on both sides with neither willing to acknowledge the human wreckage they leave in their wake.

We have all heard the sad tales of individuals who made their employment their lives, who drove to work in all kinds of weather, who emotionally assumed ownership of the business in which they worked, and suffered untold stresses to help it survive, only to be told late in life that they were no longer needed. In that dark hour, if they have neglected their relationships with God, family, and friends, it can be a moment of loss and despair that for some is impossible to endure. Far too many in these troubled times face a dark morning when everything in which they have trusted simply falls away. It is for this reason that we must always remember to place God, family, and true friends before the often futile quests of this fallen world. In the end, the vain glories of the workplace often prove fleeting, while God, family, and a few good friends are all that can ultimately be relied upon. There comes a time when our faith, our capacity to love, and the good that we have been able to accomplish along the way are all that we have to place upon the cosmic scales when our lives are weighed in the balance.[1] Although a Christian is saved through his or her belief in the atoning sacrifice of Jesus Christ, a Christian should be known by his or her love, faith, and good works.[2]

These comments do not sanction anyone to do less than their best in the pursuit of their career. To give less than an honest day's work for a day's pay is a form of stealing.[3] It destroys one's Christian witness to the world to put forth less than one's best effort. Our relationships with God, our families, and friends do, however, cry out for an appropriate life balance. Our duty to these relationships is in fact sacred. We ignore that cry at the peril of our future happiness.

Today, many of us who are members of the baby boomer generation find ourselves confronted with our own mortality and the twilight years of our parents. There is an old adage, often attributed to Mark Twain, which states, "Denial is more than just a river in Egypt." Our youth is often a delightful float trip down the sun-splashed river of life. As we move into middle age, we often fail to notice that the grade of the river is ever downward, the current grows swifter, and whirlpools, rocks, and rapids become more common. If our journey is to be completed safely, adjustments, new equipment, and portages to avoid the waterfalls of the aging process will now be required. For those who ignore the signs and realities of the aging process, the river becomes one of denial and life's journey can end in disaster much sooner than necessary. Aging gracefully is all about avoiding the waterfalls and rowing one's canoe in safety for as long as possible. Our challenge, both for ourselves and our parents, is to make the wise decisions and adjustments necessary to manage our growing disabilities, prolong our independence, and extend the length and quality of

---

[1] Job 31:6.

[2] James 2:17.

[3] Proverbs 10:26; 18:9.

our remaining time on the river of life. For those who would dispel denial and face the challenges of mortality proactively, Atul Gawande's book, *Being Mortal*, is a valuable resource.[4]

With respect to one's parents, it can be frightening when individuals upon whom we have depended in various capacities for much of our lives begin to need help themselves, though they may not want it or even be aware of such a need. The situation can be even more complex if children allow themselves to harbor resentment for disappointments, misunderstandings, or disputes that now haunt the corridors of childhood memories. There are probably few families in which parents, children, and siblings have escaped deep disappointment in each other at one time or another. It is equally safe to assume that we have all disappointed God far more. Yet, He freely forgives all who have the faith and courage to believe. Far too many family reconciliations take place over a casket when an earlier reunion could have brought great happiness to the one now departed.

As noted earlier, even the best, most qualified, of parents are ultimately just ordinary individuals subject to mistake and error on the same basis as anyone else. There are also many parents who may not fall under the category of "best most qualified." Such parents sometimes commit many sins against their children and the institution of parenthood. Today, parenthood is often entered into with insufficient thought as to the consequences, responsibilities, and obligations involved. We have become a culture far too casual both with respect to the creation of human life and the extinguishing of it. Both parent and child need to remember that we will each be judged on the basis of our behavior in this life with respect to the obligations laid out for us by God's law. Parents will ultimately be judged with respect to how faithfully they attempted to discharge their responsibilities to their children. Their children in turn bear responsibility only for how faithfully they attempt to

---

[4] Atul Gawande, *Being Mortal, Medicine and What Matters in the End* (New York: Metropolitan Books, Henry Holt and Company, LLC, 2014).

discharge their responsibilities to their parents. In other words, the children of bad parents may be injured and hurt by the experience, but they remain untainted by their parents' sins, omissions, or mistakes.[5]

We do know that it is God's desire that we honor our parents, and that our behavior in that regard can impact either positively or negatively any blessings we might hope for or anticipate.

> Honor your father and your mother, that your days
> may be prolonged in the land which the Lord your
> God gives you.[6]

Parents are to be fair with their children and bring them up in the discipline and instruction of the Lord, without unduly provoking them to anger or desperation.[7] Parents are expected to be loving, instructional, authority figures rather than pals or buddies. Parents are charged with guiding their children safely into adulthood through example, mentoring, and godly wisdom. Parents who sire children recreationally, with no intention of honoring their responsibilities as parents, commit a sin against both God and the innocent which will be judged.

The obligation of children to honor their parents, while caring for them when the parents are no longer capable of doing so themselves, can be daunting and complex on multiple levels of emotion, ability, and circumstance even under relatively optimal conditions. We all have to eventually come to terms with the fact that, no matter how much we may worry or how hard we may strive, we cannot halt or reverse the natural process and cycle of life for our parents. It is ultimately futile for us, who cannot turn back the relentless hands of time in our own lives for even one minute, to

---

[5] Ezekiel 18:20; Deuteronomy 24:16.

[6] Exodus 20:12; Deuteronomy 5:16; Mark 7:10-13; Ephesians 6:1-2; Colossians 3:20.

[7] Ephesians 6:4; Colossians 3:21.

rail against fate when our parents begin to encounter the hobgoblins of those hours closer to midnight on life's clock.

We all run a race with varying degrees of success against the grim reaper, but the outcome is never in doubt. The greatest equalizing or leveling aspect of this existence is that no one gets out alive. One can easily bash one's soul against the rocky reef-like realities of life's winter years without noticing the beautiful paradise just beyond the breakers. A child has an obligation to be there for their parents as needed, but there is a limit to what one can do. There is even a limit to what one should do which brings me to my next point.

As long as they are mentally competent, our parents deserve the respect and dignity of being permitted to make their own decisions during their last years without recriminations from us. We may disagree with some of the decisions they choose to make which should not surprise us unduly. We have, no doubt, disagreed with many of the decisions they have made since we have been old enough to be aware of them. We can all safely assume that our parents have often disagreed with many of the decisions we have made down through the years of our own lives. At this stage on life's journey, we are here not to judge, but to advise our parents as best we can and to love them.

In short, the weight of old age and disease is not entirely upon our shoulders alone, and all of the scary decisions, that eventually have to be made, are not ours to make alone. As stated, our role is to advise our parents and to love them. As long as they are mentally competent, we must allow them to chart as much of their own path as they desire. There is a tendency in such times of stress to think that we are now responsible for everything. We cannot, however, be responsible for everything as long as our parents still have their faculties and the will to use them. As life enters its final battles, there are limits to what a child can do and to the pressure that the child should place upon their parents or themselves.

When one's parent(s) do become unable to adequately care for themselves, it is important to take each day one step at a time. Jesus advised us to allow each day's worry and trouble to be sufficient unto itself.[8] If one allows one's imagination to range too far ahead of actual events, the worry and anxiety can become overwhelming. One can easily end up worrying about things that never come to pass. As long as one has faith, miracles and temporary recoveries are always possible. It really is not over until it is over. As the end approaches, in whatever form it may take, the parent is often more at peace than the child.

Those responsible for caring for their parents when the final disability occurs should, if at all possible, purchase the expertise needed to accommodate the situation as it develops. If an attorney is needed for a will and estate planning, he or she should be brought on board while the parent is still competent. Part of this process should be the creation of a Living Will and a Healthcare Power of Attorney. In the Living Will, the individual expresses their own desires, while they are still competent, regarding the extent of the measures they wish to be taken to keep them alive beyond that point when all hope for a meaningful recovery has expired. Families put incredible pressure upon themselves in times of crisis, trying to save a few dollars on such matters, when they just need to get it done and put it behind them. Frequently, the brief window of opportunity to get things like a Living Will and Healthcare Power of Attorney executed can close with surprising rapidity.

Once a parent is no longer able to even assist with his or her own care, families need to take a realistic approach to the consideration of a nursing home. Many people say that their loved one will never see the inside of a nursing home as long as they are alive and able to care for them. This position is taken notwithstanding the fact that most private homes are not designed to support the care of an invalid, and most family caregivers do not have the physical strength necessary for the lifting that is required. The cost of private nursing care, which will almost certainly be

---

[8] Matthew 6:34.

needed, can often place it beyond the means of all but the wealthiest of families.

The heroic attempt to care for a totally incapacitated loved one at home, without adequate or appropriate resources, can almost kill both the caregiver and the loved one. The stress of such an attempt can also destroy the loving memories of a lifetime as both the exhausted caregiver and the declining loved one founder. In such cases, a reputable nursing home can be a blessing that can actually extend and enhance whatever quality remains to the life of a loved one. A good nursing home is able to accomplish this by providing dietitians skilled in the dietary needs of the elderly, nursing care, physical and speech therapy, wheelchair accessible showers, and helping hands when needed for grooming and lifting.

As long as a family does its homework in the selection of a nursing home, and then visits their loved one on a regular basis to check on the care being provided, the family has nothing of which to be ashamed. In fact, they have done their best to provide the level of care now required by their loved one.

It goes without saying that anyone who can remotely afford to do so should strongly consider procuring long-term-care insurance before they find themselves needing it. We tend to think of the nursing home as a fixture of extreme old age, but accidents, strokes, and other misadventures can place one in a nursing home at virtually any stage of life. At the institution where I formerly worked, long-term-care insurance could be purchased at a very reasonable price as an employee benefit, but there were relatively few takers. Most who decline long-term-care insurance when they have an opportunity to procure it will probably live to regret their shortsightedness.

The other major challenge for children is to remember their obligation to honor the wishes expressed in their parents' Living Will. Unless the parent has clearly expressed the intent, while competent, to renounce or revoke the Living Will, an ethical duty exists to honor it. Families sometimes put tremendous pressure upon physicians to ignore the wishes and directions of their parent as expressed in the Living Will, simply because they cannot face the prospect of the death of their parent.

The desire to keep one's parent alive in the intensive care unit, once death is imminent and all hope of a meaningful recovery is gone, can amount to an act of almost supreme selfishness. Once death has approached or even occurred, repeated resuscitations can be painful and almost violent as the medical team works frantically to cheat death of its charge for a few more hours. Notwithstanding their previously expressed wishes for a natural death, the elderly are sometimes brought back from the edge multiple times, dazed and battered by the resuscitation process, even though all hope of any type of positive outcome has long since vanished. When compared with the dignity of a truly natural death, such heroic attempts can almost amount to cruel and unusual punishment. In these cases, a family's love for a dying parent can lead them into places, during those last hours, where God intended that only angels should tread.

No one should despair of the future during the sadness of a life's closing. Curiously enough, death is a natural part of the life cycle. For those who believe, death is but the doorway to the kingdom of God[9] where we will once again walk with Him in the heavenly garden as His children. It can be a great comfort to recall the following words of Jesus: "In my Father's house are many dwelling places; if it were not so, I would have told you; for I go to prepare a place for you. If I go and prepare a place for you, I will come again and receive you to Myself, that where I am, there you may be also."[10] There is something about the expression of peace upon the face of a good person of faith, who has passed to the other side, which should be an inspiration for all of us temporarily left behind.

Many times over the course of a modern life, we will be called upon by desire, ambition, convenience, or expediency to violate

---

[9] 2 Corinthians 5:8; 1 Corinthians 15:20-23; John 14:1-3.

[10] John 14:2-3.

God's law, oaths of marriage or fiduciary responsibility, and bonds of loyalty and friendship. If such failures rule our better impulse, in time all hope of honesty, honor, respect, and redemption will fade. We then run the grave risk of ending our day's forsaken shadows of what we might once have been.[11] In the end, the sad faces, of the wrongs one commits, haunt the troubled corridors of one's aging memory like so many apparitions regretting long-lost opportunities to do the right thing. Those who would pass through their final years with peace, honor, and grace must during life hold their relationships with God, family, and friends sacred.

---

[11] Matthew 16:26-27; Mark 8:36-38.

Chapter 19: Take Care of Yourself

One of the themes of this book has been that we are expected to persevere, do our best, and project a positive witness or example regardless of what the world may throw at us. Admittedly, this injunction is far easier said than done. It is particularly difficult if one is out of shape, in poor health, or no longer feels well. We should, therefore, do everything readily within our power to postpone our physical and mental decline. As Sirach[1] notes, the human body begins its decay while the breath of life is yet within us.

Properly maintaining our bodies, our physical well-being, and our mental health is, therefore, a very important obligation which we owe to ourselves, our families, and to God.[2] Yet, today most people take far better care of their automobiles than they do the body in which they reside. They then expect modern medicine to supply a pill or surgery to bail them out when they inevitably fall into some sort of extremis. The modern-day abuse of the human body is one of the main root causes of the crisis threatening to overwhelm our healthcare system.

As someone who has been both an attorney and a healthcare executive, it is my firm belief that the United States of America has the best legal system and the best healthcare system in this imperfect world. The average person will, however, be far happier and better off in the long run if he or she can avoid becoming entangled in either system for as long as possible. In the healthcare sense, this means that everyone should at least make the attempt to exercise on a regular basis, watch their eating habits, supplement their diet with vitamins when needed, and partake of periodic physicals and dental exams. The neglect of any of these pillars can ultimately undermine the foundation of one's health. As we begin

---

[1] Sirach 10:9. *Sirach*, also known as *Ecclesiasticus*, is a Hebrew treatise on wisdom located in the Apocrypha.

[2] Sirach 30:14-16.

to age, it is often the aspect of wellness which we ignore that brings us down in the end.

There is plenty of evidence in both the Old Testament and the New Testament that God cares about the physical as well as the spiritual health of His people. For example, in a time when animals such as the rabbit and the pig were often riddled with parasites, God declared them unclean and off limits to his people.[3] There are many requirements for washing[4] which were characterized as ritual washings since the germ theory had not yet been discovered. In an ancient world, which was both gritty and dirty, at least until the time of the Romans, any washing was, however, a very positive thing for which a caring and loving God provided.[5] The Biblical prohibitions against fornication, adultery, and other forms of sexuality outside of traditional marriage served to protect God's people from sexually transmitted diseases and promote the health and stability of the family unit.

In Leviticus 17:11-14 God makes it very clear that blood is critical to the life of the physical body. Notwithstanding this warning, the medical practice of bloodletting existed from ancient times until the early nineteenth century when modern mathematical techniques began to accurately shed light upon the carnage bloodletting was causing. Even a man as vigorous as George Washington succumbed to the bloodletting so popular in

---

[3] Leviticus 11:6-7.

[4] Genesis 18:4; John 13:10; Mark 7:3-4; Leviticus 11:25, 28, 40; 14:8; Numbers 19;7; Exodus 30:18-21.

[5] Centuries later, realizing that powerful factions of scribes and Pharisees had perverted laws such as those governing washing and dietary matters to effectively shut the door of heaven to the mass of humanity (Matthew 23:13), Jesus relaxed such legalistic restrictions (Matthew 15:11-20; Mark 7:14-23; Acts 10:11-15; 10:28) so that people of all nations who repent of their sins through faith in Jesus Christ might inherit eternal life as children of God; Wessel, Walter W. and Strauss, Mark L. "Mark." In Matthew and Mark. Vol. 9 of *The Expositor's Commentary*, rev. ed., edited by Tremper Longman III and David E. Garland, pp. 802-804. (Grand Rapids: Zondervan, 2012).

his day. His biographer, Joseph J. Ellis, notes that, in his final brief illness, Washington was bled four times, taking more than five pints of his blood.[6] Benjamin Rush was one of early America's preeminent physicians, and yet his adherence to the practice of bloodletting in the yellow-fever epidemics of 1793 and 1797 hastened the deaths of countess patients.[7] The very real wisdom of the Bible on the fact that the "life of the flesh is in the blood ..." was either not fully grasped, given the scientific limitations of the times, or was misconstrued, or was dismissed as mere theology that could safely be ignored by men of science. Human beings are by nature prideful creatures and often have but a dim perception of what may still be unknown. Today, voluntarily donating a small amount of blood to replace that lost due to injury or surgery in others is deemed a genuine act of charity which hastens the recovery of those who have lost too much blood.

God made another contribution to public health when He commanded that all of Abraham's male descendants be circumcised.[8] Some scientists now believe that circumcision may provide very real health benefits which include reducing (not preventing) the incidence of urinary tract infections, penile cancer, balanitis, and some sexually transmitted diseases such as genital herpes, HIV (AIDS), and cancer caused by HPV (human papillomavirus). It is, likewise, now believed by some scientists that the sexual partners of circumcised men may even experience reduced rates of herpes and Chlamydia.[9]

The fact that humankind may not fully grasp all of the benefits that flow from honoring God's instructions does not mean that such

---

[6] Joseph J. Ellis, *His Excellency George Washington* (New York: Alfred A. Knopf, 2004), 268.

[7] Ron Chernow, *Alexander Hamilton,* 449-451.

[8] Genesis 17:10.

[9] "Does Circumcision Make the Cut?", *University of California, Berkeley Wellness Letter* 30, no. 14 (August 2014):3; "Sensitive About Circumcision?", *University of California, Berkeley Wellness Letter* 32, no. 14 (August 2016): 2.

benefits do not exist. The adverse impact upon one's health from lack of exercise and poor dietary, alcohol, drug, tobacco, and sexual choices can take years to become obvious by which time the damage may be irreversible. The examples just discussed suggest that the prohibitions of the Bible are often meant to protect us from dangers which may not always be fully apparent. When faced with incomplete knowledge, many have historically leapt to the conclusion that God must be wrong or mistaken which leads us back to the issue of pride—the sin God arguably dislikes most.

God also dispensed basic public health information in Deuteronomy 23:13-14 when it was commanded that the Israelite soldier should carry a spade with which to bury his excrement because:

> Since the Lord your God walks in the midst of your
> camp to deliver you and to defeat your enemies
> before you, therefore your camp must be holy; and
> He must not see anything indecent among you or He
> will turn away from you.

This is another example of good advice, both from the health standpoint and the spiritual, which is as valid for our military today as it was thousands of years ago when God spoke through Moses. The Lord is a help and a shield to those who fear Him, for a king is not saved by a mighty army or a warrior by great strength (Psalm 33:16-20). Sometimes we forget that, regardless of how well trained and equipped our troops may be, victory ultimately comes from God.[10] Care should, therefore, be taken to abide by His laws and not to offend Him.[11]

The Apostle Paul states that he "disciplines" his body. He goes on to use the metaphor of the athlete who exercises self-control in

---

[10] Deuteronomy 20:3-4; Proverbs 21:31; Joshua 1:7-9; Psalm 20:7-8; 1 Samuel 17:47.

[11] Deuteronomy 23:9.

all things in order that he might prevail.[12] Discipline and self-control also constitute the theme of Proverbs 25:28 which compares a man without control to a city whose walls have been breached. In Proverbs 15:32, we learn that those who neglect discipline despise themselves.

The phrase often attributed to the Apostle Paul that all good things in moderation are permissible is not actually in the Bible, but it does seem to capture the essence of his thought on such things.[13] We must, however, remember Paul's additional caveat that one should always be mindful not to cause others, who might have less self-control, to stumble by one's example.[14] Paul goes on to ask:

> Or do you not know that your body is a temple of the Holy Spirit who is in you, whom you have from God, and that you are not your own? For you have been bought with a price; therefore, glorify God in your body.[15]

If one believes this is true then Paul asks why one would want to join with a prostitute?[16] He might also have gone on to ask why one would want to pollute the bodily temple with drugs, tobacco, excessive alcohol, inappropriate food, or to slowly cripple the body through inactivity. We marvel at ants that continue to gorge themselves on poisonous ant bait, even as the bodies of their fellows pile up all about them, without realizing that most of us are guilty of the same sort of behavior as we continue to engage in practices that we know prove fatal to many of our brothers and sisters. This is but another instance where one can expect neither long life nor prosperity if one ignores the wisdom of God. The Bible states that "poverty and shame will come to him who neglects

---

[12] 1 Corinthians 9:24-27.

[13] *See,* 1 Timothy 4:4-5.

[14] 1 Corinthians 8:9.

[15] 1 Corinthians 6:19-20.

[16] 1 Corinthians 6:15.

discipline."[17] There is little doubt that both Moses and Paul would have frowned on the self-indulgent hedonist or the modern couch potato.

The science of health, wellness, and fitness is constantly evolving as more is learned about the human body and the effect of one's behavior and environment upon it. Nonetheless, much of the current conventional wisdom can probably be summarized in the following basic wellness tips:

1. The old dietary advice which states that to control one's weight all one has to do is eat a well-balanced diet, including all wholesome foods in moderation, is technically true, but practically false because virtually everyone has difficulty following it successfully.

2. Diets per se do not generally work in the long run. What is needed is a *Road to Damascus* experience wherein one makes a lifestyle change that works for them and results in taking in fewer calories than the body burns. Whether one is talking about carbohydrates or grams of fat, calories do matter in the end. The lifestyle adopted must be followed consistently. This is not a six-week diet, but a basic change in the way one approaches one's lifestyle choices.

3. Apart from a few people with medical problems, there is generally a weight loss lifestyle and an exercise regimen that works for virtually everyone. Since everyone is different, what works successfully for one person may not work for the next. Something, however, does in fact work for most everyone if followed consistently with discipline. For example, some might be able lose weight on a low-fat diet, but feel terrible doing it. On the other hand, those same individuals may also be able to lose weight on a low carbohydrate/high protein diet and feel

---

[17] Proverbs 13:18.

great. Finding the lifestyle that works for you is the key. Others may get good results from other dieting methodologies and be better able to stick with one of those pathways to a healthier weight. The plan that works for you is the one that you will be able to live with for the long term. Before embarking on any diet or exercise regimen, it is always wise to consult with one's physician and perhaps even get a thorough physical examination.

4. To control one's weight, one may have to give up or at least limit something and that something may be the food that one loves and craves the most. If one curtails the food one loves the most, weight loss is almost inevitable. For many individuals that food might be carbohydrates, but for others it could easily be something entirely different. The trade-off for the loss or restriction of that favorite food is the ability to gain control of one's weight and to some extent perhaps even the aging process itself. One may not be able to take the step that one knows one has to take to regain control today, but eventually one will realize that one has to do it if one is serious about controlling one's body and physical destiny. Trading carbohydrates, or whatever the case may be, for a healthy, attractive body is ultimately well worth the trade. There is much truth in the old adage that one must learn to eat to live, not live to eat.

5. A successful weight loss/maintenance lifestyle needs to be relatively simple and easy to follow under all normal circumstances. It should be simple for one to be able to identify what one can safely eat on the diet. Those foods should be readily available wherever that person is forced to eat such as restaurants and while traveling. At most restaurants one can find food that is low fat, or low carbohydrate/high protein, or that falls within those

diets allowing more diversity, but requiring rigid portion control. The important thing is to be able to follow one's dietary lifestyle even while traveling.

6. A successful weight control lifestyle should also be one that leaves one relatively satisfied and not hungry all of the time. One will not stick with a weight loss lifestyle that makes one permanently miserable. Some individuals like the complete panoply of food and are able to control their portion sizes, so for them that type of diet works. Some prefer a low carbohydrate/high protein lifestyle because the food is available anywhere, it rarely leaves one hungry, and one can even snack provided that one eats only the foods allowed in this dietary approach to weight control. Success depends upon finding an approach that you will be able to adopt as a lifestyle. A vast number of books have been written by reputable physicians, dieticians, exercise physiologists, and other experts on the various weight loss lifestyles and physical fitness approaches over the past several decades, so information is readily available when one becomes ready to tackle the ongoing maintenance of one's own body.

7. Virtually all weight loss lifestyles make one miserable in the short run. One has to stick with the lifestyle change for several weeks to allow the body to adjust. Usually at the end of approximately two to three weeks the body will have made the necessary adjustments, psychological and otherwise, to the weight loss lifestyle chosen, and life will become much more pleasant and normal. In short, the regimen becomes routine and thereafter easier to follow.

8. If physically capable of doing so, everyone needs to pick a mode of exercise consistent with their interests, ability, health, and level of fitness, and do it regularly and consistently. As noted earlier, it is always wise to consult

with your physician before suddenly embarking on any new course of exercise. As in dietary matters, the best exercise regimen is the one that you will be willing to stick with over the long term.[18] For many, resistance training seems to afford the most health and fitness benefits for the time expended. Resistance training builds muscle which is active tissue that burns calories all of the time. Other people, however, prefer some form of aerobics. A good resistance program using aerobics to warm up and/or cool down might be the best of both worlds because research is establishing that the human body needs both resistance and cardiovascular training. More people eventually lose their independence due to loss of muscle mass and the inability to carry on the activities of daily life than virtually any other single reason.[19] It is important to both slow the natural loss of muscle mass that accompanies aging as well as maintain one's cardiovascular health.

9. Regular exercise is therefore critical for the promotion of health and the prevention of chronic health problems. Regular exercise is the only fountain of youth yet discovered that seems to produce tangible results. Having said that, it is also generally true that, regardless of the form of exercise one selects, it is difficult, given most people's demanding schedules, to exercise long enough to burn sufficient calories to avoid weight creep if one continues to eat everything one wants indiscriminately.[20] This is particularly true the older one

---

[18] See, Special Winter Issue, "Your Guide to Lifelong Fitness", *University of California, Berkeley Wellness Letter* 30, no. 6 (Winter 2013-14):1-4.

[19] *See*, Connie W. Bales, "Maintain Muscle Mass with Age and Retain Your Independence", *Duke Medicine HealthNews* 18, no.10 (October 2012): 1-2.

[20] Connie W. Bales and Kathryn N. Starr, "Diet, Not Amount of Daily Exercise, is Key to Weight Management", *Duke Medicine HealthNews* 18, no.11 (November 2012):5-6.

gets if one continues to consume large quantities of gratuitous carbohydrates.

10. With respect to weight control, most people have read something at one time or another that made the light come on for them. Such an insight is revealed in *The Protein Power LifePlan,* by Michael R. Eades, MD and Mary Dan Eades, MD. In this book, the Eades note the research establishing that many cereal grains contain opioid substances called exorphins which even in small doses can be mildly addictive. They speculate that such a mechanism could be the cause of the intense cravings many people feel for carbohydrates and associate with comfort foods.[21]

11. Based on this line of reasoning, weight control would therefore possibly be somewhat analogous to the treatment of an addiction. Obviously, this is not an addiction in the sense of alcohol or addictive drugs, but it is a powerful craving that has proven difficult for many to overcome. Most of us at one time or another become, for want of a better term, addicted to a food or food class that causes our weight to creep ever upward. If one acknowledges that one is possibly dealing with something like an addiction, then it follows that one should avoid the offending food(s) or run the risk of reviving the cravings, thus starting the destructive process all over again. Just as a recovering alcoholic cannot have alcohol, so the person serious about long-term weight control should avoid or limit their intake of the food(s) to which they know in their hearts they may be addicted. The realization of this simple truth makes long-term weight control infinitely easier and less

---

[21] Michael R. Eades, M.D. and Mary Dan Eades, M.D., *The Protein Power LifePlan* (New York: Warner Books, Inc., 2000),16; *See also,* "Feel-good Food Might Be Addictive", *Consumer Reports On Health* 24, no.11 (November 2012): 10.

painful. Once one is on the wagon, it is simply easier for many individuals to stay on the wagon rather than constantly jumping back and forth.

12. It also follows from the analogy just discussed, that one's effort to live a healthier lifestyle will be easier if one's spouse is supportive. For example, it is much more difficult for one to stop smoking if one's spouse continues to smoke in front of them or to stop bingeing on carbohydrates if one's family is constantly doing so. This takes us back full circle to the Apostle Paul's caution that one should be careful not to cause others to stumble because of one's example.[22]

The purpose of this chapter is not to ask that the reader adopt the specific conclusions discussed in the paragraphs above with respect to diet and exercise. The attempt has been made, however, to arouse interest in the vital importance of adopting a healthy lifestyle. The reader is urged to perform similar research and form his or her own conclusions while seeking appropriate input from physicians and other health professionals.

Ultimately, it is easier to be a good person and fulfill the role God has designated for us if we are reasonably fit, healthy, and simply feel well. Individuals have done magnificent and even heroic things when ill or even disabled, but most of us need every advantage we can get as we struggle to be the type of individual expected by God and those who depend upon us to do our best in this world. We are to remember that we have been "bought with a price" and are, therefore, to "glorify God in our bodies."[23]

---

[22] 1 Corinthians 8:9.

[23] 1 Corinthians 6:20.

Chapter 20: Avoiding the Bonfires of History

Since the Garden of Eden there have always been those who seek to convince us that God did not really say what He appeared to say, and that His story, promises, wisdom, and commandments are not necessarily to be taken literally. Every age has had those who have tried to keep the common man and woman from reading the Scriptures for themselves, or failing that, to destroy the belief of the common man in the veracity of the Scriptures. Since the first quarter of the twentieth century, in the push to secularize American society, there has been a concerted effort on the part of some liberal historians to revise both the character and the manner in which this nation was founded to minimize the Christian influence to which virtually all histories closer in time to the period attest.[1]

The revisionist trend noted above was decisively challenged by the towering scholarship of the Reverend Dr. Peter Lillback and Jerry Newcombe cited earlier. Lillback and Newcombe established that some liberal historians have attempted to alter history to depict George Washington as either an unbeliever or a deist when nothing could be further from the truth. The George Washington that Lillback and Newcombe rediscovered was in fact a deeply religious Christian and volunteer churchman who drew upon his Protestant beliefs to help create a new nation free of religious persecution.[2] The effort to alter the historical Washington has been complemented by a similar effort on the part of many liberal academics and theologians to destroy our faith in the truth, wisdom, and relevance of the Holy Scriptures. This attempt to extinguish the light and smother the truth is one form of the ancient evil that has stalked our souls across the ages.

---

[1] Larry Schweikart and Michael Allen, *A Patriot's History of the United States,* 96-99.

[2] Lillback and Newcombe, *George Washington's Sacred Fire,* 714.

It is a point of considerable historical curiosity that a people as devout as the Jews in the time of Jesus entrusted the position of high priest, administration of the temple, and the rituals of sacrifice to a sect of priests called the Sadducees. The Sadducees were notoriously corrupt and did not believe in the resurrection of the dead, the immortality of the soul, a final judgment, heaven and hell, or angels and spirits.[3] Jesus famously refuted their doctrine and stated that they were mistaken in their beliefs,[4] but their power persisted, notwithstanding their loss of popular respect and support, until the Romans destroyed both Jerusalem and the temple in AD 70. Today, although the edifice of Western civilization rests upon a foundation of Judeo-Christian values, ethics, and beliefs, many of our modern temples of learning, theology, government, justice, and public opinion are firmly in the control of individuals who apparently share much in common with the ancient Sadducees.

The custodians of our culture's repository of truth have traditionally reposed within the ministry, our universities, our elected officials, the judiciary, and the free press. While the United States still has many excellent servants in each of these areas, a *pattern and trend* has emerged over the past eighty years from within parts of each of these cultural pillars that reveals a distinctly secular ideological and political bias. This renders it necessary that all pronouncements from any of these quarters be filtered through the prism of each individual's faith, intellect, life experience, education, and common sense. Yes, we must dare to think for ourselves, but only after doing the necessary research. One should not be impressed, for example, when someone listens to a passage out of the Bible and says, "Well, I disagree with that." One should read the Bible and make an attempt to understand the context of a difficult passage before dismissing or condemning it. God would

---

[3] Acts 23:8; Josephus, *Jewish Antiquities* 18.1.4; Josephus, *The Jewish War* 2.8.14.

[4] Matthew 22:23-33; Mark 12:18-27; Luke 20:27-40.

not have given humanity the Bible, and protected His word across thousands of years, if the issue of eternal salvation was meant to be a matter of spur-of-the-moment opinion.

With respect to nuclear arms negotiations with the Soviets, Ronald Reagan's motto was "trust but verify."[5] Given the record in recent years from each of the areas noted above, those who are wise will endeavor to educate themselves and verify, to the extent possible, all pronouncements on matters of substance and importance that touch upon one's personal salvation, one's individual liberty, and our nation's future. The truth is always superior to ideology, and a tree is known by its fruit. The Founding Fathers planted for us the Tree of Liberty, and it has been nourished with the courage, perseverance, faith, toil, and blood of the generations since that time. It has grown healthy and strong, and its fruit has made the United States the greatest nation in the history of the world. Each new generation must take care that the Tree of Liberty is not cut down on its watch.

As noted earlier in this book, a keystone of one's cultural and spiritual literacy in our society should be a basic familiarity with the contents of the Bible. The shared experience, truth, and ancient ethnic wisdom of the Bible constitutes nothing less than the living thread that stretches back through time connecting our present lives to those of the Founding Fathers, the great figures of Western civilization, the Apostles, and ultimately Jesus Christ. This is the thread of life and hope for what we know as Western civilization. Indeed, Western civilization has always hung suspended by this slender thread of light, over a broader world often mad with discord, bedlam, rage, individual serfdom, and ancient lidless malice. It is this thread, representing the spiritual life of our civilization, that the modern antireligious secularist would gladly take shears in hand to sever like the Fate, Atropos (Morta), of Greek

---

[5] Reagan, *An American Life*, 633.

mythology.[6] T. S. Eliot once prophesied, "If Christianity goes, the whole of our culture goes."[7]

More than any other source, the Bible has influenced how Western civilization has evolved and how freedom loving individuals think. It is the ultimate source of our exuberant and unique blend of faith, compassion, hope, honesty, decency, accountability, charity, individualism, and love of liberty. The course upon which our nation has met with its unparalleled success was charted from the beginning by individuals more influenced by the Bible than any other work.[8] Those who would change the course upon which our nation has thus far traveled must first distance us from and shake our belief in the Bible. As we have seen, these processes are well underway and threaten to fundamentally alter our American way of life. Jesus calls out to us from the Bible to walk while we still have the Light, so that the darkness does not overtake us, because those who walk in the darkness do not know where they go.[9] While we still have the Light, we are to believe in it, so that we may become people of the Light.[10]

Almost as misinterpreted and misquoted as the Bible are the Declaration of Independence, the United States Constitution, and the events of American history. Every citizen has a sacred and a fiduciary responsibility to become familiar enough with these documents and our own history to become responsible custodians

---

[6] The Fates: In ancient Greek mythology, the three Fates were said to be the ever-vigilant daughters of Zeus and Themis (Night). They were Clotho, spinner of the thread of life; Lachesis, who determined each individual's destiny or portion in life; and Atropos, the eldest who could not be dissuaded and who carried the abhorred shears with which to cut the thread of an individual's life at death.

[7] Eliot, *Christianity & Culture*, 200.

[8] Barton, *America's Godly Heritage*, 23.

[9] John 12:35.

[10] John 12:36.

for future generations of the many opportunities and freedoms that constitute our uniquely free way of life.

In terms of blood, toil, and sacrifice, the Bible is one of history's most expensive books. Many good Christians have been persecuted and killed so that we might have the privilege of reading the Scriptures for ourselves and, yet, today most people rarely do so.[11] The men who translated the Scriptures and preserved them from the ravages of time and the tumults of war, heresy, and politics were heroes and their stories are inspiring. As we have seen earlier in this book, the sources of the Bible are not as obscure or open to doubt as many modern critics would have us believe. While knowledge of the ancient world is constantly advancing due to archeology and analysis of ancient documents such as the Dead Sea Scrolls, to date, there have been no new discoveries that render the speculation and theories of many modern liberal critics any more plausible than the traditional doctrines of the orthodox Christian Church.

The Bible was originally written in the languages—Hebrew, Aramaic, and Greek—of the people to whom it was being preached at that time. In the early New Testament, Mediterranean world, Greek was the international language of the masses. The primary Bible of the early church was thus written in Greek. Over time, however, Latin became the dominate language of early Christianity in the western half of the Roman Empire, so Jerome[12] translated the Old Testament from Hebrew and the New Testament from Greek into Latin by AD 404. The truth of the Scriptures remained

---

[11] The American Bible Society's "State of the Bible 2014" survey found that while eighty-eight percent of American homes contain a Bible, only thirty-seven percent of Americans read the Bible on a regular basis.

[12] Jerome: (born AD 342–died AD 420) Influential priest, ascetic, theologian, historian and secretary to Pope Damasus. Jerome was perhaps the most erudite of the early Fathers of the Church having studied in Rome, Antioch, and Constantinople and lived for many years in Bethlehem. Most famous for his translation of the Bible into Latin known as the Vulgate, but also credited with 63 volumes of commentaries, sermons, letters, polemics and other religious works.

entombed in the Latin language for over a thousand years as the Roman world crumbled, and Latin slowly became a dead language accessible only to the most learned.

The common man eventually had access to the Bible only through the clergy, acting as intermediaries, who could still read Latin. With the exception of very wealthy individuals, such as King Henry VIII, Sir Thomas More, and Queen Elizabeth I, who had the means and the desire to procure the finest classical tutors, there were relatively few in even the upper classes who could read the Scriptures for themselves. The ecclesiastical elite thus became the custodians of the Scriptures, and this monopoly gave them great power over both the common man and the upper classes. The desire for earthly power has always been associated with the efforts of those who have sought to control the interpretation of the Scriptures to suit their own ideology. During this time, there was no way for the common man to personally verify that he or she was being given an accurate account of what the Scriptures really said.

Abuses, such as the selling of indulgences,[13] arose during the period described above which eventually incited reformers like John Wyclif, Jan Hus (John Huss), and Martin Luther to ignite the Reformation. These reformers, living at different times and in different countries, demanded an end to such abuses and practices that had no basis in the Scriptures. Such calls for reform were generally met with extreme hostility. One might think a translation

---

[13] The Theory of Indulgences: The Church of that time believed that few individuals other than Jesus and the saints were good enough to merit going directly to heaven at death. Most people had to spend time in a place of temporary punishment called purgatory to properly atone for their sins prior to being admitted to heaven. Jesus and the saints had bequeathed an excess of good works called the Treasury of Merits to the Church. It was believed that the Pope had the power to transfer credits from this treasury of good works to certain individuals for the purpose of either shortening that person's time in purgatory or eliminating it altogether. The indulgence was supposed to be freely given in return for a truly voluntary contribution. The recipient should also have faith and be repentant of their sins, although this was not always properly emphasized.

of the Scriptures into the current language of the people, so that each person would have the opportunity to read the Scriptures for themselves, would be welcomed. Far from it; in those days, such a common-sense idea frequently resulted in the persecution or death of those bold enough to advocate it. In every age, there have always been powerful constituencies with a vested interest, unrelated to personal salvation, in retaining the power to convey their interpretation of the Scriptures to the common man and woman rather than allowing or encouraging individuals to study the Bible for themselves.

John Wyclif was responsible for the first English translation of the Bible, and he suffered a great deal of persecution as a direct result of this great accomplishment. When he managed, notwithstanding the persecution, to die a natural death, his body was later disinterred, burned, and the ashes thrown into the Swift River. Over one hundred years later, after the printing press had been invented, William Tyndale issued the next major English translation of the New Testament. He was subsequently burned at the stake in 1536 after a lifetime devoted to making the Scriptures available to common men and women. Miles Coverdale utilized much of the translating work of those who had come before him to publish the first complete English Bible in 1535. John Rogers, one of Tyndale's successors, finished Tyndale's work and issued a second complete edition of the Bible in English in 1537, and was burned at the stake for his efforts in 1555.

Various Bibles in the common tongue of the people appeared during this period, but making the Bible available to the common man was an extremely dangerous business until at least the reign of Queen Elizabeth I. The British theologian Brian H. Edwards summarizes the Reformation creed for which these martyrs died as simply: "Scripture alone for authority; Christ alone for salvation; and, Faith alone as the path to receive salvation."[14] The modern

---

[14] Brian H. Edwards, *The Life of William Tyndale* (DVD) (Hebron, Kentucky: Answers in Genesis-USA, 2008).

church would be much more effective and faithful to its ancient mission, of nurturing the believer and spreading Christ's true message throughout the immediate community and into the rest of the world, if it would return to these basic pillars of the faith.

Christianity and the Scriptures had thus survived the attempt of the Roman Empire to wipe them out, the fall of the Empire to various barbarian groups, the ensuing dark ages, and the attempts by the Catholic church of that time to keep the Scriptures from being made accessible to the common man. After Queen Elizabeth's time, and particularly after the publication of the King James Version of the Bible in 1611, virtually any Englishman who could read had firsthand access to the Scriptures. The English Bible in its various iterations was taken by all colonial expeditions to the new world where its precepts were absorbed and utilized in the molding of the new nation that was to one day become the United States of America.

Today, all too often, many of us live the complacent, busy, self-absorbed, trivial life of nominal Christians and indifferent citizens. As T. S. Eliot noted of similar circumstances in Protestant Europe, "the boundary between belief and unbelief is vague; the Christianity is more pliant, the atheism more negative; and all parties live in amity, so long as they continue to accept some common moral conventions."[15] Just as the people of John the Baptist's time, we presume upon God's continued blessings and special favor because we are perhaps descended from better people than ourselves.[16] Yet, the Bible teaches that each generation is judged not by its ancestry, but by whether it fears God, adheres to His word, and bears good fruit.[17] Those individuals and nations that fail to heed this wisdom are cut down and thrown onto the

---

[15] Eliot, *Christianity & Culture*, 146.

[16] Matthew 3:9-10.

[17] Ezekiel 18:1-32;Luke 3:8-9.

bonfires of history.[18] This was the fate of Israel, the Roman Empire, and most of the great nations and empires that have risen to brief glory both before and since that time.

Today, we are accustomed to thinking of ourselves as the salt of the earth, but Jesus warns that once even the salt of the earth has become tasteless, it is no longer good for anything other than to be discarded and "trampled underfoot."[19] This was essentially Rome's fate, for it was never decisively defeated as long as it was capable of fielding armies. In its last years, Rome was attacked by many, but the true causes of its fall were internal. This history is instructional for those interested in the future of those nations that make up what is today known as Western civilization.

Our culture has become so entangled by political correctness and revisionist thought, both in its universities and many of its churches, that it is beginning to lose sight of the values that truly matter which have constituted the basis for its previous greatness. Endless compromise and equivocation, with respect to the basic principles upon which both our faith and Western civilization are grounded, have the real potential to fatally weaken the entire structure. It is an immutable law of history that, once a civilization begins to doubt the truth of the values upon which it rests, decline is almost inevitable.

America has a secret weapon that may yet confound the hopes of those who hope to see the failure of our grand experiment of faith, freedom, individual liberty, competitive free enterprise capitalism, responsibility, and accountability. That secret weapon is, and ever has been, the sleeping giant of the common man with his and her innate faith, common sense, wisdom, strength, and distain for failed theories that cannot stand the test of the real world. The ability of very practical, no-nonsense, common men and women to read, study, and think for ourselves constituted the flint,

---

[18] Matthew 3:10; 13:40-42, 47-50.

[19] Matthew 5:13.

tinder, and steel that sparked the flame of our original liberty, just as it has the potential to safeguard it now. In a time of smoke and mirrors, common men and women in America can still generally discern the reflection of the truth.

As stated throughout this book, its purpose is not to force anyone to accept the conclusions reached in these pages, but rather to stimulate all who read these pages to study the original sources such as the Bible and the United States Constitution, and become informed citizens capable of thinking for themselves, rather than just repeating the information fed to us by those who have lost their way in the media, pulpit, academia, and elsewhere.

In the United States, everyone is free to believe or disbelieve anything they choose as long as they remain loyal citizens, honor the values and freedoms our civilization has fought to secure for all of its citizens, make a good faith effort to assimilate into our capitalistic culture, and refrain from harming or intimidating others. What one believes is, however, extremely important and will have eternal consequences. Life and eternity are not meant to be taken lightly.

The incredible amount of research Reverend Dr. Lillback and Jerry Newcombe completed for their book *George Washington's Sacred Fire*, makes all the more impressive their statement that "To the best of our knowledge, there was not a single founding father that denied the immortality of the soul. Not one."[20] Although he apparently rejected the divinity of Jesus Christ, even Thomas Jefferson believed in God, an afterlife of reward and punishment, and the moral teachings of Jesus.[21] Benjamin Franklin's beliefs were strikingly similar to Jefferson's.[22] While far from being a

---

[20] Lillback and Newcombe, *George Washington's Sacred Fire*, 665; *See also*, Russell Kirk, *The American Cause* (Chicago: Henry Regnery Company, 1966), 38-39.

[21] Jon Meacham, *Thomas Jefferson: The Art of Power*, 471- 472; *See also*, Ron Chernow, *Alexander Hamilton*, 659.

[22] H.W. Brands, *The First American, The Life and Times of Benjamin Franklin* (New York: Anchor Books, A Division of Random House, Inc., 2002), 706-707.

fundamentalist in his personal beliefs, Franklin believed in an afterlife and recognized the importance of God and Judeo-Christian teachings and values to the ordering of his own life, to society, and the culture of the new republic. To this end, he actively tried to dissuade his friend Thomas Paine from publishing his controversial pamphlet, *Age of Reason*, which denigrated the Bible and the traditional Christian faith.[23]

When the Founders drafted the Declaration of Independence, fought the Revolutionary War, and ratified the United States Constitution, the foundation was laid for a uniquely benevolent government. This government was intended to secure the many freedoms and rights, that devolved from the Judeo-Christian tradition, for the citizens of the United States—a way of life that protected the rights of all to worship peacefully as they chose without persecution.

---

[23] Lillback and Newcombe, *George Washington's Sacred Fire*, 473; See also, H.W. Brands, *The First American, The Life and Times of Benjamin Franklin*, 658.

Chapter 21: Faith

Regardless of intellect, education, and the assertions of credible scholarship, we are each eventually brought into the hallowed chamber of the individual heart where simple faith is required. Ultimately, the human heart must dare to wrestle with our love of science and technology for mastery of our belief in those moments when only faith will serve the needs of the human soul. When one makes the decision to render unto Caesar the things of this fallen world and to God the things of eternity, faith is born. An uncompromising and unequivocal faith is an awesome force which still has the power to transform the world like the shimmering light of a fresh dawn ushering in a wondrous new age.

The belief that God inspired[1] the individuals who witnessed, testified, penned, and selected the books contained in the Bible does require faith. This is still true even though, as shown earlier in this book, we now know that the Bible is the most faithfully preserved book of antiquity. Its truth, as evidenced by eyewitness testimony, was written down within the lifetimes of those who heard Jesus or had access to individuals who had heard and experienced Jesus. The Scriptures,[2] ancient parchments, histories, and archeology can take us a long way up the path to Jesus, but the last few miles must be traveled in faith. This is as God intended. The capacity for faith is ultimately what separates the true Christian from the false. This is one of the paramount messages of the Bible.

Our faith requires courage, loyalty, steadfastness,[3] love, and hope amongst the challenges, distractions, indifference, and even hostility of the modern world. This remains true even though our

---

[1] 2 Timothy 3:16.

[2] The Scriptures contain many prophecies in the Old Testament referring to the future Messiah, but the following could almost be taken from the New Testament although they were written as much as a thousand years before the time of Jesus Christ: Micah 5:2-5; Isaiah 7:14; 9:6-7; Isaiah 53; Psalm 22; Psalm 69:20-21; Zechariah 9:9-10; Amos 8:9; Psalm 34:20,22.

[3] 1 Corinthians 15:58.

faith has been reaffirmed, according to the wisdom of the great Pharisee teacher Gamaliel, by the simple fact that its truth has withstood the test of time (Acts 5:34-39). "Faith is the assurance of things hoped for, the conviction of things not seen."[4] The Apostle Paul stated that we are "justified through faith."[5] He proudly and defiantly proclaimed, "For by grace you have been saved through faith; and that not of yourselves, it is the gift of God; not as a result of works, so that no one may boast."[6] Without faith it is literally impossible to please God, "for he who comes to God must believe that He is and that He is a rewarder of those who seek Him."[7] In summary, it is a wise man who knows what he does not know. It is an even wiser man who knows what is ultimately unknowable— who knows where knowledge ends and faith begins. In the final analysis, faith is a choice that God calls upon each of us to make. It is one of the tests of this life without which we cannot achieve a passing score.

If followed, Judeo-Christian precepts form the framework for a fruitful, just, sane, and orderly society that maximizes individual liberty and protects more freedoms for the common man and woman than any other culture on earth. "There is neither Jew nor Greek, there is neither slave nor free man, there is neither male nor female; for you are all one in Christ Jesus."[8] When the Apostle Paul made this statement he was echoing the teachings and example of Jesus Christ with respect to women, children, and the common man. These teachings, and His example, mark Jesus, alone among the world's great religious leaders, as an individual completely apart from the conditions and mores of the times in which he lived—just as though He had come to us directly from Heaven.[9]

---

[4] Hebrews 11:1.

[5] Romans 3:28; 5:1; Galatians 2:16.

[6] Ephesians 2:8-9.

[7] Hebrews 11:6.

[8] Galatians 3:28.

[9] John 3:31-34. See also, Chesterton, *The Everlasting Man*, 122-124, 128-129.

With respect to those parts of the globe that fall within the sphere of influence of the Judeo-Christian heritage, the statement by G. K. Chesterton that with Christianity "the sanity of the world was restored" has been, against all of the odds, borne out.[10] If one objectively considers those countries in which the rule of law encourages tolerance and allows all elements of society the opportunity to participate fully and equally with respect to fundamental and identified human and property rights common to all, the list even today is short and it consists almost entirely of Christian countries. This observation is not meant to offend, but is merely one of fact. The long and sometimes tortured historical path to this point has not been easy, short, or always obvious, but its source has always been the Judeo-Christian ideal as evidenced in the West by the Old and New Testaments.

While still far from perfect, it has taken the West two thousand years of struggle to drag itself out of the mire of intolerance, bigotry, inequality, cruelty, and subjugation that still oppresses common men and women throughout much of the rest of humanity. As our own culture has been secularized and distanced from the faith, accountability, discipline, and morality of the orthodox Judeo-Christian traditions, those elements of darkness and chaos, which have been the doom of mankind throughout history, and continue to be so in the rest of the world today, have already begun to destabilize our own society. This can be seen in the disintegration of the family unit accompanied by soaring levels of violence, addiction, immorality, and unethical behavior throughout our nation and the rest of Western civilization. People of every faith from all over the world come to the countries of the West for peace, opportunity, security, and freedom. Strip away the Judeo-Christian values upon which Western culture rests and these characteristics begin to evaporate one by one. Taken in this light, the full scope of Jesus' words, "I am the way, and the truth, and the life; no one comes to the Father but through Me" takes on a powerful new meaning (John 14:6).

---

[10] Chesterton, *The Everlasting Man*, 161.

We once knew the answers to the problems that threaten to unravel our civilization. These historical solutions are grounded in the essential decency and fairness of Judeo-Christian values, ethics, morality, and hope without which nothing else in a free society works. This is why those who wish to banish the so-called social issues, and the morality they represent, from public discourse are so misguided. These rapidly disappearing Judeo-Christian values constitute the social glue and voluntary discipline that make all of our other freedoms possible. The historically rare fabric of freedom of religion, personal freedom, individual worth, private property rights, and economic liberty in which our privileged lives are draped, is both tenuous and fragile. It has from the beginning been sustained and nurtured by Judeo-Christian enlightenment, values, ethics, and morality. As touched upon in the previous pages of this book, many social, political, and economic reforms are necessary to halt the decline of Western civilization. Unless applied in an environment of Judeo-Christian values, morality, ethics, and voluntary self-discipline, such reforms, even if achieved, are doomed to ultimate failure if the primary goal is to preserve our unique culture of freedom and personal liberty.

In conclusion, this book has been about many things that comprise the components of a disciplined, accountable, and principled Christian life that each of us should attempt to live with love, faith, prudence, and wisdom. It concludes with the topics discussed above because they constitute the cornerstone upon which the structural stability of both Western civilization and the United States rely. If we allow the removal of this cornerstone, it will bring down Western civilization, as we know it, just as it brought down Jerusalem and the great Jewish temple in AD 70.[11] "God is not mocked, for whatever a man sows, this he shall also reap."[12]

Yet, while the common men and women of the Western world still think for themselves and have the willingness to study their

---

[11] Matthew 21:42-44; 24:1-2; Luke 19:43-44; Acts 4:10-12.

[12] Galatians 6:7.

faith, their history, and our shared Judeo-Christian heritage, all hope is not lost. Only God can bestow wisdom and He reserves this great gift for those who fear Him and actually seek it.[13] For those who do seek God's wisdom, He has often granted energizing spiritual renewals or awakenings that have the power to positively transform individuals and nations. In describing this process God says, "Moreover, I will give you a new heart and put a new spirit within you; and I will remove the heart of stone from your flesh and give you a heart of flesh. I will put My Spirit within you and cause you to walk in My statutes, and you will be careful to observe My ordinances."[14] Such an awakening could arouse us from our stupor and reopen our eyes to God's truth as manifest in the Bible and our Judeo-Christian past. Such an awakening is urgently needed if God's blessings are to be restored to our future.

The relentless march of our society away from our Judeo-Christian heritage, individualism, the wisdom of the Founding Fathers, and competitive free enterprise capitalism is far from preordained or inevitable. No demonstrable body of truly objective theological, historical, constitutional or economic fact supports the path down which we have traveled over the past eighty to one hundred years. The objective facts that do exist affirm the merit, utility, and overwhelming success of the values we are abandoning rather than those to which we have turned. As the Apostle Paul feared, we have allowed ourselves to be taken "captive through philosophy and empty deception, according to the tradition of men, according to the elementary principles of the world, rather than according to Christ."[15] All too often, we have ignored sound doctrine, and, in order to have our "ears tickled," we have accumulated teachers in accordance with our own desires while turning away from the truth.[16] The invaluable lessons of our long

---

[13] Proverbs 2:3-8; James 1:5-6.

[14] Ezekiel 36: 26-27; Jeremiah 31:33-34; Hebrews 8: 10-12.

[15] Colossians 2:8; *see also* Acts 28:27.

[16] 2 Timothy 4:3-4.

and successful experience are now, in the words of Edmund Burke, frequently despised as simply "the wisdom of unlettered men."[17]

As we have seen, a strong argument can be made that our journey away from our Judeo-Christian heritage, and our slow retreat from the principles of competitive free enterprise capitalism and much of the original vision of the Founding Fathers for this nation, has been, in fact, largely the byproduct of mere opinion, error, and hubris on the part of those that we have innocently empowered to make such decisions without adequate supervision on our part. While it is true that some things may be considered matters of opinion, issues that determine our liberty, economic philosophy, and personal salvation should not be among them given the hindsight of history with which we are blessed.

As has previously been noted, both false prophets and trees are known by their fruit, for "a good tree cannot produce bad fruit, nor can a bad tree produce good fruit."[18] Jesus further clarified this point when He explained, "A good man out of the good treasure of his heart brings forth good things, and an evil man out of the evil treasure brings forth evil things" (Matthew 12:35). Each one of us has a window of experience and intellect through which the orchard of life can be viewed if we are willing to pull aside the curtains and look. It is time for common men and women to examine the fruit that has fallen into their lives and start paying attention to the types of trees that have crept into our orchard — trees which threaten to rob the Tree of Liberty of its place in the sun and our faith of its place in our history. To willfully ignore the godly precedents of our past is to unleash the furies of history upon our future.

If we truly desire that our descendants be mighty upon the earth[19] as our fathers were, then we must remember that the fear of the Lord is not only the beginning of wisdom,[20] but also of God's

---

[17] Burke, *Reflections on the Revolution in France*, 58.

[18] Matthew 7:15-20.

[19] Psalm 112:2.

[20] Proverbs 9:10; Psalm 111:10; Job 28:28.

blessings if we honor God's commandments.[21] It is the upright, disciplined, and accountable people of faith that will be blessed and have the potential to restore the wealth and prosperity of God's blessings to America and the countries of the West.[22]

The ancient Judaism of the Old Testament gave mankind knowledge of the one, true, unchanging, timeless, utterly holy God; the moral and ethical standards which He has consistently demanded; and the concept that every human life has potential, meaning, and worth in the eyes of God for mankind was made in God's image (Genesis 1:26). These values, ethics, morality, and voluntary self-discipline safeguard the individual and form the foundation upon which the unparalleled order and security of Western civilization rests. The classical civilizations of Greece and Rome bequeathed to the West a primordial pool teeming with the building blocks of Western thought, law, political science, social structure, and nascent concepts of individualism and freedom. It took, however, the New Testament, hurled like a thunderbolt from the hand of God in the years after the resurrection of Jesus Christ, to quicken and animate those still waters to bring forth the liberties of mankind we know today in the West. Thus was born a humane civilization different from anything previously known in the history of the world. In this book, the faith of our Judeo-Christian legacy has been characterized as the cornerstone upon which everything worth preserving in our civilization rests. This concept has never been more beautifully or more clearly expressed than by the G. K. Chesterton, who likened the Christian creed not to a cornerstone, but to a "key" which fits the lock of the human experience and has allowed humanity to pass through a doorway into a new existence of unparalleled freedom and liberty.[23]

---

[21] Psalm 112:1.

[22] Psalm 112:2-3.

[23] Chesterton, *The Everlasting Man,* 161.

CPSIA information can be obtained
at www.ICGtesting.com
Printed in the USA
BVOW03s1847110717
489092BV00001B/120/P